Praise for
Are You Being Seduced into Debt?

"In *Are You Being Seduced into Debt?* author John Cummuta presents a challenge to the consumer mentality that seduces all of us. This book is full of real-life insights and field experience. This book is not written to inform you, but to change you."

—PASTOR BRAD E. KELLER
Cornerstone Church, Prairie du Chien, WI

"In a world where individuals and families are fighting for financial survival, John Cummuta stands as out as a giant-killer! Through reading his new book, *Are You Being Seduced Into Debt?*, you will be strategically empowered to break free from the culture of manipulation and indebtedness to an environment of real freedom and wealth-building. This is a MUST read!"

—BISHOP TONY MILLER
Destiny World Outreach

"Finally, a 21st Century *Toto* pulls back the curtain and exposes the Wizards of Manipulation, the debt conspirators. In *Are You Being Seduced into Debt?* John Cummuta not only defines our major obstacles in achieving financial security; he gives us the transportation vehicle to take us from 'over the rainbow' to the actual realization of the American dream."

—DENIS WAITLEY
Author of *The Psychology of Winning*

"*Are You Being Seduced into Debt?* is a must-read. By applying the principles listed in this book, *anyone* can find the financial relief he or she is looking for."

—DEBORAH MCNAUGHTON
Author of *The Get Out of Debt Kit: Your Roadmap to Financial Freedom* and *Financially Secure: An Easy to Follow Money Program for Women*

"*Are You Being Seduced into Debt?* is the best book written on one of the most important subjects of all. It can change your life!"

—BRIAN TRACY
Author, *Create Your Own Future* and *Victory!*

Are You Being
SEDUCED
into DEBT?

Break Free and Build a Financially Secure Future

JOHN M. CUMMUTA

NELSON BOOKS
A Division of Thomas Nelson Publishers
Since 1798

www.thomasnelson.com

Published in Nashville, Tennessee, by Thomas Nelson, Inc.

Author is represented by the literary agency of Alive Communications, Inc., 7680 Goddard Street, Suite 200, Colorado Springs, CO 80920.

Unless otherwise noted, Scripture quotations are from THE NEW KING JAMES VERSION. Copyright © 1979, 1980, 1982, Thomas Nelson, Inc., Publishers.

Scripture quotations noted AMP are from THE AMPLIFIED BIBLE: Old Testament. Copyright © 1962, 1964 by Zondervan Publishing House (used by permission); and from THE AMPLIFIED NEW TESTAMENT. Copyright © 1958 by the Lockman Foundation (used by permission).

Library of Congress Cataloging-in-Publication Data

Cummuta, John.
    Are you being seduced into debt? : break free and build a financially secure future / John M. Cummuta.
      p. cm.
    ISBN 0-7852-6330-6 (hardcover)
    1. Finance, Personal. 2. Debt. I. Title.
    HG179.C837 2004
    332.024'02--dc22

2004001596

Printed in the United States of America

04 05 06 07 08 BVG 5 4 3 2 1

This book is dedicated to . . .
Jesus, my Savior and King,
Lois, my wife and love,
Stacyann, my daughter and joy,
Adam, my son and fun,
Anthony, my son and energy,
Abbey, my daughter and light,
and
Dominic, John, Ethan, Michael, Matthew, and Nico,
my grandsons and the greatest challenges to keeping my
spending under control.

CONTENTS

∞

PART ONE
THE GREAT DECEPTION

1

YOU'RE BEING DECEIVED

∞

"I am Oz, the Great and Powerful. Who are you?"
"I—if you please, I am Dorothy, the Small and Meek."

You remember the scene. Dorothy, Scarecrow, Tin Man, and the Cowardly Lion had just walked the long corridor to the hall of the great Wizard of Oz. Frightened by the wizard's awesome face, billows of smoke, explosions, and venting steam, the timid foursome make their requests to return to Kansas, get a brain, get a heart, and be filled with courage.

The "Great and Powerful Oz" cowed them with a noisy outburst. Then—hoping to permanently comb them from his wizardly hair—he ordered them to eliminate the dreaded Wicked Witch of the West and return with her broomstick as proof.

Later, when they rose to the challenge and laid the broomstick before him, Dorothy quivered, "So we'd like you to keep your promise to us; if you please, sir."

While Oz was trying to evade the issue and send the foursome away again, Toto, Dorothy's little dog and brave hero of the story, grabbed a mouthful of curtain and pulled it back.

That's when the wizard haltingly stammered those classic words: "Pay no attention to that man behind the curtain!" And Dorothy and her friends discovered that the Great and Powerful Wizard of Oz was just a human being pushing buttons and pulling levers to create frightening images. But the images—indeed, the wizard himself—were frauds . . . illusions.

Thank God for Toto! Where would Dorothy and her friends have been without him? Probably running wizardly errands all over the Oz countryside, all in obedience to an illusion—a powerful, influential, but fake image. Which begs the question: Why did they risk their lives for the wizard? In fact, why did all the citizens of Oz do his bidding?

Because they all bought into the illusion.

And the fact that all of them could look around and see everyone else behaving as if the wizard were real made it easier for them to accept his reality. The wizard's promotion of himself, along with good old peer influence, enslaved the whole region to the illusion. Good grief, even the Munchkins and Glinda, the Good Witch of the North, had swallowed the wizard's propaganda. Remember, it was Glinda who sent Dorothy to "the great and wonderful Wizard of Oz" in the first place.

Yes . . . Toto is the real hero of this story. And . . .

I'm Your Toto

I'm going to pull back the curtain on the deception and manipulation being aimed at you by a "wizardly" group of mercenaries. These seemingly benign businesses subtly push your buttons and pull your levers to get you to do their bidding, day in and day out. And their bidding is for you to work hard, earn as much money as you can, and then give most of it to them over the course of your lifetime.

Am I serious? Are people really manipulating you into giving them your money? Well, let's look at a simple government statistic, then ask that question again.

According to the U.S. Census Bureau, of all American households age sixty-five and older:

- 79 percent are living *under* the average household income.

- 44 percent are living under $25,000 annual income.

- 19 percent live below the poverty level (two-person household).

This means nearly 80 percent of all American households will end up trying to enjoy the remainder of their lives on below-average incomes, and just under 20 percent will be scraping along beneath the poverty level. This is a disgraceful record for the richest nation on earth, and I don't think we the people could have accomplished this bad a performance without some help.

In fact, I know better because I've been both perpetrator and victim of this manipulation. I've been a component of the wizard's machinery, and I've been with Dorothy and her friends. One day, while I was happily operating in the wizard's camp, life hit me square in the face, and I was forced to question the illusion. I was put in a pressure cooker that baked the manipulation out of me, and since then I've been helping others find their way back down the Yellow Brick Road to financial reality.

In fact, not only am I going to help you stop surrendering your financial future, but I'm going to help you transform your debt into blessing—transform your bill payments into wealth investments. It's easier than you think, and it's the only way for us average citizens to end up with the retirement incomes we deserve.

So, I ask the question again: Are people really manipulating you into giving them your money? Yes!

And once you see how your wealth is subtly being stolen from you, you'll be open to a whole new financial reality. A reality where achieving debt-free financial independence is clearly possible for the average-income earner. And I want to make the point that this book is written by a regular person, for regular people. As I peruse bookstore shelves, I find plenty of financial publications for those extraordinary folks with tens or hundreds of thousands of dollars to invest, who are just looking for the best places to put those dollars to work.

These books expound on the "best, fastest, most powerful" ways to invest all the extra money *most average income earners simply don't have,* and they seem to ignore the fact that for most people, the obstacle preventing them from becoming wealthy is *not* that they're unaware of the latest investment technique . . . it's that they don't have any significant money to invest each month! And this includes relatively high-income earners, whose higher monthly expenses keep them nearly as close to the financial edge each month as their lower-income neighbors.

GERRY THE LAWYER'S STORY

In 1991, when I wrote my first book on the financial strategy I'm going to teach you in these pages, I began selling it through direct marketing. I wanted to be sure I didn't do or say anything that could get me into trouble, so I contacted a lawyer who had been referred to me as an expert on certain kinds of marketing.

Gerry and I had a cordial conversation, and he asked me to send him my book and all marketing materials for his review. I overnighted them that day.

The following afternoon the phone rang. "This is Gerry. I worked out my debt-elimination plan this morning, and I'll be completely debt-free in just over three years! My wife and I will be able to retire as millionaires well before we ever thought we could retire. I want three more copies of your book for my adult children. Just include a bill with them, and I'll pay it!"

This was more than a decade ago, so the details are a little fuzzy, but as I recall, I hardly got to say anything besides "Hello" when I first answered the phone. Finally, after nearly ten minutes of

Gerry telling me how he'd always made a good income as a lawyer but was not really doing much better than people who made a lot less money, I finally had to interrupt him to find out if my marketing materials were legal. "Oh, yes . . . they're fine."

About three years later, Gerry told me that he was debt-free and building retirement wealth. He also reported that one of his children had paid off all his debts, and the other two were close behind. Then several years ago, during one of our business conversations, Gerry mentioned that he and his wife had just purchased a winter home in Florida, something they "never would have accomplished" without the plan you're going to learn in this book.

∞

Now let's get back to those investment books I find on most bookstore shelves. They seem to ignore the fact that most people just don't want to have to learn a lot of technical stuff to achieve financial independence. They want to live their regular lives, with their regular families, but still end up financially secure . . . so they can enjoy their regular-but-happy golden years with their regular loved ones.

I believe that what most people *do* want is an uncomplicated way to achieve true financial independence using the income they already produce, without having to become a great investor like Warren Buffett or a powerful entrepreneur like Michael Dell. I believe that, like me, they want to live their lives more or less normally, enjoying their loved ones, their hobbies, and their dream vocations, without having to expend themselves in the grinding pursuit of wealth.

Does that sound like you? Would you like to achieve debt-free financial independence without having to become a different person to do it? Would you like that process to be a natural progression from where you are now, and a result of the income you're already producing? If your answer is yes, I have good news for you: You're already a millionaire in the making. All I'm going to do is show you how to end up with the fruit of your labors, instead of giving it away to a powerful combination of opponents set on taking it from you.

"Me . . . a millionaire in the making?" you ask. "Is he kidding?"

Let's do the math.

At the time of the 2000 census, the median U.S. household annual income was $40,800. We're talking household here, not individual, so if you and your spouse work, both your incomes constitute the "household" income. The average person works more than forty years, but we'll just say forty to keep the numbers round and easy to work with. Now multiply $40,800 a year by forty years. If your calculator is programmed the same as mine, that comes out to $1,632,000. This median American household is a *millionaire household*!

Your household income may be higher or lower than $40,800, so do that math yourself. And if your household's income is currently lower than this median amount, consider the fact that most people's incomes increase over their working lives, so try to estimate what your income will likely *average* over your working decades.

Just to put this in perspective for a particular occupation, I was crawling down a Chicago "expressway" one day, and to keep myself from dozing off I started reading the lettering on the back door of the eighteen-wheeler I was following. The company was advertising to recruit more drivers, and the message said, "Our average driver made $56,700 last year." Let's do the math: $56,700 a year times forty working years equals $2,268,000. Next time you meet a truck driver, be sure to give him or her the appropriate respect a multimillionaire deserves!

The point? The money's there for most regular people—average-income earners—to become millionaires. The problem for you and me is that our incomes are being systematically siphoned out of our lives. So my job is to pull back the curtain and show you who's doing that and how it's being done. Then my job will shift to showing you a simple system for redirecting your money so it builds your wealth instead of others'. You'll go from having to work for money, to having money work for you. You'll go from having no options, to having unlimited options.

And that's what this book is ultimately about—giving you the options most people never have to choose the lifestyle that best suits you: living where you want, doing what you want, enjoying the people the good Lord has put into your life. And that takes money. So this book is really a wealth-building book.

You may be uneasy with my putting the good Lord in the same paragraph with wealth-building, so let me put this issue into a biblical perspective.

A form of the word *prosper* appears more than eighty times in the Old and New Testaments. The most common Hebrew word for "prosper" is *tsalach* (tsaw-lakh'), which means "to advance, make progress, succeed, be profitable. To bring to successful issue; to experience prosperity." But, in context, it's clear that these various forms of prosperity are blessings the Lord gives his people when they follow his commands:

> Blessed is the man
> Who walks not in the counsel of the ungodly,
> Nor stands in the path of sinners,
> Nor sits in the seat of the scornful;
> But his delight is in the law of the LORD,
> And in His law he meditates day and night.
> He shall be like a tree
> Planted by the rivers of water,
> That brings forth its fruit in its season,
> Whose leaf also shall not wither;
> And *whatever he does shall prosper.* (Ps. 1:1–3, emphasis added)

> This Book of the Law shall not depart from your mouth, but you shall meditate in it day and night, that you may observe to do

according to all that is written in it. For *then you will make your way prosperous,* and then you will have good success. (Josh. 1:8, emphasis added)

The blessing of the LORD *makes one rich,* and He adds no sorrow with it. (Prov. 10:22, emphasis added). (And The Amplified Bible adds, "neither does toiling increase it.")

And you shall remember the LORD your God, for it is He who gives you power *to get wealth,* that He may establish His covenant which He swore to your fathers, as it is this day. (Deut. 8:18, emphasis added)

So, when I say I'm going to help you "build wealth," I'm talking about helping you secure God's blessings. Financial blessings . . . wealth . . . which he intends for you to both enjoy and put to work.

But, to help you achieve this wealth—and keep it—I first have to unveil those who are committed to taking it away from you. So let me tell you a story of a subtle conspiracy. A convenient arrangement among the most influential forces on the planet. A shadowy relationship designed to take most of the money you earn over your lifetime away from you. And they do this by manipulating reality to slant the financial playing field in their direction.

WHOSE REALITY IS THIS?

Have you ever wondered whether the "reality" you see and experience each day is . . . well . . . *real*? Are you sure the choices you make—particularly when it comes to your money—proceed from your own core values and needs, or are they choices you're very cleverly manipulated into making?

Are you really in control of your life, your likes and dislikes, your attitudes about the world around you? Are the TV, radio, newspapers, magazines, movies, music, and other media sources in your life simply mirrors that reflect the existing culture back to you, or are they propaganda portals that indoctrinate you to a vision of life and a set of core values that fit someone else's purposes? Is this particularly true when it comes to your financial mind-set and behaviors?

You probably believe you make self-determined consumer and financial decisions, and that's understandable, because you're supposed to believe that. But who's creating the backdrop, the value system on which you're basing your decisions? Is it possible you're being manipulated by powerful and influential forces with manipulations so subtle, you are clueless? And could it be that because everyone around you is being simultaneously manipulated, it appears you're all in step? Could it be that because everyone around you accepts this "reality," you don't question it, and therefore believe it to be your *chosen* path?

"Woof woof!" Okay . . . Toto's going to start pulling back the curtain now, and I want you to pay attention to that man behind the curtain, 'cause it's me.

That's right. I know this money-draining manipulation is ongoing, because I've been behind the curtain, working some of the machinery. But I've written this book because I've also been a trembling consumer in the presence of the wizard's awesome image.

I spent most of the last three decades behind the curtain in the marketing industry, winning a couple of high-profile international marketing awards and rapidly building my own marketing company to where it was three times elected to *Inc.* magazine's prestigious "Inc. 500" list of the five hundred fastest-growing private companies in America. Am I trying to throw my arm out of joint patting myself on the back?

Nope. I'm simply explaining that I know how the process works, and I'm going to unveil some of the mechanisms behind it so you have a fighting chance to defend yourself. Once we've established a strong defensive position, we'll move on to a powerful offense designed to turn your looming financial defeat into ultimate victory. By "victory," I mean you'll be debt-free and have all the money you need to live as you like, whether you choose to work or not. Pretty simple, huh?

THEY WANT TO USE YOU

Many of the influences pressed on our culture by the merchants, the media, the advertising industry, and the credit industry are cleverly designed to motivate you to sacrifice yourself—particularly your finances—to this collection of powerful organizations. This amoral and soulless group intends to use you like a little wealth engine—to benefit itself, not you and those you really care about.

It took a personal financial crash for me to face this truth and gain control of my future, but I don't want you to have to experience what I did to learn these important lessons. It's been said that a smart person learns from his or her mistakes, but a genius learns from the mistakes of others. I'm betting you're a genius.

WELCOME TO THE REAL WORLD

At the risk of mixing metaphors, I'm going to take on one more persona to help expose this exploitation. In addition to being your Toto, I'm also going to be your Neo. Have you seen the movie *The Matrix*? The hero, played by Keanu Reeves, helps free the world from a master manipulation being perpetrated on its people.

If you haven't seen the movie, you'll have to suspend reality a little (like you didn't with *The Wizard of Oz!*) because the setting is an unbelievable future reality. You'd also have to suspend reality to think I have anything in common with Keanu Reeves, but that's not really important for this discussion.

In *The Matrix*, nearly all the humans on earth are experiencing what they think is reality, but each person's reality is actually images and emotions being fed directly into their brain by powerful machines who got so smart they took over the planet. In fact, the humans are simply being used by the machines like batteries. They lie, unconscious, in liquid-filled pods, while their body heat and electrical energy feed and power the machines.

Human-filled pods, as far as the eye can see, from a chilling vision, but that's a pretty close analogy to our financial reality today. We're being used by a powerful coalition of economic and cultural giants who are feeding us an illusory reality, while we quietly and cooperatively feed them our wealth.

In the movie, Neo is the character empowered to challenge the machines' control over humans. He gradually frees the humans from their counterfeit, involuntary reality to their conscious, self-willed, self-determined future. So, like Neo, I'm here to tell you you're being used, like a battery, to power the operation and expansion of these mercenary giants—who have no regard for your short- or long-term financial well-being. You're being fed illusions of progress and prosperity, while the financial life is being drained out of you.

Of course, the media, a member of this coalition, would complain that they're just "reflecting reality" back to you. They'd say they don't influence or create the cultural reality, they just mirror what's already going on.

Let's examine that.

Are they just showing you what's in . . . what's new? Are they just trying to make a buck the good old capitalist way, by advertising to you what you've already indicated you want and need? Are they just making you offers you could easily refuse? Or are they creating and feeding you a cultural and peer-pressure reality that generates almost irresistible "wants" and "needs" for the things they've already predetermined to trade you for your hard-earned money? Are they training you in a set of financial behaviors designed to feed your wealth into their hands?

How about the merchants and credit companies? Are they just trying to help you enjoy a better life? Or are they subtly trading prosperity illusions for your hard-earned cash? Are they swapping short-term gain for your long-term pain? Is the price of using credit a harmless, small charge, or is it a cancer, slowly but increasingly draining the financial life from your future?

Having been an insider, I assure you their purposes are not harmless. I'll explain in more detail in a moment, but first let me tell you how I began to see what is really happening—what they're really up to.

My Story

I thought I was living the American Dream—a financially successful life, according to the way the culture commonly defines it. I was senior partner in a successful business, I had a big home in a place-to-be Chicago suburb, I drove a new gold Corvette, I had an airplane parked at the nearby airport, my wife and I took expensive vacations, and all our clothes had the right labels. We could afford it all on our monthly cash flow, so I figured this was it—I had caught the brass ring. This was the success all the books talked about.

But deep in the recesses of my mind, I worried about the fact that in spite of our healthy income, we weren't really getting anywhere. We were running in place financially. We looked good doing it, but the scenery wasn't changing because we weren't really moving forward.

Then one bleak day the sole source for the product our company was selling went out of business, and before we could recover, we were out of business too. Virtually overnight, my income went from really good to really zero. That's when I realized: I hadn't achieved anything. I had just been *renting* someone else's definition of the American Dream. I had been handing over the bulk of my income each month for the right to keep "using" all the stuff in my life, but my money wasn't really helping me "own" anything. I wasn't becoming wealthy or secure.

I was simply funneling my income to the big businesses who had sold me the illusion. They had convinced me, over time, that I "needed" the illusion . . . then they rented me the components of the illusion . . . then they let me live it for as long as I could continue the rent payments. When I couldn't make the payments, I was evicted from the illusion.

Unless you've experienced this, you may have a little trouble tracking my emotions, but I went from stunned to defensive to depressed. No sooner had it sunk in that my big income was gone, than it seeped through the fog that all my creditors still expected to be paid. It was a real shocker the next day when I went to the mailbox and found bills. Hadn't they heard I had no income?

I wondered where the sympathy and understanding were. I had played the game according to their rules, and I had played it well. I had funneled tens of thousands of dollars to my creditors, but I was still just a number. And now I was a troublesome number that wasn't cooperating with the rules of the game. I wasn't feeding their appetite for money, so they no longer had kind words for me. I was disillusioned. But, as a wise man once told me, that just meant I had lost my illusions . . . and I was beginning to see reality.

A lesser man might have folded under the pressure, but I'm here to tell you that I responded well to the challenge. I became a great salesperson.

I sold the Corvette. I sold my wife's new Oldsmobile Regency Brougham. I sold the airplane. In fact, in an effort to save the house, I sold everything that couldn't run away. Thankfully, after a couple of months, I secured a good job and we were able to hang on to the house, but my new income was nowhere near what it had been in the business, so we were perpetually behind. What followed was the worst year of my life.

You might know what it's like. You juggle the bills, put them in a hat or something, and try to pay as many creditors as you can, but it doesn't take long before you're getting those insane phone calls. You know, the ones where the person says, "Well, Mr. Cummuta, I see you didn't pay the $50 you owed us last month."

"Yeah, I know. I'm still trying to catch up from having my business crash. I don't have enough to cover everyone completely."

"Okay. Well, then we'll be needing you to catch up. So when can you send in $100?"

"Excuse me, but like I just said, I don't have enough to even cover everyone's minimum monthly payment. I didn't pay you last month because I didn't have $50. So where do you expect me to find $100?"

"I understand. So when will you be sending in the $100?"

That's how my life was for about a year. Then one morning I found myself staring in the mirror at a face that looked like a prisoner of war's. Deep, dark circles framing hollow eyes with no personality. I felt helpless and hopeless, and no matter how I looked at it, I couldn't see a way out. I had long since forgotten my delusions of financial independence and the good life. I was now on the bottom of Maslow's hierarchy of needs. It was strictly *survival* time.

Then it hit me: It wasn't the loss of income that had put me in this position. It was how I had used the money that had come through my hands. It was the debts! Yes, I had experienced an interruption on the money supply side. But what was killing me was the demand side, and I was totally responsible for having allowed all that demand to be created in my life.

Suddenly I saw the lips move on the face in the mirror: "I will never be this vulnerable again!" The mist was clearing in my fatigued brain, and I acknowledged having painted myself into this corner, living what I had been sold as the fast-lane lifestyle, much of it on credit. I was experiencing the reality that when you owe people . . . they own you. Soon the full scope of what I had done rushed over me.

I had promised away my income for years, even decades into the future. I hadn't been working for myself and my family, I had been working for the merchants and creditors. I—the one who thought he knew how the world worked—obviously didn't know how money worked. So I set to learning.

Over the next year I read every financial book I could get my hands on. I attended financial seminars, workshops, and conferences all across the country. I subscribed to over forty financial newsletters and devoured every issue. I was on a mission. And after all the study, development, and testing, I created the initial version of what is now called the *Transforming Debt into Wealth*® system. Here's how it worked for us:

We had twenty-six years left on our mortgage, along with other assorted debts. When I ran them all through my new system, it showed we could pay everything off—including the total mortgage—in just four years, seven months. It further showed that, after we were debt-free, if we invested the money we had been wasting on debt payments, we'd have over $3 million by age sixty-five. All with the *same money* we were currently bringing home.

Excited enough to jump through the roof but not wanting to jump to conclusions, I next tried my system on friends and family. Lois and I both come from large families, so we had a considerable sample base. This experiment proved the system would likely work for everyone, regardless of income or debt level. Now we were really excited, so—in less than five years—we followed our system to debt-free financial independence.

As I sit here writing this book, we have no debts, we own everything in our lives, and we live off the cash flow generated by our investments. And we accomplished this with our paychecks!

But the fact that the system worked so well and so quickly actually made us angry, because we realized how we'd been manipulated into believing we'd have to live with debt till we died. We had gone from paycheck to paycheck, handing the money over to creditors, taking for granted that we'd always have a car payment, always have a house payment, and always have credit card payments.

WE WERE MANIPULATED

A little self-analysis revealed that my desire for success and self-gratification had been used against me to entice me to overextend myself. I had been cheered on by my creditors and the other purveyors of the *success illusion,* with the mantra that "only today mattered." The images, messages, and indoctrination being fed to me said that what *was* important was what we drove, where we lived, how we dressed, and where and how often we vacationed. "Tomorrow's a million years away, and it'll all just work out somehow. Don't worry," the subliminal messages soothed. "Just keep the payments flowing!"

But when the illusion was shattered, I had to ask myself how I had become so deceived. Where did the deception begin? Had I been sabotaged somehow?

It didn't take long for me to connect the dots back to when I was just a little guy watching my dad handle his finances. He thought credit was the eighth wonder of the world. To him it was just the coolest thing that when the washing machine broke, someone would let him have a brand-new one for just $24 a month. He never thought about the cost to his ultimate wealth. That's what I learned about money at home. But that lesson was a lie. My dad was loving, funny, and generous, but he never understood money. His only goal was to bring it in as fast as it was going out, and he died young on that treadmill.

When I grew up, I emotionally reacted to having witnessed his being crushed by what I viewed as insufficient income. So I bought into the "success illusion" hook, line, and sinker. I thought that more and more money would be the solution, and that's precisely what the powers behind our culture wanted me to believe. They wanted me to work myself to death earning that money, while I progressively handed most of it over to rent the trappings of a "successful" lifestyle.

Of course, when we're on the treadmill we're told all along that we're building wealth. But whose wealth are we really building? Who's actually ending up with it?

The incident that started me asking that question happened shortly before our big financial crash. My son Adam, who was about fourteen at the time, was studying something about compound interest in school, and he asked me how it worked. So, seizing upon a teaching moment, I went to the kitchen bill drawer and pulled out the latest mortgage payment. Our payment was $1,500 a month, and I explained every number and every term. I was proud of my parental prowess.

Then, after casually staring at the payment coupon for a moment, he said, "So let me be sure I understand this right. They're charging you $1,390 to use their $110 this month?"

I ripped the coupon back from him and stared at it myself. There it was, in black-and-white: payment = $1,500; interest = $1,390; principal = $110. There was almost no other way to look at it. They were charging me $1,390 to use their $110 dollars that month, and that was sickening. I don't mean just figuratively. I mean I felt queasy, but I let the nausea subside and made the payment, because we wanted to continue living there. Later, however—after the crash—I remembered the experience, and it hardened my resolve to free myself and my family from the wealth-draining matrix.

How Much Are Your Rent Payments?

Are you just renting your lifestyle? Is the money flowing through your life, while you enjoy temporary custody of the illusion? Let's follow the dollars and find out.

You work hard each week to earn a paycheck, but whose money is in that check? Is it really yours to do with as you choose, or have you promised the bulk of it away to your creditors? Stop paying your bills for a few months, and you'll find out who really owns everything in your life. They will soon be rapping on your door, asking for the keys to *their* car or to *their* house. You might find yourself sitting and sleeping on the floor or watching that old black-and-white TV because the home entertainment center was just carried out the door.

What happens when you get a raise? Does it just get absorbed into your spending patterns without seeming to make that much of a difference? Is your spouse or other household member working? Is that really improving your prosperity?

Welcome to Oz. Welcome to the matrix. You're being used to work hard to produce wealth, but it's being cleverly diverted to make a few huge industries richer, while you get used up. When you get old, you'll eventually be thrown away, replaced by younger workers, with more wealth-producing years ahead of them. But don't you dare stop making your payments just because you're old.

"Wait," you might complain. "I'm working as hard as I can, and I'm making the best decisions I can from the options put before me. I'm trying to put a little money away in my 401(k), and we're adding a little extra to each bill when we pay it."

"Why Can't We Get Ahead?"

As I said earlier, if you're like most people, you're not getting ahead because you don't have enough available money to invest. Period.

You've likely promised away your monthly cash flow and have little or nothing left to funnel into investments. You've been subtly and deftly maneuvered into trading your hard-earned income, over your lifetime, for a rented illusion of prosperity. And now your piece of your paycheck isn't enough to build significant wealth.

And a powerful part of this manipulation is that you'd somehow be a lot better off if you just made a little more money. But the facts show that when most people realize an income increase, their spending habits absorb the additional money without a significant change in their true financial pictures. They *consume* (destroy) the additional money. It normally goes into a bigger TV, a newer car, fancier furnishings, more shoes or jewelry, more expensive recreational toys. In other words, bigger and newer versions of things they usually already have. It's *consumption* in its purest form, and it's right out of the manipulation handbook of the forces benefiting from our consumption.

The good news is, once I help you see through this manipulation, you *can* turn it around, whether or not you increase your income. Most people who follow the plan I'll lay out for you in these pages are completely debt-free—including their home mortgages—in just five to seven years. From that point on, building wealth is an almost unavoidable consequence of having so much money to invest each month.

And before you assume this is some kind of tightwad austerity program, it's not. It's obvious that you cannot spend everything that comes into your life now and somehow hope to achieve financial independence later. But neither is it necessary to spend nothing now and defer it all to the future. The process I'm unfolding here is one of *managing* spending, not ceasing it. It's about making informed, conscious purchases, based on *your* plan, not the plans of outside forces who are pursuing their interests over yours.

I've been teaching these principles for more than a decade, and I've found that when most people discover how they're being manipulated, they resist fiercely. I'm counting on that in you. What we're talking about here are learned behaviors that are working against you, but behaviors can be modified. I'm going to help you identify outside financial influences that you may not be aware of, then we'll identify and correct any consequential behaviors that are undermining your success.

You'll stop feeding the financial system and have the system start feeding you. You'll create a life and achieve goals of *your* choosing. You may end up a debt-free millionaire. It will likely be possible, no matter how impossible it might feel right now. But first, you have to let me pull back the curtain and expose the wizard. You have to let me disconnect you from the matrix and help you build a life of your own design in the real world.

The first step is to identify your opponent.

2

THE COALITION
OF FOUR

∞

There's a shadowy relationship among the four most powerful industries in our economy, and your financial survival depends on understanding that relationship. I call them the Coalition of Four. This alliance is made up of Merchants, the Advertising Industry, the Media, and the Credit Industry, and they have but one purpose—their mutual enrichment.

This group is not necessarily evil in its intent, but it is destructive in its effect. In fact, emotion is not the driving force behind the Coalition members' insatiable appetite for our money. They simply exist to grow. These industries, and the people who run them, know only balance sheets, revenue forecasts, and shareholder dividends, which all must show continued growth. The executives who manage these huge corporations are hired by the stockholders for a single purpose: to make the numbers rise, quarter after quarter, year after year.

I'm dating myself here, but I can remember comedian Flip Wilson pleading, "The devil made me do it," after getting caught doing something naughty. Well, I believe Satan takes advantage of the Coalition's natural greed and obsession for growth and uses it to keep you and me financially anemic, so we can't properly fund the work of God's kingdom or receive the blessings that come from tithing and offerings. So while the Coalition members might not themselves be evil, the devil makes them do hurtful things to us to foster the growth on which they're so focused.

You see, the principal resource these industries feed on to continue their growth is our money. They know that all money starts its journey through the economy in the hands of income earners, so the Coalition of Four cooperatively creates a culture and supporting mechanisms to consistently and relentlessly move that money from our *consumer* bank accounts to their Coalition bank accounts. Jesus put it this way in Luke 16:8: "For the sons of this world are more shrewd in their generation than the sons of light."

Let's see just how shrewd they are. We'll start with the part the Merchants play in the Coalition of Four.

The Merchants Depend on Our Weakness

Hedonism, avarice, and self-gratification lie within the workings of every man and woman. The Merchants depend on these human urges to be insatiable, and they operate on the premise that you and I will never be content with the lives we live and the things we have. We'll never have enough stuff, and we'll never tire of rewarding ourselves with indulgent experiences. So they produce endless streams of products and services, and they depend on their Coalition partners to keep us buying those products and services.

Statistics appear to prove the Merchants' assumptions correct. According to one IRS study, the number one reported reason why people failed financially was *the inability to delay gratification.* We want what we want . . . and we want it now!

In a speech to the nation while he was president, Jimmy Carter said, "In a nation that was proud of hard work, strong families, close-knit communities, and our faith in God, too many of us now tend to worship self-indulgence and consumption. Human identity is no longer defined by what one does, but by what one owns."

Mr. Carter was trying to get the American people to reconsider their "self-indulgent consumption," but he failed . . . because he was opposed by the Coalition of Four. Historian David Shi says, "He [President Carter] totally ignored the fact that the country's dominant institutions—corporations, advertising, popular culture—were instrumental in promoting and sustaining the hedonistic ethic." Mr. Shi listed everyone in the Coalition except the Credit Industry, but I'm sure he recognized their part in the process as well.

Notice his words: The Coalition is "instrumental in promoting and sustaining the hedonistic ethic." This is how they seduce us, drain our resources until we're too old to produce them anymore, then throw us away in favor of younger income earners. They don't just feed off our hedonism, our inability to delay gratification; they *create* it, *promote* it, and *sustain* it. Our weakness is their strength.

THE MERCHANTS ARE THE TAIL, NOT THE HEAD

You might think the Merchants would be the kingpins, the drivers of this unholy alliance, but they exist only to create and provide products and services the other three partners need continually in the pipeline to keep the machine running. This is an important point in helping you understand the scope of their operation. The Coalition looks at you and me as revenue sources—not people, just revenue sources. Its members look at us as manipulatable entities from which they can siphon a predictable amount of money each year, each decade, and over our lifetimes. One of marketing's vogue terms is a customer's "Lifetime Value" or LTV. Our value to them, over our lifetimes, is measured by them in dollars.

I look at my wife, and I certainly don't equate the value of her life to me in terms of dollars. When I'm playing with my grandsons, or enjoying a visit with one of my children, I don't put a dollar value on it. It would be weird or even offensive if I did. But that's because these wonderful people are valued by me in a way dollars could never represent.

The Coalition, on the other hand, has no such emotional framework within which to value my wife, my grandsons, my children, you, or me. They see each of us simply as representing a certain number of dollars over the period between our first transaction with them and the date we expire, figuratively or literally. They look at us with neither evil intent nor benevolence. They simply want to find ways to manipulate the maximum LTV out of each of us.

THE MERCHANTS ARE THE MASTERS OF MANIPULATION

To succeed in this ongoing manipulation to get our hard-earned dollars, the Merchants know they must trade something they can convince us has value . . . and *they don't really care what it is.* A product is just a *thing* to them, an object around which their Advertising Industry partners can build a perceived value, so they can brainwash us into wanting it and eventually get us to trade our dollars for it. The Merchants' principal part in the process is simply to keep coming up with *things* that can be foisted on us manipulated income earners . . . at a profit.

Just look at all the worthless, mind-numbing gadgets and widgets offered in the overnight and weekend infomercials and direct-TV commercials. These products generate untold millions of dollars for the Coalition. But take a good look at the products. Do we really *need* them? Mankind has lived perfectly well for thousands and thousands of years without infinite versions of vegetable choppers, suction storage bags, wrinkle-reducing creams, sandwich cookers, and abdominal exercisers, just to name a few. We don't really *need* those things.

It's the Coalition of Four who needs them, so it continually has something new to stuff into our lives. We obediently buy the junk, use it for a while, then shoehorn it into a closet, the attic, the garage, or the basement. No sooner have we chucked a former "must-have" item out of sight, than we're back dialing a toll-free number to order something new. Check your closets, attic, garage, and basement to see how much stuff you bought thinking you couldn't live without it. Now it's just taking up space, and the Coalition has your money. Money that could otherwise be building *your* wealth instead of theirs.

But these notorious $19.95 impulse buys are only the tail sticking out of the doghouse. The Coalition's relentless assault on your wallet, purse, and bank account runs the full spectrum of furniture, jewelry, cars, boats, houses, vacations, and anything else they can convince you that you need . . . or that you need a newer, bigger, shinier, more impressive version of. Your senses and emotions are under attack every waking moment, and even some of your dreaming moments, with seductions designed to keep the flow of your money moving into Coalition coffers.

And this ongoing seduction is necessary because Coalition members have built their business models around getting you to buy everything you could possibly need . . . then more than you need—*a lot more* than you need.

But none of us naturally want "more than enough." At least not to the extent that we'd go into debt to get it. So someone has to seduce us, whip up our emotions, and condition us to throw reason out the window and overextend financially. This is where the Merchants join with the second member of the Coalition: Madison Avenue—the Advertising Industry.

THE ADVERTISING INDUSTRY
RELIES ON YOUR NAÏVETÉ

You are bombarded with thousands of Advertising impressions a day. Over the past decade the number of commercials shown on network TV has increased by sixty-five thousand a year. To give you a dollar-value example of this Advertising onslaught, one Merchant, American Express, spends over $100 million a year on just print and TV ads. This doesn't count its radio, direct-mail, billboard, insert, e-mail, sponsorship, and other Advertising activity. And it's not the biggest Advertiser, by any means. It's a relentless assault, and it works!

What makes Advertising effective is the natural human trait of accepting things at face value. Combine that with everyone's upbringing to do what we're told, and most consumers behave like good little boys and girls who do exactly what Advertisers tell them to. Like when everyone's favorite teenage computer expert, Steven, used to say, "Dude, you're getting a Dell." After a number of exposures to Steven's good-natured urging, Dude, you were more and more likely to pick up the phone and order a Dell.

It's easy to underestimate the power this young man wielded for his handlers, and to believe he was just a randomly chosen, regular-looking teenage young man, with a happy face, recommending the virtues of Dell computers. But it's nothing as simple as that to those in the Advertising Industry. To them, finding the right person through whom to weave their web is as precise a process as selecting the right star for a Hollywood movie. Here's how it was explained in excerpts from a January 14, 2002, *USA Today* article on the most successful TV ads running at the time:

> As played by 21-year-old actor Benjamin Curtis, Steven is more than just a dude. He's something of a modern-day Tom Sawyer. Consumers both within and without his commercials are now repeating his catch phrase: "Dude, you're getting a Dell." He has wide appeal: Dell's fan mail ranges from teeny-bopper girls who want to date him, to seniors who like his Eddie Haskell charm.
>
> Curtis' star turn shows the importance of casting on Madison Avenue as well as in Hollywood. Ad agencies rely on copy, art direction and consumer research. But it all needs the perfect face.
>
> "The right cast is as important as the right message," says Paul Tilley, group creative director at DDB Chicago. "You need somebody to bring it to life." Agencies spend weeks searching for the right-

actors. First they put out a casting call. Then they hole up in conference rooms looking at audition tapes. Finally, they invite a few actors to read for the parts.

Like their Hollywood counterparts, they know when a star is born. Curtis, for example, was actually discovered by Dell's former agency, Lowe Worldwide, in New York. But once Dell shifted its $200 million account to DDB last year, both the client and the agency quickly saw they had a hit. Consumers participating in Ad Track, *USA Today's* weekly survey, think Dell made the right casting call.

"People love him and want to see more of him," says Claire Bennett, senior manager of consumer advertising for Dell.

"Steven appeals to all ages," Tilley says. The company and agency get calls, letters and e-mail asking for pictures and personal information about Curtis.

"Our business results bear out the effectiveness of these spots," says Bennett.

Business results are the *only* results that matter to the Coalition, and whatever it takes to manipulate you into buying what they're selling, they'll find it out and put it into their commercial messages. The gurus of the Advertising Industry are master manipulators. They condition us to respond to their seductions like Pinocchio dancing at the end of their strings . . . without a thought as to the consequences. But these marionettes know their effect would be significantly limited if they could work only through overt commercial messages, because you and I generally recognize unmasked Advertising as biased in favor of the Advertiser. In other words, we usually recognize that ads are not objective, so their influence on us is reduced by good old human skepticism.

Madison Avenue knows this, so it orchestrates another Coalition partner to foist supposedly unbiased messengers on us. Enter the third Coalition member, the Media, to create a world where it appears important to have the products or services being pushed by the Merchants and Advertisers.

THE MEDIA CREATE YOUR EMOTIONAL "NEEDS"

The Media's part in this four-legged wealth destroyer is to create a "reality" in your mind that generates an apparent "need" for products and services the Coalition is selling.

Have you ever wondered why you like to wear certain clothes? Look at what your favorite TV show characters wear. Look at what your favorite music artists wear. Look at what all the beautiful people in your favorite magazines wear. Look at what the most popular people at school or work wear. Look at what *their* favorite TV show characters wear. And so on, through as many levels as you'd care to track.

Have you ever wondered why you started drinking cappuccino or designer bottled water? Look at what your favorite TV show and movie characters drink. Look at what your favorite music artists drink. Look at what all the beautiful people in your favorite magazines are drinking, and what the articles in those magazines tell you is cool or healthy or "in" to drink. I'm not debating the health benefits of drinking clean water. But I am asking you to consider why you might feel the "need" to pay more than a dollar-a-bottle for designer water rather than get 33-cents-a-gallon refill water at Wal-Mart or other discount stores.

Have you ever wondered why you love the car you either drive now or are dying to buy? Look at what your favorite movie characters drive. Look at the images of the people in the commercials advertising the car. Do you want to be like them? Look at the sexual implications of owning that car. If you're a man, are the Advertisers trying to make you think the car will transform you into a studly chick magnet? If you're a female, are they trying to make you think the car will transform you into a hip, sophisticated, mature woman . . . or into a hot, sexy, young woman?

Would you have felt the "need" for these things had you never seen them used by celebrities or seductively advertised as if they will turn you into a more desirable person?

SYNERGY: THE POWER OF ADS AND MEDIA WORKING TOGETHER

Have you ever noticed how the clothing, cars, furniture, fashions, hairstyles, and lifestyles in your favorite movies and TV programs are also being advertised around and during those shows? Have you also noticed how similar ads simultaneously show up on your favorite radio stations and in your favorite magazines? Have you ever noticed how the movies, TV shows, and magazine articles cooperatively create or promote a certain culture . . . then the Advertisers offer you the components of that culture through interweaved commercials?

These synergistic scenarios are orchestrated by the Advertising Industry to create just the right images and emotions—images and emotions that will make you want the things the Coalition is selling. Like combination punches in a boxing match, the effect of seeing your favorite celebrity wearing a certain style of clothes or driving a certain brand of car, then seeing the same clothing or car offered in an adjacent commercial, is overpowering. It literally creates a subconscious emotional reality that says, "I have to wear and drive what I see my favorite celebrities wearing and driving, or I'll be hopelessly out of style. Everyone will think more of me if I'm in step with what the images in the Media are showing as trendy."

The Advertising Industry coordinates this campaign, directing the Media's influences over us. They work directly with the Merchants, who have "new and improved" products and services to sell to us. As I said earlier, these products and services are mostly just more "stuff." Stuff that's no better or more valuable than the "stuff" we already have. It's just more "stuff" they can sell us because they want more of our money.

So the Advertising Industry tells the Media how these products and services are to be featured in TV shows, music, movies, magazines, Web sites, and so on; then they complement and reinforce these exposures with adjacent Advertising designed to get us consumers to pull the trigger and buy. The Media are dependent on Advertiser dollars for their survival and prosperity, so they play their part in the Coalition and help their partners separate us from our money.

Every time you see a commercial during your favorite show, you're watching the Merchants and Advertising Industry pay their Coalition partners in the Media to influence you and me to desire the things the Merchants are advertising. When you or I make the purchase, those dollars go to the Merchant, who then pays the Advertising Agency, who then pays the Media in which the product was advertised. Each partner gets its piece. And when you see a brand-name product in a movie, that didn't happen by accident either. When you buy the product, that money goes to the Merchant, who then pays the Advertising Agency, who then pays the movie producer (Media) for the product's placement in the movie.

Products and services show up being used by the movie's hero or heroine. They show up in our favorite TV shows. They're sung about in songs. They're reported about in the news. They're featured in our favorite magazine articles. We, of course, think it's coincidence that we're seeing a product or service highlighted everywhere. More likely we don't think about it at all. The fact is, however, something's happening in our subconscious.

We naturally want to be like those we admire, so our subconscious moves us to emulate them. We try to look like them, buying the clothes, jewelry, tattoos, piercings, and hairstyles they wear. We try to drive what they drive. We try to eat and drink what they eat and drink. We try their recreational activities. We gradually modify our value sets and lifestyles to be more like theirs. This direct approach is only the first wave the Media use to influence us to buy the lifestyle, products, and services the Merchants and Advertising Industry are selling.

THE POWER OF THE PEER

The second and more subtle wave of attack on our emotions is based on the peer power of those around us . . . who are also trying to emulate the cultural icons du jour. To be liked, we feel we have to be *like* those around us, so we conform. We are followers following followers, and all the following costs money. We have to drive a car like our peers'. We have to dress like our peers. We have to take the same vacations. We have to buy from the same Web sites. This "keeping up with the Joneses" is an American national pastime, and it's a major wealth destroyer, because the Joneses are on the wrong road. They think they're having fun, but they're going broke feeding the Coalition's insatiable appetite for money.

The Joneses go to school—and pile up student loans and credit card debt. They get married and furnish their place on credit. They finance the purchase of a car at least as good as their neighbor's. Then it's a video-equipped minivan when the kids come along. They charge vacations and weekend getaways on whatever credit card isn't maxed out yet. They buy their kids every fad . . . with credit cards. They move into a bigger house about every seven years and trade cars every three to four years. They live their lives owning practically nothing, while owing nearly everyone.

The average American household members earn nearly $2 million over their working lives, but they give nearly all of it away trying to keep up with or impress their neighbors. In other words, they do it for pride. Please believe me: Using money in an attempt to buy status or to prop up a low self-image is the worst possible investment. As the Bible says in Proverbs 16:18, "Pride goes before destruction." The Merchants end up laughing all the way to the bank, and you end up crying all the way to the poorhouse, or to an early grave.

If the Joneses—and everyone trying to keep up with them—could only see the utter fruitlessness of this pursuit. You can never achieve victory in this competition because, in the midst of your pride-motivated buying, the Media keep raising the bar, telling you that you need new things, different things. You wouldn't want to be caught dead in last year's things. And did you notice the guy across the street already has next year's thing? It's a synergistic and nearly irresistible web of motivators designed to keep you buying and buying, and after a while this process exhausts your income.

You eventually run out of cash. You can no longer afford more than you really need. That's where the fourth Coalition member, the Credit Industry, steps up, ready to "help" by lending you the money to continue buying more than you need.

CREDIT COMPANIES—THEY MAKE IT POSSIBLE FOR YOU TO SACRIFICE YOURSELF

All the manipulation plans of the Advertising Industry and Merchants would not get very far if you had to pay cash for every purchase. If Merchants took only dollars or checks, they could sell you only things you really need and could afford. If you had to pull greenbacks from your wallet or purse for each purchase, you'd think too much and the impulse would wear off. So the money changers are right there in the temple, ready to advance you the amount you need for each transaction . . . for a "slight" fee, of course.

They say, "Give us your future, and we'll lend you the money to buy this thing you think you need right now."

IT WASN'T ALWAYS THIS WAY

The Coalition relationship between the Merchants and the Credit Industry is a twentieth-century phenomenon. A long time ago, when I was buying my first car on payments, I remember remarking to my uncle Jack how convenient General Motors made buying a car, by having General Motors Acceptance Corporation (GMAC) financing available right there at the dealership. Uncle Jack, who had worked for GM for many years, said, "You probably think General Motors is in the car business, but the only reason they make cars is so they have something to lend you money on. General Motors is in the money business." I laughed because I thought he was just being clever, but about a decade later GM came out with its GMAC MasterCard, and the curtain began slipping back to reveal the wizard.

General Motors Acceptance Corporation, established in 1919, repre-sented the beginning of the end of thinking that you couldn't buy some-thing until you could actually afford it. Up until that time, people didn't buy a car until they had saved up the money to pay the full price. All of a sudden GMAC made it possible to put down a percentage and make "small monthly payments," with a "small finance charge attached." Sounds sort of harmless, doesn't it?

Then, in 1950, Diners Club introduced the first credit card, and that began the spiral down to our present credit-based consumer society. One by one, more credit cards appeared, first offered by individual Merchants, then through banks as VISAs and MasterCards. People flocked to them because the cards appeared to enhance their lifestyles. But that was a lie. Using credit could never improve your lifestyle in a million years. Using credit, as an individual consumer, is a losing proposition—it can only diminish your lifestyle because it turns the power of compound interest against you.

COMPOUND INTEREST WORKING AGAINST YOU

Albert Einstein was once asked what was the greatest invention he'd seen in his lifetime. His answer: "Compound interest." Why would the man many consider the most intelligent who ever lived view something as common as compound interest to be a great invention? Because, much like creation itself, compound interest makes something out of nothing.

The American Heritage Dictionary defines *compound interest* as "inter-est computed on the accumulated unpaid interest as well as on the orig-inal principal." In that one short phrase lies the key to building wealth. What fascinated Einstein, and what excites every wealth accumulator in the world, is the idea that the interest I earn this month is itself earning interest next month. The following month, both this month's interest and next month's interest are earning interest. It's compounding!

How powerful is that? Let me show you.

In 1626 settlers purchased the island of Manhattan from local natives for $24 worth of beads and trinkets . . . and most people assume that to have been a pretty good deal. However, if the settlers had instead put that $24 in an interest-bearing account, compounding at just 8 percent annually, as of early 2003 it would have grown to $272 trillion. With $272 trillion, you could buy the island of Manhattan, including all the buildings, and have change left over to pick up a few smaller cities you might like to visit from time to time.

Yes, compound interest is powerful. Your problem is that when you have credit debt, you're on the *paying* side of compound interest. Its power is working against you. It is diminishing your financial resources, not multiplying them.

Today the average American household is paying more than 92 percent of its after-tax income on debt payments. In 1946 that was only 4 percent. The average American household is carrying a total of $8,123 in debt on credit cards alone. This doesn't count what it owes on cars, boats, the home, or any other noncredit card purchases. If this average household were to make just the minimum required payment on each monthly credit card bill, it would take thirty-seven years, six months for it to pay off the $8,123 . . . and the payments would total $21,117. That means, for borrowing $8,123 on credit cards, the family will pay back the $8,123 plus $12,994 interest!

The interest cost is greater than the amount borrowed. See the power of compound interest? See the damage caused by being on the wrong end of that power? Remember, *compound interest is always making someone rich*. In this case, it's the credit card companies.

Let's look at it a different way. Imagine yourself as a little business, and your monthly income is the business's revenue. In essence, when you use credit you're saying to the credit company, "I'm taking you on as a partner and giving you part ownership of the business. I hereby promise that a percentage of all the money *our business* makes from this point forward will belong to you, and I'll faithfully send you your share each month." The more credit offers you accept, the more partners you take on. And the more you use each credit source, the higher percentage of your income you're promising to that "partner." After a while, *your* percentage of your income is pretty small. You become a minority partner in your own business . . . your paycheck.

USING CREDIT WILL *NEVER* IMPROVE YOUR LIFESTYLE

Another way to understand the damage of using credit is to realize that when you decide to use financing of any kind as a financial tool, you are *choosing* to pay a higher price for everything you buy. You're saying, "I'm choosing to pay *price plus interest,*" while the people living cash-based lifestyles will pay only the *price* for each thing they buy.

Let's suppose you and a friend make the exact same income. You choose to use credit to get the things you want, while your friend decides to avoid credit and buy everything with cash. What you'll experience is something like the race between the tortoise and the hare.

For a brief period at the beginning of this race, you will *appear* to be winning, because you'll initially be able to run out and buy things you want, even if you can't really afford them. Whereas your friend will have to save up to buy the furniture, the stereo, whatever those purchases are. It won't take long, however, before you start experiencing what I call "credit-forced income degradation."

You and your friend will each be bringing home the same amount of money, but *you* won't own all of your income because you spent the early part of this financial race taking on partners and promising them chunks of it each month. Now you have to slice up each paycheck and hand the pieces over to those "partners" to whom it's committed. You have to live on whatever's left over.

Your friend, however, is not so encumbered. All of his paycheck still belongs to him, and this is where the tortoise passes the hare, never to look back. From this point on, *your friend will always be able to buy more things than you* because every penny of his income is still his.

Of course he has normal living expenses, like food, utilities, housing costs, and taxes, but so do you. So those expenses cancel out. However, these expenses highlight a growing difference between your credit-based strategy and your friend's cash-based strategy.

Let's again suppose that you both rent your housing. Assuming you'd both like to eventually buy a home, who do you think has the better chance of being able to save up a down payment? Obviously, your friend will be the first into a home. And since he will have no other debt obligations besides his mortgage, he'll be able to quickly pay it off.

So a handful of years down the road, your friend will not only live in his own home, but he'll actually own it. His net worth will include the full value of his home, he'll have no debts, and he'll be rapidly investing for retirement . . . while you'll still be trying to scrape together a house down payment with the few dollars you have left each month after paying your credit partners.

I could extend this story with endless examples of how your friend will be living a superior lifestyle to yours *because he chose to live on cash rather than credit,* but I believe the point has been made. It is *impossible* for credit to provide you (as an individual, not a business) with a better long-term lifestyle. The impression that it can improve your lifestyle is a lie that millions of Americans and consumers around the world fall for every day. It's one of the Coalition's greatest deceptions, and the credit card is its most destructive form.

WHEN A COMPANY GIVES YOU A CREDIT CARD, IT'S NOT REALLY *GIVING* YOU ANYTHING

It's amazing to watch people when they get a new credit card. They think the credit limit is an endowment. They feel and act as if someone has given them that amount of money, like it was a gift or inheritance, and they use it like disposable income. What a trap this is.

Let's say this person makes $35,000 a year, and one day she receives a credit card with a $2,500 limit. She immediately feels like she's a $37,500 income earner! And it doesn't take long before she's spending that $2,500 as if it's part of her income. In comes another partnership.

After a while this unfortunate consumer has to live as though she makes *less* than her actual income of $35,000, because now a portion of that income belongs to her new partner, for years into the future.

I call credit cards "consumer cocaine" because they're pushed like drugs, and people use them like drugs. If you're anywhere in the vicinity of "creditworthy," your mailbox is regularly populated with credit card offers, and these offers seduce you with low-interest or even no-interest introductory periods. The offers are designed to give you the impression the companies are offering "FREE Money!" But these offers are no different from the schoolyard pushers who offer kids free drug samples to get them hooked.

Credit cards are pushed like drugs, and credit cards are frequently used like drugs. You've had a tough week at work, and you deserve a treat, so you stop at the mall (a crack house for credit junkies). You slap down the plastic and give yourself a quick feel-good. But then when the bill comes in, you feel bad . . . so you go back to the mall for another feel-good. Of course, that makes the next bill go up even more, so it will take a bigger feel-good to overcome the hangover from the last one, and on the cycle goes—just like the cycle of a drug addict's life. It's scary.

But the analogy doesn't end there. Just as with the schoolyard drug pusher, once the introductory period is over, up pops the interest rate and you're forking over more and more of your hard-earned dollars to the Coalition. If you have a strong stomach and a good magnifying glass, read the fine print on the next credit card offer you receive. Look at what happens to the interest rate after the introductory period. Then look at the interest rate for cash advances. Then look at what happens to the interest rate if you're late with just one payment. Then look at some of the fees they'll charge you for using the ATM or if you make a late payment, bounce a check, or make any other possible mistake.

Yes, credit cards are consumer cocaine. They're pushed like drugs, frequently used like drugs, and they have long-term punishing effects like drugs. But as powerful a Coalition tool as credit cards are, their financial effect can often pale in comparison to your mortgage.

THE BIGGEST CHUNK OF INTEREST GOES TO YOUR MORTGAGE LENDER

If you total up the 360 monthly payments in a typical thirty-year mortgage, you'll find that you're going to pay back almost three times what you borrowed—one time for the money you borrowed, and two more times for the interest the Coalition is siphoning out of your life. But the problem is really worse than that, because we rarely stay in the same home for thirty years.

According to the National Association of Realtors, the average family changes homes about every seven years. This means most folks will have at least three homes over their lifetimes:

- Starter

- Step-up

- Ultimate

The problem is that in the early years of a mortgage, most of your monthly payment is interest, so after seven years you will have paid off only about 8 percent of the principal. This means after twenty-one years you'll be in your third house . . . and you'll still owe 92 percent of what you borrowed on it. Many people compound this already difficult situation by borrowing against the relatively small percentages of the houses they actually own. By taking out home equity loans and lines of credit, they give away the little net worth they have in their homes to debt obligations.

However, by following the simple principles I'm going to show you in this book, in that same twenty-one years, you can own your home and have hundreds of thousands of dollars in investments. Hundreds of thousands of dollars of wealth that can pay you income each month, instead of hundreds of thousands in debt that will continue to cost you money each month.

Think carefully about what I just said.

By using your income the way I'll show you, you could own your home and be debt-free with hundreds of thousands of dollars in investments. Or, by using *the same income* the way you're likely using it now—the way the Coalition of Four wants you to continue using it—at the end of *the same timeline,* you'd still owe 92 percent on your third home mortgage and have next to nothing in investments. Not to mention the fact that you'd probably also have car loans, credit card balances, and so on.

Which scenario would you pick, seeing that both can be accomplished using the income you bring home right now, over the *same* time period?

And don't be misled by apparently "low" mortgage interest rates. At the time of this writing, mortgage rates are relatively low, but the rates you see advertised are deceptive numbers because of a magic formula called amortizing. *Amortize* is defined in *The American Heritage Dictionary* as: "To liquidate (a debt, such as a mortgage) by installment payments or payment into a sinking fund."

Talk about a "sinking" fund. When you sign on the line for a mortgage, you dive into a sinkhole of major proportions. Just look at your monthly payment coupon and note what portion of that payment is interest. That's the rate you're really paying. Remember when I was teaching my son about compound interest, and I discovered that $1,390 of my $1,500 monthly mortgage payment was interest? I was literally paying 92.6 percent interest!

Most people who feel good because they have 7 percent or lower mortgages are really paying 92 percent or more interest, month after month. Then they refinance or buy new homes and start over again at the highest interest end of their loans' amortization schedules. If you have a 7 percent mortgage loan, you would indeed pay only 7 percent interest—*if you paid the entire balance off in the first year.* But since you use the nice loan company's amortization, you'll be paying more than 90 percent interest for a long time to come.

Whenever I mention paying off mortgages at a seminar, people will invariably raise the objection that they don't want to lose their mortgage-interest tax deduction. First of all, you continue to enjoy the deduction all through the mortgage payoff period. But more important, the mortgage-interest tax deduction is a bad deal, so don't worry about losing it.

I remember when I first told my accountant I was going to pay off my house. He said, "Don't do that, John. It's the last tax shelter left for the average guy."

Well, I thought about what he said because he was a CPA and a smart guy. But after I chewed on it a while, I said, "Tony, you're telling me to continue paying $1 of interest to the mortgage company, so I can save 28 cents in taxes (I was in the 28 percent tax bracket). It seems to me I'd be 72 cents ahead by paying off the mortgage company so I don't have to give them that interest dollar, and just paying the government 28 cents. That way I'd get to keep 72 cents instead of 28 cents."

He stared off in the distance for a moment, then sighed. "I never looked at it that way before."

Here was an extremely qualified and successful tax consultant, but the advice he was giving me was nothing more than what his CPA professor in school had told him, and what all his CPA newsletters were telling him. Of course, all those newsletters were written by other CPAs who had CPA professors telling them the benefits of the mortgage-interest tax deduction.

These well-intentioned professionals were all just parroting what they'd heard for years. But I'm telling you, you'll be money ahead by paying off your mortgage and just living with your taxes. We'll talk about ways to legitimately reduce your income taxes in a later chapter, but for right now, just take my word on this one.

COULD YOUR $100,000 MORTGAGE REALLY COST YOU NEARLY A THIRD OF A MILLION DOLLARS?

If you still need any motivation to pay off your mortgage, let's say you borrowed $100,000 to buy your home. With a typical mortgage, your thirty years of payments will total nearly a quarter million dollars (at 6 percent interest). But since you have to make those payments with after-tax dollars, you'll have to earn somewhere around $300,000 before income taxes are taken out, so you can net the $216,000 you'll need to make all your mortgage payments. *That means you have to earn nearly a third of a million dollars . . . to pay off a $100,000 loan!*

But that's not the worst of it.

If you follow the plan I'll lay out for you in later chapters, you'll have that mortgage loan paid off in an average of four to five years. For most folks, that means the mortgage is paid off about two decades early . . . eliminating around twenty years of mortgage payments.

Let's assume you're one of these people, and your mortgage payment in this scenario is $600 a month. You would then have twenty years to invest that $600 a month, instead of sending it to the mortgage company. Compounding at 8 percent annually over those twenty years, the $600-a-month investment would grow to $353,412. So . . . instead of *costing* you nearly a third of a million dollars of income, the same monthly payment could *build up* to more than a third of a million dollars in your retirement investments.

And you'd own the house!

Which plan sounds better to you—the Coalition's or mine? I suggest my plan, because the Coalition's plan will unremorsefully use you up, grind you into dust, then throw you away.

THE CYCLE IS ENDLESS

The Merchants want to sell you more than you really need. The Advertising Industry helps them by creating in you the "need" for more than enough. The Media cooperate by creating a culture that supports the Advertising Industry's campaign to create the need for more than enough. And when you exhaust your money, the Credit Industry is right there, letting you consume your future as you buy more than enough.

Again, let me say that I'm not advocating a life of drudgery and self-denial. You may have to defer some things or scale back from the more-than-enough versions the Coalition wants you to buy in the near-term, but I am not promoting an austere, monklike lifestyle. I'm promoting a self-directed lifestyle. A lifestyle of deciding for yourself what's really important enough to have now . . . and what's important enough to wait for a little while. It makes all the difference in the world.

In this chapter I've talked a lot *about* the brainwashing and manipulation the Coalition uses against you. Before we begin turning your finances around to build your wealth instead of the Coalition's, you need to understand *how* this brainwashing and manipulation work, so you can adequately defend yourself. That's what we'll cover in the next chapter.

3

WE'RE BRAINWASHED INTO BEING "CONSUMERS"

"Consumer," from the root word consume:
"To waste; squander. To destroy totally;
ravage [as in]: flames that consumed the house;
a body consumed by cancer."
(The American Heritage Dictionary)

If we extrapolate the financial application of this definition, a "consumer" is a "wealth destroyer," which casts an interesting spin on the oft-quoted "Consumer Confidence Index." It's really the "Wealth Destroyers' Confidence Index." Think about that. If you're trying to find an indicator to tell you the health of your personal economy or how you should be using your finances, do you really think following the Wealth Destroyers' Confidence Index is a good idea? I personally don't care how confident the wealth destroyers are.

Yet, if you watch TV or read the newspapers, you quickly see that the stock market, layoffs, lending rates—nearly every economic indicator—are dramatically influenced by the Consumer Confidence Index. Consumers propel the economy; or, more correctly, the wealth generated by consumers and passed along to the Coalition propels the economy. So, you have to ask yourself if the economy is a valuable guide to you as you decide how to use your money.

Here's what I believe: The state of *the* economy—fueled by wealth destroyers—is not nearly as important to you as the state of *your* economy. I experienced my financial crash during the rip-roaring late 1980s, when—much like the late 1990s—everything was going up, up, and away. The news on TV was rosy, and most boats appeared to be rising with the tide. I, unfortunately, was stuck in a submarine. *My* personal economy was diving at maximum rate, so I enjoyed no solace from *the* economy.

The purpose of this book is to help you focus on *your* economy. And the first thing I hope you agree with is that being a good consumer is a bad thing. My goal is to help you get *your* economy to a place where it's impervious to gyrations in *the* economy.

Just Say "No" to Being a Consumer

We so easily and dutifully accept the label "consumer" because we're indoctrinated to consume. That's our job in the Coalition's plan. We are to consume—totally destroy—our finances, in order to enrich the Merchants, Advertising Industry, Media, and Credit Industry. It's our consumerism that oils the conveyor belt between our bank accounts and theirs.

Jessie H. O'Neill, in her book *The Golden Ghetto: The Psychology of Affluence* (Hazelden, 1996), cites that:

- Per capita consumption in the United States has increased 45 percent in the past twenty years.

- During the same period, quality of life as measured by the index of social health has decreased by roughly the same percentage.

- The average workingwoman plays with her children forty minutes a week—and shops six hours.

- Ninety-three percent of teenage girls list shopping as their favorite pastime.

We have become the consumers the Coalition members want us to be. We now identify success and enjoyment with spending money. Buying things has changed from an occasional necessity to a regular recreational activity, and few recognize how dangerous that is in the long run. With medical advances dramatically lengthening our lives, the long run could be a lot longer than it was for our parents and grandparents, and that time won't be much fun if we have no wealth left to enjoy it. Our long run could end up being decades of passing out shopping carts at Wal-Mart or hamburgers at McDonald's if we fall into the "consumption trap" set for us by the Coalition of Four.

Now, I'm not proposing that you never buy anything that might bring you immediate pleasure or enjoyment. However, I am proposing that you beware of buying things simply because the *process* of shopping and buying things brings you pleasure and enjoyment. Spending money just to make yourself feel better is more expensive than most personal incomes can bear. And what happens when your income can't bear it? You continue buying with money borrowed from the Credit Industry. So now you're not only giving up your present income, you're promising your new credit partners decades of your future income as well.

Consumption is self-defeating. Overconsumption by use of credit is financial suicide. But reversing this process does not mean total self-deprivation. It means thoughtful choices. It means spending today while thinking about tomorrow. The term isn't "deny." It's "defer."

You know, the way your parents or grandparents did it. They knew they couldn't have it all now *and* have it later too. And they knew that using credit was like putting a gun to your head with the chamber loaded.

COMPARE TODAY'S CONSUMERS
WITH THE WWII GENERATION

Those who grew up in the late thirties and forties, called the "Greatest Generation," hardly used credit. Even when it was offered by a local merchant, these financial conservatives lived by the code that "if you cannot afford to buy it with cash, you can't afford it." They had watched their parents' generation be crushed by the Great Depression, an elongated superrecession caused—at least in part—by an overleveraged economy. Too much credit, especially on Wall Street.

The people of the Greatest Generation watched their relatives, and often themselves, become dispossessed because they couldn't make the mortgage payment. Many packed all that was left in small trailers or on the roofs of cars, and begged their way from town to town, looking for work. Having experienced the worst of credit's "benefits," they wanted nothing to do with it. They had to *know*, with certainty, what was theirs—what no one could take away from them. It was a security issue.

And it still is.

It's just as easy to have the mortgage company repossess your house today as it was back then—and you'd be just as homeless. One study indicated that the average family is only two paychecks away from insolvency. This means that should they fail to bring home the next two paychecks, they'd be out of reserves and falling behind. It wouldn't be long before the finance companies came to collect such things as cars, furniture, appliances, and even the house if they went a few months without making a payment.

I don't know about you, but I never liked living that close to the edge. In the back of my mind I always knew that should I get sick or become temporarily unemployed, it could all dissolve, and I could literally end up homeless. That actually happened to many highly educated professionals and blue-collar workers in the recent 2000 recession. One day they lost their jobs, and within a few months they were packing up what belongings were left after their creditors had taken back anything of value. These people were stunned, scared, and back at the bottom of the ladder. Too bad that when they were employed, they didn't use their money the way their grandparents did.

While many today might feel their grandparents deprived themselves, living less-enjoyable lives, just a glance at their generation shows a high percentage who retired well, even by today's standards. I think of my wife's grandparents. They both worked blue-collar jobs, retired in their early six-ties, and have (so far) lived three decades taking two or more cruises a year. They own their home and several other pieces of real estate, and—while not extravagant—they don't live deprived lives by any measure.

"But it's a different world today," asserts the Coalition.

It sure is! But is it a better one?

Why is it that today's consumers, who—even factoring in inflation— bring home many times the money their parents and grandparents did, never seem to enjoy the contentment experienced by earlier generations? And if that's true, why then don't today's consumers adopt the values that worked so well in the past? Where did the consumer mentality come from? Is it a recent development, or is it simply the harvest of earlier seeds? Let's get into the Way-Back Machine and find out.

CONSUMPTION AS A RECREATIONAL ACTIVITY— A NINETEENTH-CENTURY INNOVATION

In the 1870s, visionary retailers like John Wanamaker in Philadelphia and Marshall Field in Chicago planted the first Coalition of Four seeds by cre-ating luxury department stores. This was the beginning of shopping as a recreational activity; it was an experiential outing for women who had pre-viously enjoyed few opportunities to be out and about on their own. These stores gave them a place to hang out, and they were the obvious ancestors of today's shopping malls.

In the 1900s, Advertising became an art form and exploded into every area of American life. The advent of mass production made many more Merchant products available, and the Advertising Industry was needed to make people believe they "needed" the new goods. Citizens were told by both government and industry leaders that consuming made them good Americans. Economist Simon Nelson Patten declared in 1907 that the "new morality does not consist in saving, but in expanding consumption."

As I mentioned earlier, right after World War II, Diners Club introduced the credit card, and the Credit Industry fueled the era of impulse buying. Impulse buying is one the most destructive forms of consumption because it represents pure consumption with little or no real value in what's purchased. We joke in this country about impulse buying, saying things like, "Shop till you drop." My wife, Lois, once had a refrigerator magnet that boldly proclaimed, "If you think money can't buy happiness, you don't know where to shop."

But finding a place to shop shouldn't be that hard because, since 1957, the number of shopping centers in America has increased from two thousand to over thirty-one thousand. Women frequently get the impulse-buying rap because most of the people you see in malls and shopping centers are ladies—but men's impulse purchases are usually more dangerous, like boats, cars, power tools, golf clubs, and the like. I remember saying to Lois, "I only bought one thing this year!"

"Yeah . . . but it was an airplane," came the reply.

All this lightheartedness about impulse buying creates the illusion it's harmless. This fantasy is perpetrated and perpetuated by the Media and the Advertising Industry. As Mr. Patten the economist indicated, they'd have you believe it's downright un-American not to be an impulse buyer. The problem with being a good impulse-buying American, however, is that it leaves you with unneeded junk, and it leaves the Coalition with your hard-earned money. Not an equitable trade.

Of course, deep down inside, most people know that impulse buying is not really a good thing. So why do they do it?

One of the chief causes of impulse buying is stress. You've had a tough week, so you stop at the mall on the way home. Your fatigue is high, so your willpower is low. You need to give yourself a little reward for your diligent labor or for putting up with the jerk at work or whatever, so you stop off at the mall on the way home, plop down the plastic, and take home your latest piece of unneeded junk. It seems so harmless. But the cumulative effect on your wealth potential is devastating.

And stress shopping becomes a pattern. The more your bills go up from stress shopping, the more stressed you are . . . so it's off to the mall for another treatment. This is using shopping just as drug addicts use drugs. It's a way of getting a quick rush to make the bad feelings go away. But after a while, it takes more and more shopping because there's more and more pain. Short-term gain . . . long-term pain.

Of course, the Coalition wants it to be as hard as possible for you to resist your buying impulses, so it makes buying opportunities plentiful and convenient. Malls are grazing pastures for impulse buyers, and now you have shopping channels and infomercials on TV, and the bottomless World Wide Web, all available to suck money out of your wallet or purse. These portals to poverty make it too easy to hurt yourself financially, so you have to be doubly diligent against impulse buying.

You're in a battle—against powerful external forces as well as powerful internal weaknesses.

THAT'S WHY YOU HAVE TO WATCH OUT FOR THE CIA (CONVENIENCE, INDULGENCE, AND APPEARANCE)

CONVENIENCE

Paying money instead of exerting a little effort. This category includes such things as paying for simple car maintenance and cleaning instead of dirtying your own hands; buying restaurant, take-out, or frozen meals instead of cooking less-expensive home-prepared ones; paying a landscaper or the kid down the street to mow the lawn instead of doing it yourself; taking clothing to the laundry that could be cleaned at home; and similar options.

INDULGENCE

Here's your classic impulse buying. Buying things or experiences to "make yourself feel better." These expenditures might include clothes, jewelry, electronic gadgets, or whatever you tend to buy on your end-of-the-week junkets to the mall. Maybe a manicure, pedicure, facial, couple of drinks, dinner at that expensive restaurant, or other exchange of your dollars for a brief "warm and fuzzy."

In your heart you know the feel-better never lasts, and you're just helping pave your path to the poorhouse with these little feel-good experiences, so I strongly suggest you take a hot bath instead. Millions of people waste thousands of dollars a year on indulgence.

APPEARANCE

Appearance is *keeping up with the Joneses*, buying things to impress other people. Please believe me, they won't be impressed if you end up in poverty. The only thing that really impresses most people is success, and chasing the Joneses takes you directly to failure. There's no return on money invested to impress people. You might as well just give them the money . . . they'd be a lot more impressed.

How to Fight the Impulse to Buy

When you see an offer for something you think you want, don't immediately buy it. Instead, write down the information and phone number or Web address. Then set it aside for three or four days. After this cooling-off period, read the note and see if you still can't resist the offer. I can tell you from personal experience, as well as reports from many others, that there's a better than 90 percent chance you won't feel the buying urge anymore. In fact, you'll probably wonder what you were thinking because the product or service will seem so frivolous or unimportant.

This is why the commercials give you all that "if you call in the next ten minutes" baloney. Or they say they'll send you two of the product instead of just one, or throw in some free bonuses, if you'll just pick up the phone right then. They don't want you thinking about it for three or four days. They don't want you thinking about it for three or four minutes. This part of the commercial is what's known as the "Call to Action." They want you reacting, not reflecting. They want you sending them your money without thinking because they know your thinking will work against their purposes.

Don't worry about missing out on bonuses or two-for-the-price-of-one offers by not calling within the specified time period. The fact is, with TV and radio commercials the advertisers have no way of knowing whether you responded within a certain amount of time from seeing the commercial. You'd get the bonuses if you waited ten days rather than the ten minutes they stipulate. They're just trying to get you to pull the impulse trigger. It's the same thing with the "Supplies are limited," or the "While supplies last" ploys. Believe me, supplies are limited only to the number of people who order the product. If the Coalition gets more orders than it has inventory . . . it'll make more inventory!

Advertising is a seduction . . . and seduction wears off over time.

One more thing about impulse buying. Ask yourself whether you're a person who attaches self-esteem to the ability to impulse buy. When we decided to make the spending changes I'm asking you to consider, my wife got emotional because part of the way she identified our prosperity was in her ability to slap down a gold card at all the right department stores. Self-image should have nothing to do with being able to do self-destructive things such as impulsively spend money. If you connect your self-image to impulse buying, you're probably reacting or responding to something in your childhood or younger years. I know that a lot of my spending was in response to growing up in a lower-middle-class home where we never could seem to afford things we wanted. If you're playing any of these mind games, figure them out and put them to rest. They're only working against you.

EATING YOUR FUTURE ALIVE

If the Coalition can't get to you through offers of convenience, indulgence, and appearance, or through your uncontrolled impulse buying, it will attempt to siphon money out of your life through your stomach. Many people *consume* thousands of retirement dollars just eating out.

Let's look at an example. Simply going out to a $5 lunch each workday, instead of bringing something from home, can cost $100 or more a month. If that $100 were invested instead of digested each month—over a forty-year working life, at an average 8 percent return—it would grow to nearly $350,000. That's more than a third of a million dollars of future wealth gobbled up.

Or suppose you spend $50 going out to dinner each weekend. Over the same forty years at 8 percent interest, that could turn into $698,202 in increased retirement wealth instead of expanded waistline girth. Of course, there's also the harmless $3-a-day latte, cappuccino, or whatever your particular beverage weakness happens to be. Over forty years, you're drinking up $230,407 of retirement wealth. That's nearly a quarter million dollars, which could've bought you endless retirement lattes, fading away like the foamy residue in the bottom of a throwaway cup.

"What's left?" I can hear you cry. "He's taking away all my binkies and blankies."

No . . . I'm not trying to *take* anything away from you. I'm just telling you how much it really costs. I fully acknowledge that you're likely to buy a fast-food lunch or cappuccino in the future. I stop at Starbucks myself from time to time, but I'm conscious of how much I'm spending. I make a *conscious decision* that a hot cup of go juice today is worth the expenditure's future effect on my investments. And that's the real point. Money is printed to be spent, but most people spend it unconsciously, without any consideration of the long-term consequences. They rarely weigh the value of a dollar's momentary current effect versus its multiplied future effect. I won't let you be one of those people.

DON'T GIVE YOUR RETIREMENT
TO THE MOUSE

If you watch TV, especially if you have kids who force you to watch their channels, you know that Orlando is the center of the universe. We're told, in thousands of little ways, that if we don't go and see Walt's place, we're some lower form of life. But Walt's place and other places that have ridden his coattails over the past quarter century in central Florida are *expensive*!

And the Big "O" isn't the only costly vacation destination. You're being continually wooed by cruise lines, resorts, states, and destination cities. If you have money, they want you to deposit some of it in their zip code. And whatever you do, don't think about how much it will really cost you!

Just for fun, let's run a few numbers. Twenty years of $1,200-a-year vacations will cost you just under $60,000 of retirement wealth. How? Because that $100 a month over twenty years, put into investments returning 8 percent annually, would grow to $58,902. Over forty years, the same vacations cost you $349,101 of retirement wealth. Of course, it's unlikely you could do the Mouse visit for $1,200, so let's bump that up to $2,500 a year (even this would require staying in low-end hotels). Over twenty years, you're giving up $122,516 in retirement wealth, and over forty years, the retirement cost of these vacations jumps to $726,130.

Again, I'm not trying to say you shouldn't take vacations. I'm just pointing out how much they can cost, in case you'd like to consider some less-expensive, closer-to-home options. There are really great state parks, theme parks, historical landmarks, and other recreational attractions in every part of America, or wherever you live, and they cost a lot less than those we see promoted on TV. Yet the memories they produce can be just as vivid. Remember, a vacation need not be about buying your children's love for another year with an expensive visit to their favorite Saturday morning TV character. It can also be about teaching them the value of money. If you ingrain responsible financial behaviors in them, you'll be giving them something far more valuable than pairs of mouse ears for their dresser tops.

I do believe vacations are important, both for recreation and family bonding. I just don't believe they have to be costly, Coalition-brand spending orgies. And I concede that one trip to Mickey's place may be unavoidable in a family's life, but making it a habit can completely sabotage your financial future. Especially if you do it on credit.

TERRILL AND SUE'S STORY

Terrill and Sue Webster are a couple in their mid-thirties who live in central Florida. Both work at Disney World, Terrill in the Transportation Department and Sue in the Market Place souvenir and gift shop. They got information about my debt-elimination system in the mail one July. "I was skeptical at first," says Terrill. "It seemed too good to be true, but somehow I couldn't bring myself to throw it away. Finally, I showed it to several friends, and they suggested I give it a try."

They managed to squeeze a few extra dollars out of their monthly income and began using the Accelerator Margin™ (explained in Chapter 5, Step 3) to speed up their bill paying. They focused first on one bill, then another. They had a VISA card with a $950 balance. They paid it to zero. They had another VISA with a $3,000 balance, and paid it to zero. A $1,000 school debt was quickly banished. A credit card from JC Penney's with a $200 balance was dismissed. The loan for Sue's Ford Escort quickly dwindled from $6,000 to zero.

Today, Sue and Terrill are beginning to plan their investment program. "It's amazing. Suddenly we have all this money coming in, and neither one of us has had a pay raise," says Terrill.

"It's not like we were on an austerity program," says Sue. "We buy the same items we did before; we just find them at better prices. We operate a little differently, but the quality of our life hasn't gone down. If anything, it's improved."

Terrill agrees: "Definitely! We even feel better. We're more relaxed and we have more time to do what we want. I'm spending more time than ever on the golf course and in the pool. I lift weights a few times a week, and Sue and I like to take hikes together. The best part is that I don't have to feel guilty, because I'm keeping my finances in as great a shape as I am myself."

∞

USING CREDIT TO CONSUME JUST INCREASES AND PROLONGS THE DAMAGE

If you think a quarter-million-dollar lifetime latte cost is high, or that a vacation cost in excess of $1.2 million of retirement wealth is incredible, just pay for these things with credit cards and see how the cost mushrooms.

Look at the house you live in. Now look at the houses the executives of VISA, MasterCard, and Discover live in. How many people could comfortably retire on the billions of dollars these Coalition members take in each year?

Using credit just makes things cost more. Whether the purchase is responsible or irresponsible, you pay more for it if you use credit because you're paying the price plus interest. Anyone buying the same thing for cash pays only the price, so cash buyers pay less than you. That's why someone making the same income as you can live a *better* lifestyle using cash than you can using credit.

This is the Credit Industry's big lie. It perpetuates the myth that using credit enhances your lifestyle, when that's impossible. Using credit can only diminish your lifestyle. It'll show happy, sometimes ecstatic people slapping down their credit cards to buy life's so-called "priceless" experiences. What they don't show you—unless it's a debt counseling commercial—is the fruit of a credit-based lifestyle: stress, fatigue, depression, marital dissonance, and often physical illness. Using credit isn't "priceless." It has a price . . . and that price is high.

OKAY . . . WE'RE CLOSE

We're close to implementing your customized financial solution. The one that will immediately begin reversing the flow of money—from out of your life to back into your life . . . with interest. The solution that could literally leave you a debt-free millionaire at the end of your working life. But, before we start working the numbers to get you completely out of debt and building real wealth, we have to consider just one more mind-set issue.

I want to deprogram you from the Coalition's work-yourself-to-death-for-them value system and give you the opportunity to develop a new paradigm, a new life view. One of your own choosing, based on your own values. One that fits *your* likes, dislikes, and loved ones. One that uses your energy for *your* ultimate good, and not the good of the Coalition.

This may sound scary or even weird, but it can truly be the most exciting and rewarding part of the process because it gives you one of those rare "blank slate" opportunities to rechoose both your life's destination and the paths you want to travel to get there. So please open your mind and turn to the next chapter, as you prepare to take your biggest step out of the matrix.

Part Two
A Midcourse Correction

4

A CHANCE TO
REDESIGN YOUR LIFE

❦

An unseasonably warm, mid-April Wisconsin day was forming when I first sat down at my computer to start this chapter, and cabin fever began arm-wrestling with responsibility. For a pilot with his own plane, it doesn't take much of a day to believe the world would look better from five or six thousand feet. But this was an unusually nice day getting its early morning legs, and I decided I couldn't miss it. So I shut down the computer, flipped on my sunglasses and flying hat, and it was off to the airport.

As the hangar door climbed up its cables, sunshine washed in. It was just as wonderful as I had imagined, with a warm south breeze rolling across the tarmac. I fired up the Lycoming engine. It was a day made for pilots. A day not to be trapped in a nine-to-five job. A day to be a free man who can choose what to do and when to do it.

I'm obviously back at the computer now, but with an even stronger resolve that you should be able to enjoy the freedom I do. The freedom to shape each day however seems good to you. The freedom to do work that fulfills you or enjoy avocations and hobbies that make you warm inside. But what kind of work would that be? And what hobbies would give you joy, if you had time to take pleasure in them?

Is it difficult to come up with quick answers to these questions? Are you having trouble even envisioning unscheduled recreational activities, impromptu time with loved ones, or even the possibility of such freedom in the life you now live? Then maybe you need a new life!

That's the power of becoming completely debt-free and building true financial independence. When you've finished implementing what you'll learn in this book, you'll find yourself in that rare human circumstance of having the freedom to make almost unlimited choices. You'll be clear to define whatever life you desire for the balance of your years.

Of course, that new definition should be sensitive to God's leading and the feelings of significant people in your life, but the principal obstacle of "having to stay in this rat race because I have to pay the bills" will be gone! You won't have to make as much money because you won't need as much money . . . so you'll have the option of redesigning your life and lifestyle to fit however hard you want to work, or whether you want to work at all. Maybe you'll work just as hard but end up with a lot more money. Whatever fits you and those you love . . . it's your choice . . . and that's the point.

In fact, that's the full goal of this book—to give you back options and the freedom to dream dreams you may have long since buried because you had to pay the bills. I want to give you that glorious and infrequent second chance. The chance to do the "if onlys" you may have been convinced were lost forever. Go ahead and dream again, then . . .

REDESIGN YOUR LIFE

Take a deep breath, clear your mind, and ask yourself these questions:

- If I could completely redesign my life—wipe the slate clean and write a new life plan from scratch—what would I do?

- What would I be?

- Where would I live?

- What would an average day be like?

- How would it be different from the days I live right now?

- Would I continue living in the city or area where I live now, if I could live anywhere I want?

- Would I continue working the job I work right now, if I didn't have to work, or if I could get along on a lot less income?

- How would I change my life, if I could start fresh?

As outside-of-the-box as these questions might sound to you right now, I encourage you to start answering them, or at least considering them, because this chapter will reawaken dreams long buried and birth new dreams you may never have considered possible. Creating a new life-paradigm is the most exciting transformational step this book offers you. You can literally redesign your life!

"Why," you might ask yourself, "should I be defining a life today that I won't get to live until some tomorrow several years in the future?"

There are two answers to that question. First of all, have you ever seen those before-and-after pictures on a diet product commercial? Sure you have, and you know exactly why the Advertisers show them. Because they want you to mentally compare the "after" pictures to your current "before" waistline. They believe the "after" images will motivate you to buy their product and eventually make the lifestyle changes necessary to achieve "after" results in your own body.

Well, the new life I'm asking you to design—before you even start the process to achieve it—is the "after" picture of your life. You're living in the "before," and you need that "after" image to hold in front of you as a carrot, to motivate you through the necessary steps to get there.

Second, you won't have to wait as long as you might think to begin feeling the "after" effects of the program I'm going to teach you in this book. I've taught these principles to hundreds of thousands of people over more than a decade, and in most cases they've experienced real financial improvements in the first few months—improvements that relieved financial pressure, lightened their loads, and, in a very tangible sense, began their journeys to their "after" lives.

BILL AND ANNE'S STORY

Back in 1994 I received a letter from Bill and Anne Boylan. It came from Rapid City, South Dakota, a wonderful community, but not one of the more tropical locations in America. At the time, they projected they would be debt-free in three years, nine months following my plan, compared to more than fifteen years had they continued paying their debts the way their creditors wanted them to. And they estimated my plan would save them over $80,000 in interest.

Recently I got an e-mail from Bill. In part it said:

Dear John,

I want to thank you for the principles you taught my wife and me. Our children have followed them, and are all doing well financially—as are we.

I just wanted to let you know my wife and I are now taking the next step in our wealth-building plan . . . moving to a wonderful barrier island off the coast of Alabama in the Gulf of Mexico. Life on our island is wonderful—and very inexpensive. We are completely debt-free, will remain so during our upcoming move, and plan to remain debt-free and wealthy the remainder of our lives (we are in our early sixties now). We thank God for you! And we thank you for all you taught us about freedom from debt and building wealth.

Bill and Anne Boylan

SO WHAT'S STOPPING YOU?

Ask average persons if they'd continue living the lives they live today if they won the lottery, and you'll most assuredly get "No!" for an answer. It's not that they necessarily hate everything about their lives, but most people would take advantage of their new financial independence to re-examine whether things they spend their time at—like their jobs, for instance—are so fulfilling that they'd do them even if they didn't have to. According to every survey I've ever seen on the subject, many people would leave their current jobs and many would change locations—if they could only afford to.

Another way to say this is that a lot of people work at jobs they don't particularly like—to pay their bills—while they dream of different occupations they wish they could be doing. Or they slog their ways through each day, in neighborhoods, cities, or states they really don't like, while they dream of completely different environments or regions. Or their time and energy are sapped working to pay their own bills, while they wish they were free to donate time and money to community or religious programs centered on other people's needs.

What's stopping these people from fulfilling their wishes and dreams? Their debts!

If you ask them why they don't just make the life changes they wish they could, they'll tell you, "I can't afford to. How would I pay my bills?"

To which I have to respond, "What if you didn't have any bills beyond food, utilities, and taxes?"

That changes the picture, doesn't it? And I'm going to show you the mechanics of how to eliminate your debts—*all* your debts—in the next chapter. But an even more important process must take place before you start your financial transformation. First, you have to decide where you want this journey to take you, so your financial plan can be tailored to that destination. And that destination will, indeed, affect the route and dura-tion of the journey. If you're determined to live like Bill Gates, it will take a lot harder and longer journey to get you there. But if you want to end up living a simpler country life, that could be accomplished with an easier and shorter journey.

While this might seem like a simple, personal choice, you have to ask yourself whether the Coalition of Four would have a preference for you . . . and might it be trying to influence your selection?

THE HIGH PRICE OF THE FAST LANE

The fast-lane life is a creation of the Coalition of Four. For reasons I've already explained, the Coalition members want you earning more, so—as a fast-lane consumer—you can afford to feed more money to them. They want you living hard. They want you playing hard. They want you consuming without conscious thought, all the while believing you've achieved success. Been there, done that, got the credit card slips.

The fast lane is painted to look like a desirable goal, but many who've clawed their way into this lane—thinking it would provide freedom and happiness—are increasingly feeling trapped there. According to a Yankelovich Partners survey for Hilton Hotels, six in ten Americans say they are pressed for time, and nearly 70 percent say they feel stressed; 31 percent report they feel guilty even when relaxing. They work high-pressure jobs because they pay enough to support their fast-lane high expenses. But the fast-lane high expenses come mostly from living in the fast-lane area of cities where the fast-lane jobs are, and from wearing the fast-lane clothes and driving the fast-lane cars required to look the part. So they're working the jobs because they pay enough to cover the cost of living near the jobs and working the jobs. And around and around they go.

Maybe it's time for them to redesign their lives.

I was on a fast-track paradigm when everything crashed around my ears. But, with the benefit of 20/20 hindsight, I can see that I really didn't fail, my *paradigm* failed. Think of a paradigm as a recipe. If you follow a recipe designed to produce a cake, you'll end up with a cake. If you follow a paradigm designed to suck the financial life out of you, while trading you some illusions of prosperity along the way, you'll end up with a financially depleted life and some expensive, rusting toys. The Coalition calls this paradigm "Success."

I learned three critical truths about success through my "Valley of Death" experience:

1. It's hard to *achieve* and *sustain* the kind of wealth it takes to live the Coalition version of a successful life. It requires a heavy price in time, energy, and relationships.

2. Achieving that lifestyle does not usually make people less stressed or more joyful.

3. It's a lot easier to achieve a much more enjoyable and sustainable lifestyle with a change in paradigm.

THE COALITION FINANCIAL SUCCESS MODEL

This is the financial model most Americans dream about and think they're working toward. They believe—because they've been brainwashed by the Advertising Industry and the Media—that to be successful and happy they need luxury cars, preferably foreign, big houses in the right subdivisions or neighborhoods, the right labels in their clothes, and the spending habits of Congress.

This model is the most expensive way to live. It forces you to pay the maximum amount for everything in your life because you're buying the highest-priced versions of everything. That means you're going to have to work especially hard to make all the money it will require to live out this model, and that takes a lot of time. Time that your money won't be growing into resources for you to live off of at some future date. Time you won't be spending with your spouse and other loved ones. Time you won't be living the relaxed, stress-reduced life you really wish you were living.

Time you won't be free to answer the call God has placed in you to invest yourself in something beyond yourself . . . in his name.

When I realized how expensive this model was, I finally understood that true financial wealth is not shown by my income statement, but rather by my net worth statement and my calendar. Real wealth is not how much money is flowing *through* my life, but how much is accumulating in assets I actually *own*. That's the dollars-and-cents of it. But, in practical terms, the truest measure of wealth is time. How long can I go without working . . . without producing income to live on? That's real financial independence, and that's what the high-consumption, fast-lane lifestyle prohibits most people from ever achieving.

The little, white, paid-for *Che*vette in the driveway suddenly made more sense than the gold *Cor*vette with its $549 monthly payments. Less than a year after downsizing to the Chevette, I purchased a three-year-old Pontiac Bonneville for cash and have never driven a "beater" since then . . . but all my subsequent vehicles have been cash purchases. They all went directly to my net worth statement as owned assets.

As I developed my Transforming Debt into Wealth® system, I also began to realize that our big "Coalition success model" house was not worth its cost. So Lois and I moved to a slightly farther-out suburb, into a much less-expensive but really nice home. This immediately reduced our mortgage balance by $100,000. In addition, we enjoyed much lower property taxes, and I could even put a TV antenna on the roof if I wanted to. We had more property, we lived next to regular people (not counting the guy across the street), and our much lower monthly payment freed up a ton of money for debt elimination and then wealth-building.

We eventually went rural, moving to southwest Wisconsin, 150 miles from any big city. Out here it's much cheaper to find a nice home for far less than in urban areas, with three-bedroom homes still available for under $100,000. We bought thirty-seven acres of rolling farm fields and woods for less than $500 an acre, and because we weren't married to the opulent house model anymore, we put a modest two-level cedar home on the property, then quickly paid it all off. Over the following years we gradually finished the walk-out basement, added a room, and built a three-car garage, but only as we saved up for each improvement and could pay cash.

Once the homestead was done and paid for, we began investing.

With our two paychecks it took us less than five years to pay off all our debts. From that point we were able to invest an average of about $4,000 a month over the following seven years in the stock market and commercial real estate. Today we live completely off the proceeds from our investments, and I don't have to work another day in my life if I don't want to. And even when I choose to work, like writing this book, I have the freedom to shut down the computer and go fly my plane whenever I like. Sure, the plane is a 1966 model and there are newer, flashier, more-expensive ones to be had, but they don't fit my paradigm, my redesigned life. My paid-for 1966 Cherokee Six is in great shape, it gets me up in the air and on to my destination just fine . . . and I think it's beautiful!

DID I LOWER MY EXPECTATIONS?

Some might say that all I did with my paradigm shift was lower my standards—that I caved in by not sticking with the big house near the big city in the fancy suburb with all its expensive cultural accoutrements. I dealt with that for a while, but over time I came to understand I really didn't want that "rich" model. I knew I was expected to want it, but, in my heart of hearts, it really didn't hold that strong an attraction for me. It did in the beginning, but as I looked around at the rich people I was trying to catch up with and emulate, I saw a lot of shattered lives, hollow smiles, broken marriages, battered dreams, bratty kids, and prescription drugs. If money could buy happiness, where was theirs?

However, letting go of that success paradigm was still weird at first, kind of what I'd suspect it's like to detox from drugs or alcohol. It took time for the Coalition of Four influence to wear off. But as it did, Lois and

I began to clearly see what kind of life *we* really wanted—not what kind of life the Coalition wanted us to want.

In the process I believe we actually *raised* our expectations. We ended up achieving a wonderful lifestyle, and we can sustain it for a fraction of what our old paradigm would have cost. We live in a nice home with a breathtaking view. We drive dependable four- and five-year-old vehicles that look new because we take care of them. We have the airplane—not the biggest or fastest—but it gets us to fun places, and it's paid for. And our taxes are lower because we're not helping support a high-income area's infrastructure. The truth is, we live where most overworked, overstressed city people come to get away from it all for a week or two.

And because we shifted our paradigm, we achieved it all much faster than we could have back in the rich Chicago suburb. Plus, we can fly or drive to the city and enjoy any of its cultural offerings any time we want. It's a nice place to visit, but I'm glad we don't have to live there.

You Might Be Able to Make This Transition Today

Some people who bought their homes a couple of decades ago for a fraction of their current value have enough equity that they could sell them, use the proceeds to pay off all their other debts, and still have enough left over for down payment on rural homes. Then, if they have sufficient income streams at their new locations, they could accelerate the payoff of their new country homes and end up totally debt-free in a handful of years—a feat that would likely have taken them a decade or more back in the city. This isn't your typical scenario, but I've seen it happen.

IS THIS PARADIGM SHIFT HARD TO SWALLOW?

It may seem so at first, but let me be clear that I'm not trying to push you into moving to Mayberry. I'm simply posing it as an option. Remember, this is about giving you back options in your life, and changing your tempo and environment is an option you may want to consider. But if you're one of those people who can't fall asleep without traffic noise outside the window, or if the idea of stepping out your front door and seeing no one scares you, then just design your new life model to fit the environment that suits you. But make it a lifestyle of *your* choice, not of the Coalition's choice.

For example, if you're a confirmed city person, you can live in or around most big cities in modest neighborhoods or in obscenely expensive ones. I suggest the modest end of the spectrum. My sister lives inside the city limits of Chicago in a very nice, relatively quiet, and reasonably priced neighborhood. But within a few minutes' drive, she can be passing houses that cost more than the gross national product of many Third World nations. If you find yourself compelled to live in one of these monstrosities, you'll likely end up working till you die just to make the payments.

As long as that's a conscious decision that appeals to you, go for it. Of course, your loved ones will stand at your funeral, remembering how they barely knew you because you were never home but saying how grateful they were that you let them live in the empty caverns of your big house. Not!

More likely, they'll be lamenting that you died early trying to make mortgage payments that they're now stuck with. It's a loser's game, trying to look rich.

COULD STATUS OR SELF-WORTH BE STANDING IN THE WAY OF YOUR MAKING THIS CHANGE?

If you're spending your hard-earned wealth trying to look "well off," you're playing Monopoly by the Coalition's rules. It's the bank, remember? And it'll end up with all your pretty colored money. Glance around the board at the other players—the people you're trying to emulate or impress. If you could crawl into their lives, you'd find that they're barely hanging on to their own trappings of status. And even if you somehow surpass them, the Coalition will be right there, mercilessly and relent-lessly pushing you toward even loftier competition. You'll never have enough.

But what if competing with others is not the thing that's driving you? What if it's your own past you're contending with? Could you be running away from childhood poverty rather than toward adult prosperity?

Do you feel yourself striving to achieve material status in reaction to early life deprivations? Then let me assure you that attempting to buy your way out of a materially poor childhood just promises a materially poor old age. The best revenge for living a deprived youth is to get rich, and the key to achieving millionaire status is not to spend money like TV and movie millionaires. Real millionaires don't waste any money trying to look like millionaires.

Or maybe you're one of the many people who strive to *feel* wealthy out of a sense of insecurity, either financial or personal. I'm not a psychi-atrist or psychologist, but I can tell you this: You cannot spend your way into being a more secure person. In fact, mounting bills and debt obliga-tions will just make you more insecure. On the other hand, knowing there are hundreds of thousands of dollars in your accounts can chase away many of life's bogeymen.

LEARN TO BE A CONTRARIAN THINKER

The key to a truly wealthy and financially secure life is managed spending and consistent wealth-building . . . exactly the *opposite* of the way the Coalition wants you to use your money. It's this contrarian thinking that will get you to true financial independence. You have to be able to do the opposite of what the culture and Media are screaming at you to do. It's like getting yourself free from Chinese handcuffs.

Have you ever played with Chinese handcuffs? They're a little flexible tube woven from bamboo, into which you insert one finger from each hand. Once the fingers are installed, the harder you try to pull your hands apart, the tighter the tube grips the captured fingers. The only way you can free yourself is by pushing your hands toward each other—the exact opposite of the direction you instinctively want to move them. That philosophy is the core tenet of this book.

If you want to become a millionaire, you have to move in the opposite direction of your natural instincts to buy the big car, live in the big house, and wallow in the platinum-card lifestyle. If, however, you're intent on living large and lavishly today, and you're content to deal with the consequence later, my plan won't be of much use to you. Just get yourself a subscription to *Hedonism Monthly,* and a big term-life insurance policy, so when you have the early heart attack your heirs won't have to pay the price of your short-term thinking.

People in the fast lane relentlessly work themselves, for forty or more years, to get to where you can get to in five to ten years simply by following the right recipe—the right paradigm. Because of its higher price tag, fast-laners must work harder to earn a higher income to reach and sustain their Coalition lifestyle. But the higher their income goes, the more the government takes, which means they have to work doubly hard to make even more money, so they can give more to the government and the Coalition . . . and here comes the early heart attack.

But with a new, less-ostentatious paradigm, you can achieve financial independence on a lower income, so the government's share would be smaller. Remember, you can spend only *net* dollars—dollars left after taxes and debt payments. So, if you eliminate debt payments, you can live on less. And if you earn less, the government takes a smaller percentage. The result is that you can actually live on a reduced income but still enjoy nearly the same net dollars as you would living a much higher-income, higher-tax, debt-ridden lifestyle. It worked for Michael Phillips.

MOVING OPPOSITE TO THE HERD

Michael Phillips was one of the youngest vice presidents of the Bank of California, but he changed his paradigm and quit his high-paying job.

I'll let him tell you why, in these excerpts from an interview in *Health World Online* (www.healthy.net):

Quitting the banking business was just the final step of a long process that began when one of my clients—who knew what I needed better than I did myself—sent me away on a cruise ship. I was thirty-one years old, and I'd never had a vacation in my life. I was nervous, tense, and stressed—a typical superachiever. I'd never in my life been able to just sit still and do nothing.

Once I was on board and realized that there was literally nothing to do, I just about had a nervous breakdown. It was the beginning of a big change for me—a big change in the way I thought about myself, about money, and about the world, [and] once I thought through why I felt so driven to make money, I realized that my job was keeping me from getting what I really wanted.

It came down to the things everybody wants—freedom, respect, health, security for my family, and security in my old age. I had been thinking that money would help me get these things, but in fact, it was keeping me from getting them. I realized that because I wanted freedom, and thought that money could get me freedom, I had ended up working in a job where I had very little freedom to do the things I really cared about.

I decided the best thing I could do was to start right now to do the things I really loved, and to spend as much time as I could with the people I really cared about. Of course a person wouldn't necessarily have to quit his job to do that—he or she could just begin to realize that they are not working primarily for money, and make their decisions accordingly. If you reduce the amount of money you have to earn, you'll have a lot more freedom to do the things you love, and more freedom to spend time with the people you love.

Mr. Phillips said it very well, and I can honestly add that being debt-free and having sufficient income from my investments to live indefinitely without working is much more enjoyable and stress-free than life ever was when I had the pedal to the metal in the fast lane.

Are you looking to make the changes Mr. Phillips and I made . . . or are you on the other end of the spectrum, feeling that you're living below your potential and wanting to add more action, productivity, and success to your life? Whatever you see as the goal for your redesigned life, it's time to define that goal—that new life. Here's a recipe.

SIX STEPS TO REDESIGNING YOUR LIFE

STEP 1: ACCEPT 100 PERCENT RESPONSIBILITY FOR WHERE YOU ARE NOW, AND WHERE YOU'RE GOING

Even though the Coalition manipulated your spending habits, it won't do you any good to point fingers and play the blame game. If you transfer your life's financial quality control to outside forces, you're condemning yourself to a life where only those outside forces can make improvements. But if you take responsibility for your life, you have *response-ability*, which is the ability to proactively respond to your circumstances, on your own, without anyone's permission or help. That means you can unilaterally choose a new destination for your life and a new route to get you there.

But you first have to admit to yourself the reality of where you are and how you got there. Certainly, the Coalition of Four seduced you, but no one put a gun to your head and said, "Make this purchase with a credit card." You made the choices that brought you to your current reality, even if those choices were simply to be passive while someone else mishandled family finances.

If you find yourself struggling with this self-responsibility admission, you may be imitating Cleopatra's pet crocodile—living in "de Nile." Denial is the great paralyzer. A state of nonreality disables you from taking remedial action, dooming you to the worst possible consequences of your reality. You may *wish* things weren't the way they are, but those wishes are just symptoms of denial. Wishing won't change anything.

You may also feel, because you've been victimized into your current financial predicament by the Coalition of Four, that your situation is obviously unfair . . . so truth, justice, and the American way will somehow make it all come out right in the end. This is also classic denial—mentally curling into the fetal position, sucking your thumb, and hoping all the bad stuff just goes away. I know I'm being blunt here, but I wouldn't be serving you if I let you pull the blankets over your head and hide from reality. If, from time to time, I grab you by the shoulders and give you a good shake, it's in love. I care about you, and I know that breaking free from emotional inertia isn't easy.

To make progress, you have to face reality. If you wish something in your life were gone, there's only one way you can make it go away: You have to face it to erase it. Then it's 100 percent up to you to create a new reality to replace the erased one. Waiting for outside forces to solve your problem is a helpless and hopeless posture. Believe me, no matter how difficult your finances or your life may seem to you now, the fastest way to reverse the situation is to run directly at your problems and whip them in the shortest possible time. Sitting in the dark fretting about them just makes the monsters get bigger in your mind.

God puts it this way: "I call heaven and earth as witnesses today against you, that I have set before you life and death, blessing and cursing; therefore *choose life,* that both you and your descendants may live" (Deut. 30:19, emphasis added).

Okay . . . assuming you've overcome denial and are willing to face your reality, it's time to evaluate that reality. Ask yourself, "Is my current financial life strategy working for me?"

If your answer is no, here's the fact you must accept before we can go any further: *If you continue to do what you've always done, you'll con-*

tinue to have what you've always had. This is not only logical, but it's an inescapable law of the universe. Some have gone so far as to say that the definition of insanity is to continue doing the same thing but expecting a different outcome.

You see, life operates on the Law of Cause and Effect, or "Actions and Outcomes." Every time you've taken an action in your life, it has produced its corresponding outcome. And every time you've taken the same action over the years, it has produced pretty much the same outcome. So, if you don't like your current situation—your current set of outcomes—it will take new actions to produce new, more desirable outcomes. These new actions will be the building blocks of your redesigned life strategy.

The Bible reinforces this cause-and-effect law with the familiar phrase "You reap what you sow." Notice that *you* reap, not others. While your irresponsible sowing may negatively affect others, you cannot avoid being its principal victim. Notice that you *reap.* There is no opting out of the consequences of your actions. Notice that you reap what you *sow.* You are continually sowing with the actions you take, and your seeds lead either to successful outcomes or to failure, depending on what those seeds are. If you sow corn seeds, you'll reap corn. If you sow apple seeds, you'll reap apples. No one would ever expect to sow corn seeds and reap apples. If you have the right seeds, the quality of those seeds determines the quality of your harvest.

By the way, choosing to do nothing automatically sows seeds of failure. You will unavoidably reap a failure harvest.

STEP 2: BEFORE YOU BEGIN DEFINING YOUR REDESIGNED LIFE, CHECK YOUR ASSUMPTIONS

Most of your financial assumptions have likely been deposited in you by the Coalition of Four. For example, most consumers assume that using credit will enhance their lifestyles, when that is mathematically and logically impossible. The Coalition has also labored to deposit in you the belief that a life worth living will include luxury cars, big houses, and lots of expensive recreation. And it's likely conditioned you to believe that you'll have a car payment and mortgage payment till the day you stand before your Maker. Deal with these assumptions before you start the design process.

To produce a successful strategy for the person you see in the mirror each morning, your life redesign must be built on assumptions that are born out of *your* values, desires, and abilities. One size does not fit all, and you must pursue only a life strategy that will closely fit you and those who will share it with you. This is not as easy as it might first sound, because your Coalition of Four indoctrination has been so powerful, persistent, and penetrating. You must question your every impulse to be sure it is self-directed.

STEP 3: FACE YOUR FEAR

Fear of change and fear of taking bold steps can paralyze you, leaving you unable to move in a new, better direction. Fear may even inhibit your ability to conceive of a new life.

How is it possible to know that a change would be good for us, yet be afraid to make that change? Our ever-active imaginations tell our minds that the unfamiliar places we're thinking about going are filled with monsters and booby traps. So we feel safer where we are, and we're reluctant to stick a pinky outside our comfort zone. The monsters aren't there, and any booby traps are usually well marked.

American philosopher Will Rogers is quoted as saying, "In my life I've experienced many terrible things . . . a few of which actually happened." He was testifying of our common human tendency to overestimate the difficulties we face. We mull them over and over in our minds until we build them up into horrifying goblins determined to destroy us. But psychologists tell us that the vast majority of things we fret over never happen. However, the stress we feel while experiencing the horror in our minds is very real. That's why we fear these things.

For example, your mind will probably overestimate the pain of depriving yourself of credit cards, or of leaving the area where you live, or of changing occupations; while the reality would likely be an exciting new adventure in your life, an adventure of your own design, not of compulsion or deception. Sure, there are uncertainties ahead of you on any new, uncharted course. I'm not promising there won't be surprises and difficulties. But wouldn't you rather deal with uncertainties on the path *you've* chosen than those awaiting you on the road the Coalition is pushing you down?

The fear of being different also can sabotage your efforts to redesign your life. Rejection is the number one fear reported to psychiatrists and psychologists. Why might you feel the fear of rejection if you chart a new course for your life?

Up to now you've just been one more cow in the herd, living like the bovines around you, wearing the Coalition of Four brand, so you've felt "acceptable." But now I've upset the apple cart—excuse me, the hay bale—and asked you to move in an obviously different direction. This starts your fear of the other cattle's reactions to the new you. What will they think? They're headed for the slaughterhouse, and you're headed for the hills. How will they feel about you when they've been reduced to Coalition porterhouses, and you're comfortably grazing in a field of your own without a care in the world?

"Maybe," a voice whispers inside, "it would be better to be slaughtered while still being accepted as one of the herd, than to escape but be an outsider. It's a sad thing to be a rejected cow."

Yes, and it's even worse for humans.

What will friends and family think? Will your success make them uncomfortable? Getting out of debt and taking long-range control over your finances is somewhat like succeeding on a diet. While you might expect everyone in your crowd to be happy for you, the fact is that your success may only highlight their failures. When an overweight person begins succeeding with a diet, almost without fail some of the overweight people in her life start hitting her with friendly fire—sabotage. They'll suggest, "Just one piece of cake," or "Pizza and beer won't hurt just this one time."

Unfortunately, you need to be aware that similar emotions may arise in some of your friends and family who are financially out-of-control. When they see you getting a handle on your finances, rapidly paying off all your debts, and redesigning your life, it may make them feel inadequate in these areas of their own lives. This inadequacy can manifest in unkind words or even avoidance. They may even accuse you of having gone off the deep end. Just remember that it won't help them for you to slide back into your previous, financially doomed existence just to make them feel better. The best thing you can do for them is to succeed and keep them abreast of your success, with an open offer to help them achieve the same changes if they wish.

STEP 4: ANALYZE YOUR PRESENT LIFE STRATEGY AND ITS OUTCOMES

What aspects or outcomes of your current life, particularly your financial life, don't you like? For each answer to this question there is a cause—a seed you sowed—either actively or passively. Some of these issues may have surfaced in Step 1, when you were taking 100 percent responsibility for your life, but I want to delve a bit deeper here.

This analysis will be challenging because it may seem unfair in some situations. But I'm asking you to try not to deny accountability here because even if you did little more than simply *allow* things to get to where they are, you are accountable for that reason and to that extent. This is not to say it's all your fault, but you must be brutally honest about what you did to contribute to the outcomes you're living with. Were you too quiet? Did you allow things to happen that contributed to your problems? Did you do things yourself that led to your current life situation? Tell it like it is . . . in writing! This is not just a therapeutic mental exercise. You're creating data you'll use to sow better seeds for future harvests. Keep this list available for periodic review, to keep you from repeating mistakes of the past.

Now look for Coalition thinking. What untruths have been programmed into your assumptions, values, and judgments by the Coalition of Four? Think of your mind as a computer. It can do only what its programming allows or instructs it to do. In other words, its output can be no better than its input. Garbage in—garbage out.

The Bible says it another way in the twenty-third chapter of Proverbs: "As [a man] thinks in his heart, so is he" (v. 7). What thoughts are creating or limiting your reality? These are your "controlling thoughts." They define and confine your life. They determine the seeds you believe you can sow, and thereby the harvests you believe you can reap. For most people, their controlling financial and lifestyle thoughts have been programmed into them by the Coalition of Four.

Analyze the way your mind reacts to various situations and stimuli. Are those reactions Coalition-friendly? Then they're probably the result of Coalition programming that's directing the way your mind evaluates the risks and rewards associated with how you use your money. That Coalition thinking will inevitably create a reality designed to enrich the Coalition at your expense.

Ask yourself, "What are my controlling thoughts about . . ."

- Where I live?

- What I do for a living?

- What kind of home I live in?

- Whether or not I use credit cards?

- How wealthy I believe I could become?

- How I believe family and friends view my financial capabilities?

- Whether I see my home as simply where I enjoy living or as a statement about how successful I am?

- Whether I buy cars to make a statement, either to myself or to the world?

- Whether I shop recreationally?

- Whether or not I can say "No" to myself?

- Whether I truly believe I deserve to be debt-free and prosperous?

Add to this list whatever questions would help shed light on your current situation, because it's honest answers to such questions that will equip you to create different outcomes, to effectively move to the step we've been working toward since the beginning of this chapter: designing your new life.

STEP 5: DESIGN YOUR NEW LIFE

Now that you are in conscious control of the thinking patterns that generate your lifestyle, you have the leverage to think your way to a life of your own design, rather than the one the Coalition has in mind for you. Redesigning and achieving this new life will require you to establish and maintain the new controlling thoughts you identified with your answers to the questions in Step 4. These new controlling thoughts must be solidly defined and continually reviewed. That's why they must be committed to in writing.

Write in detail about:

Where you will live. If you're not happy with where you live right now, decide where you want to live and incorporate that controlling thought into your redesigned life strategy.

What you will do for a living. Will you live off your investments? If you'll continue working but don't like your current occupation, describe how you will qualify for and obtain employment in the occupation you desire. You may also consider taking the opportunity afforded you by debt-freedom to start and build a business of your own.

What kind of home you will live in. Make sure your definition of your ideal home is not one indoctrinated in you by the Coalition of Four. Consider how comfortable and maintainable your new home will be as you grow older in it.

What kind of car you will drive. Will your vehicles simply provide transportation, or will you pay thousands more to buy status or some other egocentric and short-lived benefit?

How you will manage your spending. In the next chapter I'll introduce you to a spending plan designed to develop what I call your *Accelerator Margin*™. But the important fact to remember at this point is: If you can't afford to buy something with cash, you can't afford it. And that brings us to most people's biggest spending-control issue—credit cards. Assuming you remember that credit cards cannot possibly improve your life, you shouldn't be including them in your new life strategy. If you have to make an exception for business travel and expenses, establish controls to protect yourself from undisciplined misuses.

What you will do for recreation. How often will you do it? Do you enjoy that activity now? Will you need any training to get reasonably good at it? Will participating in it require substantial amounts of money?

Elements of your present life you want to minimize or eliminate. What changes will you have to make to minimize or eliminate those elements? Do they involve others? If so, to what extent will you respect others' interests?

The principal feature in your redesigned life that is not present in your current life. What changes will you have to make to develop this feature in your life? How committed are you to its achievement? This could be something as simple as a physically fit body, or as involved as a college degree.

How all this will provide a more rewarding life for you and your loved ones. Remember, this is not about just you. Beware of allowing disagreements over finances or your life-redesign strategy to destroy relationships. Don't lose what money can't buy, while chasing the things money can buy. We're potentially talking about a whole-life makeover here, not just a financial tune-up, and your whole life includes the other lives God has put into yours. Lead, don't push, your loved ones toward your new life strategy. Explain your every thought . . . then *listen* to their feelings. Try to find ways to address their concerns. Sit on the same side of the table and put your interests and their interests in front of both of you. Look for ways to come as close as possible to accommodating all the interests, rather than sitting across from one another, playing tug-of-war. And continually highlight the benefits they'll enjoy from this accommodation. Remember, everyone's favorite radio station is WII-FM: What's in it for me?

Why you want to make these changes. If you're looking to create a life that will make you "feel" a certain way, identify the feelings you're seeking and explore all possible ways to achieve them. Then sort through that list for the least expensive and intrusive ways to realize your desired feelings. Be sure you're moving *toward* what you want, not just away from what you don't want. No one ever achieved anything great by running away.

Now at first blush this might sound selfish, or in some way unharmonious with a non-self-centered Christian walk, but actually the life you're planning here might be the one you "feel" God is calling you to live. And don't forget, he wants to give you the desires of your heart (Ps. 37:4), so it's okay to have some wholesome desires in your heart for God to give you.

The point here is, if you can't answer the "Why" question in a way that has traction to you, you won't persist in the changes necessary to accomplish the new life you're designing.

How badly you want your new life. Do you want it badly enough to discipline yourself to follow a plan that will get you there? There will be times when your desire for a new life will be the only thing keeping you on the beam. That's why you want all the answers to these questions *written down,* because the flames of your desire will require periodic fanning to keep them ablaze, and reviewing these written controlling thoughts will provide the wind.

STEP 6: IT'S TIME TO TAKE ACTION

The number one key to your success is your ability to take action. Intentions have no currency, no value to the world, to those around you, or to the quality of your life. The best-laid plans, hopes, and dreams are of zero consequence without action.

But action alone is not sufficient. It has to be the right action, and that's what the systems I'm teaching you in this book will lead you to take. It has to be focused action, and that's the key to my *Cascading Debt-Elimination System*™ (explained in the next chapter). Its power comes from focusing your money to overwhelm and eliminate one debt at a time. Yet when you finish this book and you have all the knowledge I can convey, it'll still come down to your ability to take action.

As the book of James tells us in chapter 1, verse 25, if you want to be blessed in what you do, you need to be a "doer." For example, many dream of paying off their debts, but Bill and Anne Boylan took action and are now enjoying their Gulf Coast island life.

Action. That's the key. You can agree with everything I write in this book, underlining and highlighting all the good stuff, showing your spouse the things you "should do," but if you don't take action, it won't matter what your attitude is about what I've written here. A great attitude isn't enough. You need PMA^2.

You may have heard the term "PMA," which stands for Positive Mental Attitude. Back in the seventies and eighties, PMA was considered the foundational success truth—the principle from which all other success concepts flowed. If you maintained a Positive Mental Attitude, you were unstoppable. Success could not escape you. Yet over several years as a PMA disciple, I witnessed people who maintained a Positive Mental Attitude that could light up a small American city, but they never achieved much. The missing ingredient? Action.

That's why I added another PMA—Positively Massive Action—to the success formula. If you multiply your Positive Mental Attitude (PMA) by focusing it through Positively Massive Action (PMA) you get PMA^2, and that will produce a successful outcome. You'll achieve your goals and out-distance any competition because your competitors are just standing there with their positive attitudes glowing. Without action, all the positive expectation in the Milky Way galaxy won't accomplish a thing.

And your action will accomplish a lot more, a lot quicker, if it's massive. That's why the principles you'll learn in the next chapter and beyond are based not on doing a little here and a little there, but on focusing massive financial action—first on your debts, then on your wealth-building. Massive action produces massive, extraordinary results.

Okay . . . are you ready to take action, dump your debts, and get started? Yes? Then turn the page.

5

SIX STEPS TO FREEDOM

∞

Welcome to the real world," Morpheus whispered.

Neo faded in and out of consciousness after being flushed from the Matrix and hauled aboard the *Nebuchadnezzar*.

"He still needs a lot of work," Dozer sighed.

Over the following weeks they surgically removed connections that had wired Neo's body into the Matrix. Connections that had allowed the machines to manipulate his mind with illusions of a self-directed life, while in reality he had been their slave, feeding his life energy to the Matrix. Acupuncture and electric shock therapy stunned his atrophied muscles back to life. His eyes struggled with the light; he had never used them before.

Welcome to your real world. In this chapter I'm going to surgically remove connections that have wired your soul into the Coalition of Four. I'll also help you shock back to life intellectual and emotional muscles that are capable of making self-directed financial decisions. Muscles that have atrophied from lack of use because the Coalition was making those decisions for you, while feeding you an illusion that the choices were your own—choices that were good for you.

Your financial eyes will be opened, seeing some realities for the first time. It's likely that in many ways you have never used clear, unmanipulated financial vision before.

We Have to Disconnect Your Soul

When I refer to your "soul," I'm talking about your mind, will, and emotions.

For most of your life, your soul has been connected to the Coalition of Four at many levels. It's had emotional cables coupled to your self-image, to your sense of self-worth, to your perception of relative success in all areas of your life, to self-measurements of your professional and financial progress versus that of friends and family, to your definitions of a desirable man and woman, to your definition of an acceptable lifestyle, to your beliefs about how money should be used, and to many other "ports" to your mind, will, and emotions.

I'm going to perform informational surgeries to remove those external connections between you and the Coalition. From this point forward you're going to follow your own mind, will, and emotions to the redesigned life of your choice—not the Coalition's choice. There are six steps in this process—just six steps from where you are today to your new, redesigned life:

STEP 1: Assess where you are right now.

STEP 2: Manage your spending.

STEP 3: Create your Accelerator Margin™.

STEP 4: Pay off *all* your debts.

STEP 5: Build your wealth.

STEP 6: Live your redesigned life.

STEP I: ASSESS WHERE YOU ARE RIGHT NOW

The beginning of your journey, from where you are now to complete debt freedom and your redesigned life, is a list of your current debts. This is a snapshot of your present financial condition.

List all your debts on a sheet of paper. All you need is the name of the debt, the total outstanding balance, and the minimum required monthly payment (see Fig. 1). If you're in the habit of adding a little extra to the payment of any debt, don't do that on this list. Include only the minimum payment required by the creditor.

FIGURE 1

Name of Debt	Total Outstanding Balance	Minimum Monthly Payment
VISA	$1,132.76	$22.66
Car 1	$12,350.00	$671.90

The sample list in Figure 1 shows only two debts. Your list will likely be longer than this, probably a lot longer. You should include every debt that can be paid off, regardless of interest rate. Even if no interest is currently being charged, include it on the list. And don't bother trying to put the debts in any particular order. I'll be taking you through a little mathematical exercise that will prioritize them for you. Do not include expenses that are ongoing and can never be paid off, like utilities, rent, and food.

The next step in assessing your financial starting point is to figure out where the money *not* dedicated to the above debt payments is going. On what are you disposing your "disposable" income? How are you "consuming" it? The easiest way to accomplish this step is to keep a Spending Journal for at least two weeks, preferably for a month. The purpose of the Spending Journal (Fig. 2) is to capture all your nondebt spending, but particularly cash expenditures. Just write the five column headings— What, How Much, When, Where, Category—across the top of any sheet of paper or day-planner page, then capture your expenses, line by line, below them.

FIGURE 2

What	How Much	When	Where	Category
___	___	___	___	___
___	___	___	___	___

Why is this Spending Journal necessary? Typical consumers visit ATMs or cash checks at the beginning of the week, and by the end of the week they're heading back for more. But if you ask what happened to the money they got a few days earlier, they're hard-pressed to account for it. This disappearing money is disappearing wealth, because when I describe your Accelerator Margin™ in Step 3, you'll see a much more powerful use for it than what it's accomplishing for you now.

You'll notice the last column in the Spending Journal is labeled "Category." Tracking expenditures by category, such as food, recreation, gifts, clothing, and so on, will help you see what types of products or services you tend to spend your money on. This can give you insight into what part each spending category plays in your soul—your mind, will, and emotions. When you see a concentration of spending in one or more categories, try to explain to yourself what need this spending fulfills, and what other less-expensive ways there might be to fill that need.

Remember, you're taking 100 percent responsibility for your financial life now, and it's crucial for you to get a handle on where and why you might be using money to take the place of something else in your life. When you identify such a need, and decide for yourself what might be a more appropriate and effective way to meet it, you're improving both your lifetime financial picture and your emotional well-being.

STEP 2: MANAGE YOUR SPENDING

The heart of this chapter is to get you completely out of debt, but you can never hope to achieve that goal if you won't first stop making new debt. That just makes sense, doesn't it? Well, the key to stopping new debt is eliminating those little debt-makers in your wallet or purse. It's time to become a plastic surgeon and cut up your credit cards.

"Aaahhhh!" I can hear you scream from here. "Why not just cut off my right arm?"

Removing your right arm won't help much, unless that's the arm you usually hand over your credit cards with, but removing the credit cards will make all the difference in the world. Credit cards are just consumer cocaine, and you can't kick the habit if they're right there in your purse or wallet. If you truly intend to become debt-free, you have to stop using credit. If you're going to stop using credit, why do you need credit cards? Believe me, I've heard every excuse ever uttered as to why you should be able to achieve debt-freedom while still carrying around your credit cards, and not one of them is worthy of the ink it would take to print here.

Let's just use Jesus' test and judge the tree by its fruit (Matt. 12:33). Look at the "fruit" that carrying credit cards has given you up to now. If you continue carrying them, you'll continue getting the same result. If you carry credit cards, you'll use them. If you use them, you'll spend money you otherwise wouldn't because using credit is easier than using cash or a check. Even if you promise to pay off the full balance when the bill comes in, you'll still be paying for purchases you wouldn't have made if you hadn't had the credit card handy, so you'll still be "consuming" your wealth and transferring it to the Coalition.

This whole credit card argument is just like people trying to quit smoking. What could possibly be their justification for continuing to carry cigarettes? The only reason people who are trying to quit smoking would want to carry around cigarettes would be because they know ahead of time that they're going to cheat, so they need some butts at the ready.

It's exactly the same logic for someone who intends to stop making new debt. The only possible argument for continuing to carry credit cards is that you know you're going to cheat, so you'd better have them handy. But I'll say it again: You can't keep charging up credit cards and expect to become debt-free and build wealth. It's just not possible. And you can't expect not to use credit cards if you have them. That's also not possible.

When you identify a behavior in your life that just doesn't work . . . doesn't get you the result you want . . . why would you keep doing it? Credit cards don't get you the affluence they seduce you into believing they will. They're liars. They're really stealing affluence from your life. So why would you want to keep using them?

I concede that cutting up the cards can be emotionally challenging, but it's doable. My wife, Lois, cried when we set ourselves up over the wastebasket, scissors in hand. The cards had become part of her view of her "lifestyle," so it wasn't just the cards she was cutting up, she felt her lifestyle falling to the bottom of the wastebasket. But notice I said she "felt" she was cutting up her lifestyle. Here we are in the area of the soul again. The mind, will, and *emotions.*

Emotions are deep waters, but they are discernible by the owners if they're just honest with themselves. When she thought about it, Lois was able to see the emotional connection between the credit cards and her perception of her lifestyle. After she reminded herself that she could still buy things at all her favorite stores with cash, she realized her lifestyle would not be dealt a fatal blow. She would naturally be more conservative in her purchases because using cash or a check has that effect, but she would still be able to enjoy the "experience" of shopping without the cards.

Lois weathered the experience of having the cards disconnected from her soul rather well. But I remember a woman who couldn't quite take the leap.

She was at a seminar I was teaching in Chicago. After I had made all the arguments I've made to you so far in this book, I said, "Okay . . . are you ready to let go of your credit cards?" I scanned the audience and saw most of the heads nodding, but I caught one near the back of the room swinging dramatically from side to side.

I asked if there was something I hadn't explained clearly. She told me I had made my case quite convincingly, but she could not cut up her cards. It was wild. We went back and forth, with my making more and more arguments about the fruitlessness of her pretending she would ever get ahead with her finances if she continued using her cards, and her saying she completely agreed with me but couldn't cut them up. In the end I got her to agree to "try" cutting up one card a month and "see how it felt."

There we are with the "felt" thing again. "Feeling" we need credit cards is strictly the emotional result of the Coalition having fed us that lie for parts of our childhoods and all of our adult lives. You don't need credit. You shouldn't even want credit. Credit only makes things cost more. Why would you want to pay more for everything? Cut up the credit cards.

There's One Exception. The "just in case" excuse for keeping your credit cards comes from a fear of the unknown. A fear that some necessary expense will come up that's beyond your current cash-flow capabilities. So I do recommend that—in the beginning—you keep *one* no-annual-fee credit card in a safe place. This is to quiet the "just in case" emotion so you can sleep at night. Here's what you should do.

As I said, pick one of your cards that charges no annual fee to hang on to. You don't want it to cost you money even though you're not using it. *You're going to pay this card off according to the process I'll describe in Step 4, and you're not going to charge anything more on it—except if a bona fide emergency requires its use.* To assure its emergency availability only, I want you to put the card in a place where it won't be handy to use impulsively. My suggestion is that you clean out a metal soup or vegetable can, drop the card in it, fill it with water, and put it in the freezer. This way it will be available for a genuine emergency, but not very handy for impulse buying. The metal can will keep you from thawing it in the microwave, and by the time it thaws out naturally, so will any impulse that prompted you to reach for it.

And don't memorize or write down the account number and expiration date.

Important: When you send in the last payment for each credit card you're paying off, include a signed note telling the company to close the account. This way it won't send you a new card when the old, cut-up one expires.

"But I Need Credit Cards for Business." This is a legitimate concern, but I don't believe credit cards are the only answer. If you need plastic for business transportation, lodging, meals, and entertainment, my first

choice is the basic, green American Express card. It's a charge card, not a credit card, so you're required to pay the full balance each month. This card should be used for business purchases only. If you allow yourself to make personal purchases with it, you're vulnerable to begin counting on the "thirty-day float" between when purchases are made and the bill comes due. So, if you don't need it for business . . . you don't need it.

For personal purchases I recommend a debit card. This card is available from your bank and often doubles as an ATM card. It looks and works just like a VISA or MasterCard, but the money comes directly out of your checking account, just as if you wrote a check, so you can't spend money you don't have. This provides a measure of self-discipline not present in a true credit card.

Since a debit card deducts money from your personal bank account, I do not recommend it for expenses you might incur as an employee in someone else's business. If your boss expects you to use your own plastic and later be reimbursed, I'd again recommend the green American Express card as my first choice. If that's not an option for some reason, then get a no-annual-fee VISA or MasterCard and commit to never using it for any personal purchases.

If you try carrying regular credit cards, even if you intend to pay the full balance monthly, you'll make purchases you otherwise wouldn't, because research has shown that consumers will spend an average of 30 percent more in a given buying situation if they're using a credit card rather than cash or a check—even if they intend to pay the full amount when the bill comes due. Those unnecessary, often frivolous purchases will diminish your financial potential.

And, of course, if you have a credit card with an open balance, you'll always be vulnerable to a well-timed temptation, such as a vacation offer, a new coat on sale, a new piece of furniture that would look "perfect" in your living room, or any of a billion other possibilities. If you have credit cards handy, your soul will burn until you use them. The easiest way is to just get rid of them.

Develop a cash mentality. Since you're not going to use credit anymore, you're going to have to fit your emotions back into your income. Remember, the illusion that credit gets you more of anything is just a lie. It only makes everything you buy with it cost more. So getting back to a cash mentality will eventually release you into a better lifestyle, where everything you buy is cheaper because you're only paying the price, with no interest to increase it. Of course, when I say I want you to develop a "cash mentality," your soul might overreact and interpret that to mean "Don't buy anything—ever!"

That's not at all what I'm saying.

The financial life plan I'm unfolding in this book is *not* a nonspending system, it's a *planned spending* system. My purpose in these pages is simply to put you back in control of *what* your money is spent on, and *when* you make those purchases. Instead of spending in reaction to Coalition stimuli, you want to be using your money, like a good steward, to efficiently and effectively move you toward your life goals. That takes spending control.

In Step 3 I'll introduce you to a spending control system. But first I want to help you defend yourself from the temptations wooing you to be an out-of-control spender.

Decode the Advertising. The Advertising component of the Coalition of Four is populated by some of the most clever people on the planet. They connect to your soul through various Media like TV, radio, magazines, and movies, and then they use those connections to make you want things. After repeated exposures, your desire builds until you're ready to buy what they're selling. Then they get you to pull the trigger by manipulating you into acting now rather than later.

How do they do all this without your being conscious of it?

Well . . . they know how you're wired. Mostly because they wired you, but also because they know how your soul works. The Advertisers use your mind to get at your emotions, and then they get the two of them to overpower your will. The tool the Advertising Industry uses to describe this process is called AIDA.

AIDA stands for Awareness, Interest, Desire, and Action. This is the sequence your mind, will, and emotions go through from first becoming aware of a product or service to being unable to stop yourself from buying it. And it's the sequence Advertisers cleverly manipulate you through to sell you things you don't really need. Here's how it works.

When you first see a product or service offered, you become *aware* of it. This can actually take several exposures, but Advertisers know who they're after with a given product or service, and they know where to place their ads to get multiple, reinforcing exposures into your mind. You might first see an ad in a magazine. Then, when the same product is advertised on TV, using the same words and images, it reinforces the first exposure. Maybe it will take another TV commercial or maybe the related radio commercial to sufficiently plant the product or service in your mind, but sooner or later that's accomplished.

Once your awareness is activated, your mind begins considering the ideas set forth in the Advertising message, and the ad's argument starts lifting the product or service from something you're just aware of to something you're getting *interested* in. This process may be further reinforced by a billboard you pass on the way to work with the same images as the magazine, TV, and radio ads, or you could hear yourself mouthing familiar ad phrases, like "Dude . . . you're getting a ____." It's all reinforcing the effect on your mind. And now your mind is enlisting the help of your emotions as your interest builds.

Then one day you wake up and realize you *desire* the product or service. This is after your mind and emotions have been attacking your will, teaming up to overcome every objection the will poses, beating it down until—in a weak moment—it surrenders. This moment frequently happens when a commercial or other Advertising message gets to the "Call to Action" we discussed earlier.

This is the "if you call in the next ten minutes" part of the commercial. The Advertiser always has some hook built into the process to force you to act now rather than think it over. Whatever bribe it's found to tip the scales, it'll throw it in at the emotional peak of the ad.

In the store it's the limited-time special price. "The sale ends today. We're not going to restock this model, so if you don't get it right now, you'll never be able to get it at 25 percent off!" Advertisers know what works. These calls to action are designed to trigger the built-up Awareness, Interest, and Desire you're carrying from previous exposures to their messages, and they're frequently irresistible. But you must learn to see how you're being manipulated and resist!

Decode the Cultural Influencers. These influencers are less obvious than overt commercials, so you'll have to be more observant to catch them. But don't take them lightly . . . they're at least as deadly to your financial well-being as TV, radio, magazine, newspaper, billboard, direct-mail, e-mail, and point-of-purchase Advertising.

Observe your own emotions when you're watching a movie or TV show. Not the commercials, but the program itself. If you feel yourself starting to want something the character on the screen has, note it. If you feel yourself wanting to emulate a behavior of a character on the screen, note it. Then ask yourself if there could be any financial consequences to these new desires. Would you have to buy the product you see the character on the screen using or wearing? Would emulating the character's behavior result in your spending money in ways you don't now?

What's the point?

The point is that the Advertising Industry is not only working through the commercials to influence you to buy things, it teams up with its Media Coalition partners to use popular programs, characters, and stars to create Awareness, Interest, and Desire for everything from clothing to cars to trendy refreshments. You see your favorite TV celebrity using something, wearing something, talking about something, driving something, being attracted to people who use, do, or have something, and pretty soon you find yourself *desiring* it. It's not an ad, but it works like one . . . and the Advertisers know it.

In fact, the Coalition's cultural influencers are in many ways more powerful than Advertising because they have the appearance of unbiased, third-party endorsements. But they're not endorsements by just your friends and family, they're coming from celebrities you admire and want to be like. Just look at how music celebrities influence fashions. Shania Twain and Britney Spears expose their navels, and millions of young women quickly spend billions of dollars on new jeans that will share their belly buttons with the world.

It's seductive, and it's happening to you every day. But you're becoming immune because knowledge, as they say, is power, and you now have the knowledge to perceive the Coalition's cultural influencers for what they are, which empowers you to resist them. You can see what they're doing as if you're watching an old 3-D movie, and you're the only one with the colored glasses. In fact, it won't be long before you'll be able to intuitively sense when they're pulling your strings. And when they do, just shout at the screen, "I'm not your puppet! You're wasting your time."

If you have children, it's never too soon to begin pointing out these influencers to them. Help them decode the ads and influencers aimed at their age-group. They have less experience and maturity than you, and they are more easily led down the Coalition's path. Because they're more sensitive to being accepted by their peers, they're more susceptible to cultural influencers promoting products and services on TV, radio, billboards, and in magazines aimed at young audiences. They should at least learn to make up their own minds, rather than having them made up for them by others.

What About the Influencer Next Door? Of course, it's not only your favorite celebrities who have influence over your mind, will, and emotions. Observe your feelings when someone you know gets a new car. If you break out with a case of ride-envy, ask yourself why. Then ask yourself if you really believe that by having an identical or comparable car, the quality of your life would be significantly better, say, a year after you got it.

The best day I ever had with my Corvette was the day before I picked it up. The anticipation was way better than the reality. In reality, it eventually became just my car, the vehicle that got me to work or to the supermarket. But that reality came with $549 monthly payments.

So, when people you know cave in to a car commercial or the smell of rich Corinthian leather, remind yourself that they've been captured by the Coalition. More important, from your perspective, remind yourself that—once they were captured—they became unwitting operatives for the Coalition, and their assignment is to get you and their other friends, family, and acquaintances to buy the same or a comparable car.

Just as with cultural-influencing celebrities, this is a part of the great deception. The Coalition manipulates you directly through Media and Advertising, and indirectly through peer pressure. Whether it's a coworker who buys new clothes, a cousin who buys a new house, a neighbor who buys a home theater, or any other peer with any other "gotta have" item in our culture today. Each is unknowingly working on *you* for the Coalition.

I remember when I overheard a young lady during a break at one of my seminars several years ago. She was busily working for the Coalition, telling anyone who would listen about the new car she had just bought. I walked over and asked her how much she had paid for the car.

"Twenty-five thousand dollars," she said.

I smiled and asked, "Would you have agreed to buy the car if the salesperson had asked you to pay $29,000?"

"Of course not!" she huffed.

"How much are your monthly payments?" I asked.

"Six hundred twenty-two dollars," she answered, a little less confidently.

"How many months did you finance it for?"

"Forty-eight months." It was practically a whisper.

"Let's do the math," I said, moving toward the marker board at the front of the room. "Six hundred twenty-two dollars a month times forty-eight months, equals a total of $29,856. You've agreed to pay almost $30,000 for that $25,000 car, without the salesperson even asking you to."

The True Cost of Using Credit. You might be thinking that it sure was a waste for her to give the finance company that extra $4,856 in interest payments, but that's not the worst of it. In giving that money to the finance company—to make it wealthier—she denied herself its use to increase her own wealth. If she had put that money into a retirement account earning 8 percent annually, it could have built up to $23,924 in twenty years. So, in effect, she wasn't losing just $4,856, she was losing $23,924. That means the real total cost to her lifetime wealth of that $25,000 car could be $48,924!

This is the way I want you to look at every finance charge in your life. It's not just some little percentage added onto a purchase. It's many dollars that could have become many more dollars, had they been invested for *you* rather than contributed to the Coalition. It's also the way you should look at every discretionary purchase. The true cost of anything you buy is not just its price, it's what that amount of money could have become had it been invested instead.

But why didn't the young lady recognize she was paying more than $29,000 for her $25,000 car? Because she fell into one of the Coalition's most powerful and seductive wealth destroyers . . . the Monthly Payment Trap.

The Monthly Payment Trap. The Monthly Payment Trap is a place in your mind created by Coalition indoctrination. It's a place where the true cost of a pending purchase no longer applies. All that matters is, "Can I afford the monthly payment?"

You don't think about the total cost of the transaction, or how it might affect your long-term wealth. You base the purchase decision solely on whether the monthly payment or the increase in your credit card payment will fit within your monthly cash flow. If it does, you buy. But as soon as you hang up the phone or carry the purchase out to your car, you might as well get a marker pen and write "Victim" across your forehead. You've just become a casualty of a well-orchestrated campaign to transfer your money—for months and years to come—to the Coalition.

You have to learn to stop thinking monthly and think *lifetime*. It's not important whether you can afford the monthly payment. What's important is how much the purchase will cost in total—the total cost of all the monthly payments until it's paid off—because that's the amount of money that will actually leave your life. And since you'll make a finite amount of income over your lifetime, the more you give away, the less will be left over for you and your loved ones.

This monthly mind-set is the grand assumption upon which nearly all the Coalition members' deceptions are built. Once they have you thinking monthly, they can get you to swallow a mountain of debt and unnecessary purchases. They feed it to you one bite at a time, sometimes literally, because many of today's consumers are buying groceries and fast-food lunches with credit cards. Once again, future financial resources are digested instead of invested.

Now that you understand how to manage your spending rather than unconsciously let the Coalition manage it by remote control, it's time for the main event . . . the hinge on which your whole financial turnaround will swing. We're going to get you completely out of debt, and the key to that process is what I call your Accelerator Margin™.

STEP 3: CREATE YOUR ACCELERATOR MARGIN™

In Step 4 I'll explain my Cascading Debt-Elimination System™ for rapidly paying off your debts, but to maximize the power of this formula you'll want to focus as much monthly cash flow as you can on the process. To do this, you need to minimize other expenditures as much as is practical, so the focus of your resources is on debt elimination. When you minimize your expenses, the percentage of your income left over each month—the money we'll use to melt away your debts—is called your Accelerator Margin™.

In essence, as you develop your plan to minimize your expenses in order to maximize your Accelerator Margin™, you're creating a Managed Spending Plan. Earlier I promised I'd show you a simple method for managing your spending, and this is it.

Turn to Appendix A for a moment. It's called the Accelerator Margin™ Finder Form. This form consists of two simple tables. Together they represent a basic family cash-flow planner. The first table, under the section titled "Step 1: Total Household Income," will help you organize and account for all your income sources. The second table, under the section titled "Step 2: Reducing Your Monthly Expenses," will help you organize and minimize your spending.

As you fill in the numbers you'll be accomplishing two things:

1. You'll be developing a spending plan that will help you control how much you intend to spend each month in each of the listed expense areas. As each month passes, you can compare your actual expenditures to the amount you planned to spend in each area. It will be obvious if any corrective action is necessary.

2. You'll be calculating your starting Accelerator Margin™.

If you'd like a more comprehensive system for managing your spending and working out your Accelerator Margin™, you can download an Excel workbook of spreadsheets, called the *Personal Financial Statement*, from my Web site: www.johncummuta.com. It contains separate worksheets for all typical expense areas and income sources, and it automatically calculates and summarizes all the numbers.

Now, my Cascading Debt-Elimination System™ will work even

with an Accelerator Margin™ of zero, but it will work a lot faster with extra money to prime the pump. Each Accelerator Margin™ dollar can save you several dollars of interest, which can then multiply into many dollars of eventual wealth. That's how you transform your debt into wealth.

The goal I want you to shoot for is an Accelerator Margin™ of at least 10 percent of your monthly net income. That means, if you bring home $3,000 a month, your Accelerator Margin™ goal would be $300 a month. That may sound astronomical to you right now, but I'm going to help you locate where that money may be hiding or, more likely, leaking out of your life.

What do I mean by money "leaking out of your life"? Well . . . remember the last time you got cash from the bank? How long did it last? On what did you spend it? If you're like most folks I know and those who attend my seminars, you don't even remember. How often do you have to replenish your "carrying money"? How about when you go grocery shopping? Do you frequently leave the store with more than you planned on buying? Do you regularly stop for gourmet coffee or cappuccino? Do you go out to lunch most workdays instead of bringing something from home? Do you practice retail therapy, where you stop at the mall after a hard week to buy yourself a little reward?

These are all common and expensive money leaks—leaks that are likely costing your present and your future far more than you realize.

Now, before you start thinking I'm asking you to live like a monk who's taken a vow of poverty, that's not the plan. My whole purpose in writing this book is to help you have an affluent and comfortable life . . . for all of your life. But there is that *reality* thing we have to take into account. If you've overspent your income up to now, you're not going to be able to reverse your situation without some temporary self-discipline. If anyone tells you that you can, he'll probably lie about other things too.

You have to make some grown-up choices here. Choices to throttle back on some of your self-indulgences now, so you can enjoy many more self-indulgences later. Just a $5-a-day lunch eats up $100 a month. That $100 would make a considerable contribution to your Accelerator Margin™ and could eventually produce many thousands of dollars in your investment accounts. In fact, over a forty year working life, at 8 percent interest, that $100 a month would build to $349,101! You'd be growing your wealth instead of your waste line. I'm confident that, once you see the power of each Accelerator Margin™ dollar, you'll be more aggressive about your spending than I would have nerve to suggest.

Here are some other areas to look for Accelerator Margin™ money:

- Using grocery coupons can save you 10 percent or more on your monthly grocery bill. They're available in local newspapers and on the Internet. Do a search on "grocery coupons" or "grocery discount coupons," and watch how many sources come up.

- You have to ask yourself whether the weekly movie at the theater, the premium TV channels, the greens fees, the weekly dinners at restaurants, or whatever your recreational expenditures might be, are worth their cost when compared to those dollars going into your Accelerator Margin™. I'm not talking about doing away with entertainment, but there's a less-expensive alternative to almost every entertainment activity.

- Review your insurance policies to see if you're paying for coverages you don't need, such as overlapping medical coverage. If you have a cash-value life policy, consider replacing it with a much lower premium term policy that would give you the same death benefit. Consider raising your deductibles to their maximums on your home-owner and auto insurance. This could reduce your premiums by as much as 40 percent.

Consider canceling any credit life insurance policies you bought to cover credit purchases. These are very expensive insurance policies—and the creditor, not your heirs, is the beneficiary. If you want insurance to protect your heirs from having to pay off your debts should you die short of paying them off yourself, just get a term life insurance policy with a death benefit sufficient to cover the total of all your debt balances. Once the debts are paid off, you can cancel the policy.

If your home loan has mortgage insurance on it, you can tell your lender to cancel it if your equity is at least 20 percent. This will noticeably reduce your monthly mortgage payment.

- Cancel and get refunds on all extended warranties that you've paid for. For example, if you bought a three-year extended warranty, and you're only in the first year, you should be able to cancel it and expect a refund for the unused portion. If the company won't give it to you, someone at your state's Insurance Commission would likely be interested in hearing your story. Extended warranties are rarely used because most modern products will break within the first year if they're going to break before their normal life expectancy. The first year is almost always covered under the manufacturer's warranty. Why pay for coverage you'll likely never use?

- I recommend you stop saving money and put it in your Accelerator Margin™. You'll get a higher return on investment for money used to prepay debt balances than you will in any savings account. The reason is: When you prepay the outstanding balance of any debt that charges interest, you get an effective Return on Investment (ROI) *equal* to the interest rate the debt charges. So paying off the balance of, say, a 15 percent credit card gives you a much better return than putting that money into a savings account paying 2 percent.

If you're contributing to a 401(k) or 403(b) account, continue contributing only as much as your employer will match because you're effectively getting an immediate 50 percent to 100 percent return on that money, depending on the percentage of your employer's match. If you're currently contributing more than that, reduce your contribution to the match point and put the rest in your Accelerator Margin™ until after your debts are gone.

- Shop outlet stores, and shop them right after seasonal changes, so you can enjoy the extra reductions on the previous season's products. You'll be amazed how much less you can pay for name brands. My wife, Lois, who has a black belt in shopping, recently picked up a Liz Claiborne skirt that carried an original price tag of $119. She got it for $9.95 because she was buying this winter skirt in the summer at an outlet store. Following this strategy can buy you new, high-quality clothes and other household goods at prices comparable to those charged for used items in consignment and resale shops.

- Rent infrequently used tools and equipment. As a tool guy, I know how deeply this one can cut, but it really makes little sense to pay $100 or more for a tool you may use only once every year or two and can rent for $20. If you get into larger power or garden tools, the difference between a purchase and rental becomes even more dramatic.

- Repair breakdowns in your car and home as soon as possible. These things never improve with time and will only cost more later.

- Be vigilant in not wasting energy to overcool your home in the summer or overheat it in the winter. Try to adjust your clothing rather than the thermostat.

- Don't use your TV for background noise. A radio uses a lot less electricity.

- Assess your gift giving. Could you cut back to only close relatives? Could you cut back on the expense per gift? Could you replace some gifts with homemade items, like cookies or something you crafted? Could you offer to baby-sit or help around the person's house rather than buy her something she probably doesn't need anyway? It all counts.

- Assess your vacationing. Do you have to visit the Mouse House in Florida or California? There are a lot of great close-to-home recreational opportunities, no matter where you live. State and national parks offer many memory-making destinations, and every area has its theme parks and special attractions, which tend to be much more affordable.

- Resist the "might-as-wells." This is when you're buying one thing, so you "might as well" buy one or more associated products or services. This frequently happens when we're replacing a piece of furniture or doing some minor redecorating. The might-as-wells can really swell your spending.

Don't lie to yourself. Remember, you'll be the principal beneficiary if you diligently pursue Accelerator Margin™ money, and you'll be the big loser if you lie to yourself and continue unnecessarily dribbling away your money.

Get creative. I'm sure you can think of many more areas where money is leaking out of your life. Areas where you could make small adjustments that would pay big dividends in your Accelerator Margin™ and your eventual wealth. As I mentioned earlier, you should use the Accelerator Margin™ Finder Form in Appendix A to help you locate opportunities to reduce your spending and thereby increase your Accelerator Margin™.

Finally, give yourself a break now and then. Enjoy an indulgence to reward yourself for paying off a big debt or achieving some other important milestone in the process—just make it a reasonably sized one. Then get right back on your debt-elimination plan.

And speaking of debt elimination . . . we're finally there!

STEP 4: PAY OFF *ALL* YOUR DEBTS

The Cascading Debt-Elimination System ™ is a little engine that eats debt alive and rapidly frees up more and more of your monthly income, to increase your Accelerator Margin™ and to give you a continually increasing financial cushion that can handle many of life's little unexpected challenges.

This debt-elimination process is simple yet elegant. It's based on a concept similar to what the military call "massing of forces." What we're going to do is prioritize your debts and then focus all your Accelerator Margin™ on one debt at a time, destroying it completely before moving on to the next one. While you're focusing on this one debt, you'll make only the minimum required payments on all your other debts.

This massing of your Accelerator Margin™ against one debt at a time accomplishes two things:

1. It pays off each targeted debt quickly, giving you a sense of momentum and motivation.

2. It rapidly recovers the monthly payment amount from each eliminated debt and adds it your Accelerator Margin™, so subsequent debts can be paid off even more quickly.

Prioritizing Your Debts. The first step is to prioritize your debts in payoff order, so we know which debt to focus on first, second, third, and so on. In Figure 2, near the beginning of this chapter, you listed your debts, their outstanding balances, and minimum monthly payments. In Figure 3 I've added one column to that list.

FIGURE 3

Name of Debt	Total Outstanding Balance	Minimum Monthly Payment	Division Answer
VISA	$1,132.76	$22.66	
Car 1	$12,350.00	$671.90	

The new column is labeled "Division Answer." What does that mean? It means I want you to divide each debt's outstanding balance by its minimum monthly payment, and put the answer in the "Division Answer" column. And use only the minimum payment required for each debt. If you usually add extra money to the required payment when paying a bill, don't do that here. Just use the minimum payment listed on the payment coupon or bill.

FIGURE 4

Name of Debt	Total Outstanding Balance	Minimum Monthly Payment	Division Answer	Payoff Priority
VISA	$1,132.76	$22.66	50	2
Car 1	$12,350.00	$671.90	19	1

Now that you've done the math, write the number 1 in the Payoff Priority column next to the debt that came out with the lowest Division Answer (Car 1). This will be *the first debt you'll pay off.* Write the number 2 by the next lowest Division Answer debt (VISA), and so on through all your debts. If you end up with two or more debts with the same Division Answer, rank the debt with the lower Total Outstanding Balance ahead of the other(s).

You're now ready to start eliminating your debts. Look at Figure 5. Here's where you'll see the power of your Accelerator Margin™. Let's assume the $300 a month Accelerator Margin™ we talked about earlier. Car 1 is the number one priority debt, so you'll add the $300 Accelerator Margin™ to its normal $671.90 monthly payment for an Accelerated Monthly Payment of $971.90.

FIGURE 5

Name of Debt	Total Outstanding Balance	Accelerated Monthly Payment	Number of Months to Payoff
Car 1	$12,192.12	$971.90	13

Now simply divide the debt's Total Outstanding Balance by this Accelerated Monthly Payment. The answer is 12.5 months. But since you don't make payments in fractions of a month, it will take thirteen monthly payments to completely eliminate the Car 1 loan.

The second debt in our example is the VISA bill, with a Total Outstanding Balance of $1,132.76. For its Accelerated Payment you'll add the increased Accelerator Margin™ of $971.90 (original $300 Accelerator Margin™ plus the $671.90 former Car 1 payment) to the regular $22.66 monthly payment for the VISA bill. That would give you an Accelerated Monthly Payment of $994.56. Divide $1,132.76 by $994.56 and you get 1.1 months, which in reality is two months (Fig. 6).

This rolling of the monthly payment from each paid-off debt down to the next priority debt is why I call it the Cascading Debt-Elimination System ™. The elimination of each debt adds its monthly payment to the Accelerator Margin™ and cascades it all down to accelerate the payoff of the next-priority debt, and so on until they're all gone.

FIGURE 6

Name of Debt	Total Outstanding Balance	Accelerated Monthly Payment	Number of Months to Payoff
Car 1	$12,192.12	$971.90	13
VISA	$1,132.76	$994.56	2

So, in our example in Figure 6, the total time to pay off these two debts will be approximately fifteen months. Imagine . . . in just over a year you'll have paid off a car that probably had about two years of payments remaining, and a credit card that you would likely have been charging up and paying down for the rest of your life. In a typical scenario, all non-mortgage debt is usually gone in two to three years. And in most cases it doesn't matter how many dollars we're talking about. Here's why.

Lenders lend you money based on what are called "ratios." These ratios compare your income with the total payments your combined debt load requires to service it each month. So your total monthly payments cannot exceed a certain percentage of your monthly income—usually somewhere around a maximum of 40 percent. This means that if you have high monthly payment obligations, you likely have a high income to qualify for that debt load. Conversely, if you have a lower income, you'll likely qualify for a debt load relative to that income—because your payments and the income you have to pay them with must fall within the ratio requirements of your creditors.

This means, whether we're talking about big numbers or not so big numbers, the debt-to-income relationship will be approximately the same. Which means that the Cascading Debt-Elimination System™ will be able to pay off your debts in the same time frame as someone in a much different income strata with the same payments-to-income ratio. Another way to say that is: The system will work for you, no matter what your debt load, because the income that qualified you for those debts is sufficient to accelerate their payoff.

Important: Each time you send in a payment with the Accelerator Margin™ added on, include a signed note telling the creditor to deduct everything above the required minimum payment for that month from the *principal balance* of the account, and *not* to apply it as prepayment of regular payments.

Once you've followed this process for each of your debts in their prioritized order, all you have to do is add up all the "Months to Payoff," divide that total by twelve, and you'll have a close approximation of how many years it will take you to achieve *complete* debt freedom. For example, if the total "Months to Payoff" for all your individual debts add up to sixty-six months, you'd divide that by twelve and come out with 5.5 years. That's just five years, six months.

After more than a decade of teaching people this system, I've found that most households are debt-free in five to seven years, including their mortgage. This is usually twenty to twenty-five years sooner than they would've accomplished the same goal following their creditors' monthly payment plans.

The other exciting result of following my Cascading Debt-Elimination System ™ is that it will save you thousands of dollars in interest charges you would have paid had you followed the creditors' payment schedules. In fact, if yours is an average-income household with a home mortgage, you could well save more than $100,000 in interest.

To help you see how this might work out for you, I've put together three representative households:

- The first has an annual income of $30,000. The family's debts are:

  > MasterCard 1: $950

  > MasterCard 2: $1,703

  > VISA: $1,120

  > Discover: $390

  > Department Store: $785

  > Car: $5,250

  > They're renting, so there's no mortgage.

  > Their take-home pay is roughly $2,000 a month, so their Accelerator Margin™ is $200.

- The second has an annual income of $60,000. The family's debts are:

  > Mortgage: $100,000

  > MasterCard 1: $1,700

> MasterCard 2: $3,287

> VISA: $1,550

> Discover: $850

> Department Store: $1,122

> Car 1: $12,350

> Car 2: $7,250

>Home Equity Loan: $23,530

>Their Accelerator Margin™ is $400.

- The third has an annual income of $150,000. The family's debts are:

>Mortgage: $220,000

>MasterCard: $2,400

>VISA 1: $2,780

>VISA 2: $1,995

>Optima: $960

>Discover: $3,280

>Department Store: $453

>Car 1: $27,000

>Car 2: $12,400

>Student Loan: $27,332

>Their Accelerator Margin™ is $875.

Watch the power of the Cascading Debt-Elimination System™:

- The $30,000 household is debt-free in one year, three months, saving $1,246 in interest, and the family's left with $635 a month to save for a house down payment. At 8 percent interest, that could build to more than $46,000 in five years.

- The $60,000 household is debt-free, including its mortgage, in six years, saving $146,076 in interest. The family is left with $2,795 a month to invest, which would build to $511, 334 in ten years, and more than $1.6 million in twenty years, at 8 percent average return.

- The $150,000 household is debt-free, including its $220,000 mortgage, in seven years, saving $150,163 in interest. The family's left with $4,704 a month to invest, which—at 8 percent—would grow to $860,761 in ten years and nearly $2.8 million in twenty years.

Let's work through the $60,000 annual income family's plan to see how it works. We'll tie all the steps we've covered in the debt-elimination process in one sample plan.

FIGURE 7

Name of Debt	Total Outstanding Balance	Minimum Monthly Payment	Division Answer	Payoff Priority	Accelerated Monthly Payment	Number of Months to Payoff
Mortgage	$100,000	$733.76	137	9	$2,794.73	36
MasterCard 1	$1,700	$34.00	50	6	$1,678.54	2
MasterCard 2	$3,287	$65.74	50	7	$1,744.28	2
VISA	$1,550	$31.00	50	5	$1,644.54	1
Discover	$850	$17.00	50	4	$1,613.54	1
Dept. Store	$1,122	$33.66	34	3	$1,596.64	1
Car 1	$12,350	$671.90	9	2	$1,562.98	8
Car 2	$7,250	$491.08	15	1	$891.08	9
Home Eq. Loan	$23,530	$316.69	75	8	$2,060.97	12
					Total Time:	**72 mos.**

This is all accomplished using the *same* money the members of household are bringing home now. The same money they're using to pay the same bills. If they follow the Coalition way, they'll pay on their debts for decades, getting nowhere and ending up burned out, used up, with little hope of ever retiring. But my debt-elimination system focuses their income to obliterate debts and free up monthly cash flow to produce real, take-it-to-the-bank wealth. No smoke, no mirrors, no dependence on rocket-science investment techniques. Just a simple redirecting of their income to short-circuit their debts and build retirement wealth.

Of course, this will work only if you *stop* creating new debt. That's the reason I had you cut up your credit cards. A diet won't work if you keep stuffing Twinkies in your face, and this debt-elimination plan won't work if you keep stuffing purchases on your credit cards and other financing balances. What I'm trying to help you see is that there is a whole better lifestyle out there. One where you never have to experience credit hangover and guilt. One where you literally never use credit again for the rest of your life. I've shown you how it worked for my sample households . . .

Now It's Your Turn. Take the time right now to do these calculations on *your* debts. They're not complicated. Just use the blank Calculating Your Debt Payoff form in Appendix B. It contains complete, step-by-step instructions. As you pay off each debt, add its payment to your Accelerator Margin™, then add that total to the next debt's monthly payment to give you the new Accelerated Monthly Payment that will quickly eliminate that debt. Once you've calculated the number of months to pay off your individual debts, just add them up and divide by twelve to find the number of years to your total debt-freedom.

There's no time like the present. Why not just do it—now?

Welcome back. How many years did you come up with? Isn't it exciting to know how quickly you could achieve total debt freedom?

Now, before you read any further, I want you to write on a piece of paper "Debt-free by (date)." This date will be based on how many years and months your debt-elimination plan came out to. Later, when you have a few minutes, make copies of this "Debt-free" statement, sign them—you're making a contract with yourself—and hang the contracts or place them in strategic locations around your house and space at work to keep you focused on your goal and your commitment to achieve it.

How Accurate Are These Simple Calculations? This is a common question after people see how quickly a lifetime of debt can be melted away, so I want to address it before we talk about wealth-building and living your redesigned life.

My purpose with this "pencil and paper" version of the Cascading Debt-Elimination System™ is to show you how quickly your debts can be paid off, without having to put you through an advanced mathematics course to make my point. The steps you just executed will give you a reasonably close approximation of the payoff timeline for each debt, as well as the aggregate total payoff timeline for all your debts. But the simple formulas we're using in this book do not take several complex factors into account and therefore are not absolutely precise. The good news is that these complex factors tend to pretty much cancel each other, so the simple calculations I explained above usually come out well within 10 percent of the precisely calculated timeline.

That's close enough for our purposes, especially considering that even a precise calculation would be only an estimation based on nothing changing in your financial life over the full debt-elimination timeline. In reality, you may receive a raise, which would shorten your timeline, or you may experience a setback, which could lengthen the timeline. If these simple calculations say you'll be out of debt in five years ten months, and the precise calculation is six years one month, will those three months really make much of a difference compared to the twenty-five or more years it would take you to do it the way your creditors have their billing set up?

If absolute precision is important to you, you should get my

DebtFree™ for Windows software. It does all these calculations and more, with exact accuracy. It'll even print out your complete month-by-month debt-payment schedule, along with a host of colorful charts and graphs showing how soon you'll be debt-free, and how soon you'll be wealthy enough to retire. To order DebtFree™, just visit www.johncummuta.com on the Web.

Okay . . . you're debt-free. It's time to build your wealth!

STEP 5: BUILD YOUR WEALTH

Building wealth is a natural consequence of eliminating your debts, because you now have maximum monthly cash flow available for investing. Many people mistakenly think they're unable to build wealth because they don't know the "secret investing methods" of the rich. But the real reason their nest eggs aren't developing is that they simply don't have any money to invest each month. It takes regular, periodic (usually monthly) contributions to your investments to build a wealthy and secure future.

Once you're debt-free, you'll have a lot of money to invest each month, and that will produce rapid results. You could stuff it in a mattress or bury it in your backyard, and you'd still end up with more in retirement than 90 percent of your fellow income earners.

For example, let's look at the $60,000 annual income household I used earlier as an example of the Cascading Debt-Elimination System™. As we saw, the household members paid off their $153,639 total debt load in just seventy-two months (six years). In doing that, they eliminated debts that had required a total of $2,394.83 in monthly payments. At the beginning of the process, this family had used the Accelerator Margin™ Finder Form (Appendix A) to free up a $400 monthly Accelerator Margin™. So, at the end of their six-year debt-elimination journey, they have that $400 Accelerator Margin™ *plus* the $2,394.83 in recovered monthly debt payments, for a total of $2,794.83 a month to contribute, invest, spend—whatever they choose.

We'll say they decide to contribute $300 a month to their church and worthy charities and add $200 a month to their spendable budget for recreation, gifts, and unexpected opportunities. That leaves them $2,294.83 a month to invest. Now we'll see the power of actually having a significant amount to invest each month. At a growth rate averaging 8 percent, in ten years this investment would grow to $419,830. In twenty years it would mushroom to $1,351,702!

And keep in mind, they are able to accomplish this with the *same money* they are now investing in their creditors' profit margins! Same money, just a different destination.

In the next chapter I'll cover investment basics in detail, and then show you some specific approaches to investing your newfound cash flow in relatively safe and sound securities. I'll also give you information to help you select a good investment adviser, if you'd rather not handle your own investing. In this chapter I just wanted to show you where wealth-building happens in the process, and how it's an almost unavoidable consequence of getting rid of your debts.

STEP 6: LIVE YOUR REDESIGNED LIFE

The other natural result of paying off your debts is that you'll be able to begin enjoying the life that you, as an individual, were designed to live. After you've saved up sufficient resources to where working is optional, you'll have unlimited discretion to invest your life in whatever you feel called or born to do! You'll no longer be trapped by having to "pay the bills," so you'll be free to take your life in any direction you choose.

In the previous chapter you began the process of redesigning your life. In this chapter I simply want you to see how, once you've paid off your debts and have begun to build wealth, you'll be in position to decide just when that redesigned life should start. You may want to target a certain wealth accumulation threshold as the trigger for beginning your new life, or, if you're prepared to continue earning an income in your redesigned life, you could begin it immediately.

This is the ultimate benefit of all the work you've undertaken to get here. You can now be the *you*, you were designed to be. You can live life on your own terms, not the Coalition's. You and your loved ones can be the prime beneficiaries of all your hard work.

Now let's turn to Part 3 and build your wealth!

PART THREE
YOUR WEALTH DESTINATION

6

BUILDING WEALTH—
THE UNAVOIDABLE
CONSEQUENCE

∞

When the tornado released Dorothy and Toto, their touchdown left us with an important principle: If your house crushes a wicked witch, you'll have an abundance of Munchkins. A similar, and perhaps more germane principle of life is, if you pay off all your debts, you'll have an abundance of money every month. It's inevitable. And, if you don't lapse back into a credit-based lifestyle, becoming wealthy is almost unavoidable. So I'll assume you're in complete agreement with me, and that total debt elimination is your goal, so you can enjoy the inevitable consequence of money accumulating in your life.

Don't misunderstand me on this point. I'm not saying that money is the most important thing in life. I'm over a half-century old, I have an inexpressibly good relationship with God, I've been married to the same incredible woman for more than three decades, I have two fabulous children and six tireless grandsons who love their grandpa (or Bumpa or Papa). I know what the most important things in life are.

What I am saying about money is that your life, however filled it is with the more important things, cannot help but be diminished by a lack of money—especially in your older and more vulnerable years. So let's not quibble about the importance of money. It's just a tool, but it's a necessary tool to live a reasonably comfortable, secure, and fruitful life on this planet. As the Bible says in Ecclesiastes 10:19, "Money answers everything." What the full verse actually teaches is that you can party and drink to try to forget your troubles, or you can be a good steward of your financial resources and be able to deal with your troubles . . . with cash! Of course, everything is ultimately in God's hands, but he gives us dominion (responsibility) for our lives here, and he expects us to do what it takes to have enough money to handle this life. If we don't wisely steward our money, we become vulnerable as so many have been in recent years.

Here's how it was reported in a September 2002 *New York Times* article:

> Almost three million people nationwide have been out of work for at least 15 weeks, up more than 50 percent from a year ago. Half of them have not worked in at least 6 months, the Department of Labor said. Many people who have not worked in months have begun spending retirement savings that were already diminished by the stock market's fall. Others are considering low-wage jobs that pay a fraction of their old salaries. In either case, their stretches of unemployment could define their financial futures for years to come.

I know how these people feel. I've been there. I've had a good income disappear, only to be replaced by a smaller one . . . months later. I've experienced the journey through shock, guilt, frustration, self-diminishment, and resignation. But I came to realize that much of my grief was self-inflicted. I had greatly complicated my situation by having spent practically all my income and promising away even more through debt, while saving practically nothing.

I am committed to not leaving you in that same vulnerable state. In this book I intend to give you every argument for building up a nest egg that can sustain you no matter how long you live and even bless your heirs when you're gone. I want you to have so much money that your contributions at church will empower your pastor to dream new ministry dreams. I want you to be able to feed the hungry, clothe the naked, house the homeless, and still have a fabulous life yourself. That's what money's for. It's a power to do good, for others and for yourself. Let's face it: You can't take it with you, and if you make the right choices before you go, all the expenses have already been paid on the other side anyway.

Wealth is neither good nor evil. So building wealth is neither good nor evil. Assuming you're a good person, you'll put your money to good use, so putting wealth in your hands will be good for you as well as those around you. Agreed? Okay, let's get to it.

THE SECRET INGREDIENT: MONEY

There's no magic formula to building wealth. All it takes is money. And once you've paid off your debts, you'll have exceptional positive monthly cash flow, so you'll have wealth's main ingredient flowing into your life by the thousands each month. Regardless of how you invest this cash flow, attaining wealth will be almost inevitable. Now, if you're reading this and saying, "I barely make enough to keep the lights on, and he's talking about saving thousands a month," then you have a problem I'll deal with in the next chapter. In Chapter 7 I'll focus on helping you increase your income, but for now let's just stay on the track we've started down.

Most people who go to a financial planner or investment adviser for help to get rich find out the math won't work with their meager savable monthly resources. "People are saving blindly," says Don Blandin, president of the American Savings Education Council. "They're simply trusting that they're putting in enough without doing the calculations. But half the people who have taken the time to calculate their retirement-income needs say they realize they have to save more if they hope to retire when they want." Mr. Blandin's statement, from a March 2002 *Forbes* magazine article, may be one of the great financial understatements. The truth is, most people will have to save a *lot* more than they currently do, and they'll have to start as soon as possible.

A front-page *USA Today* article in the late 1990s proclaimed that the average baby-boomer household would need $1 million in its retirement portfolio to be able to continue its working-years lifestyle after it got the gold watch. We'll give these average household members the benefit of the doubt and say they already have $100,000 of their $1 million saved up, and they have twenty years left to put away the other $900,000. If we assume they'll be able to realize an annual average growth of 8 percent, they'll have to start putting away $861.29 *every month* for those twenty years to make it. If they haven't saved anything yet, they'll have to put away $1,697.73 every month for those twenty years.

But how is the average household going to come up with an extra $861.29 to $1,697.73 a month? By following my Cascading Debt-Elimination System ™, as I explained it in the previous chapter.

The average home-owning household that follows my system to debt-freedom will be able to invest more than $2,000 a month and still have nearly a thousand discretionary dollars left each month! This is after the family pays for food, utilities, insurance, and property taxes. That's the power of first getting completely debt-free, then building wealth.

IT'S ABOUT NET WORTH

As I've already said, true wealth consists of a lot more than just money and material things, but if we confine this discussion to the financial component of wealth, the best measurement of material or financial wealth is your net worth statement. This is an expression of *what you own minus what you owe*. If you own a $250,000 house but owe $200,000 on it, your net worth in that house is $50,000. You may "look" like a quarter-million-dollar home owner, but the numbers tell the real story.

And a sad new reality, with the proliferation of home equity loans, is that many people in this situation surrender the meager $50,000 they do own, and their net worth sinks to zero. They're being seduced into exchanging what little wealth they've accumulated in their home's equity for a few toys, a vacation, a little remodeling, or paying down credit cards, which they will probably just charge back up again.

But if you learn to think net worth instead of monthly cash flow, you'll be able to turn the process around and begin building real wealth. When you think net worth, you see that building wealth is simply increasing what you own and eliminating what you owe. So you begin building wealth from the very first month on this program! When you pay down balances on your debts, you're owning more of whatever you bought with that borrowed money, so you're increasing your net worth. You're actually building your wealth by paying off debts.

Debt elimination is always your first and best investment. You get a guaranteed return on every dollar used to eliminate debt balances. No risk, just an increasing net worth plus the savings of future interest dollars you'll never have to pay. But once your debts are paid off, it gets a little more complicated.

THREE WAYS TO BUILD YOUR NET WORTH

The easiest way to build your net worth is to inherit wealth. This, however, is the most difficult route to riches because choosing your parents and other relatives has always been problematic. It's the timing issue, you see. They always have to exist before you do, so you end up having to settle for whoever they turn out to be. They either have money or they don't when it's their time to pass their net worth on to you.

Another way you can build your net worth is by adding to it through your own income-producing efforts. The Cascading Debt-Elimination System ™ explained in the previous chapter assumes a constant income amount over the debt-elimination period, but that's completely under your control. You can open the spigot wider and let more money flow into the process, further accelerating your journey to debt freedom. Once your debts are gone, an increased income means increased wealth production.

It's that simple. As I said, I'll be covering ways to increase your income stream in the next chapter.

The third way to build your net worth, and the one we'll focus on in this chapter, is to let other people do it for you. These people may contribute to your wealth by paying you compound interest, or by building the value of a business in which you own shares. These two methods apply to traditional investing in CDs, money markets, stocks, bonds, and other investment assets. An additional way others can contribute to your wealth is by being tenants in real estate you own. We'll examine both paper securities investing and real estate investing in this chapter, but first let's establish a target for your investing endeavors: your wealth-building goal.

WHAT'S YOUR WEALTH-BUILDING GOAL?

That depends on your expected PEL (Post Employment Lifestyle) and your employment termination date or employment reduction date.

Your Post Employment Lifestyle will obviously have a huge impact on how much monthly income you'll need in retirement to sustain it. That's why earlier chapters were devoted to helping you see through the Coalition's attempts to seduce you into struggling toward a highly materialistic, difficult-to-sustain PEL. Expensive cars, boats, oceanfront getaways, and the like are money-draining mirages the Coalition members want you chasing until your last breath. Don't be another of their pitiable victims. Decide for yourself what you *really* need to enjoy your golden years and target that PEL.

Of course, you don't have to have a PEL at all. Maybe you don't plan to retire in the conventional sense. You may want to stay active. Even so, there will come a time when you won't want to work as hard as you do now. You may want to cut back on your hours or change professions to something you always dreamed of doing, something that would be more like play than work. Or you might want to do volunteer work—work that would satisfy your heart as well as your personal desires.

The point is that whether your goal is complete or semiretirement, it will have a price tag. So, if you're asking yourself when all this can happen, the answer is: It all depends on how much monthly income you feel you'll need from your investments to live the PEL or Reduced Employment Lifestyle of your choice. Many people who are disciplined in their investing can retire five to eight years after they're debt-free. But, again, that depends on the amount of income they decide they'll need in their PEL.

Once you've determined your annual PEL income target, it's an easy process to see how much you'll need to accumulate in your retirement savings to pay you that annual amount without reducing the principal. Just divide the *annual* amount you believe you'll need by .06. The resulting number will be the Total Savings Goal you would need to accumulate in your investments, assuming these investments would earn an average of 6 percent annual interest, dividend income, rental income, or capital appreciation. For example, if you feel you'll need $60,000 annual income to support your PEL, divide that by .06 and you'll come up with a Total Savings Goal of $1 million. You'll need to build your investments up to $1 million, so at 6 percent a year, they'll pay you $60,000 annually without reducing the $1 million principal amount.

But now the question becomes: How long will it take you to build up your investments to the Total Savings Goal you've determined you need? The following table (Fig. 8) will help you estimate that. The first column shows various Total Savings Goals. Find the one closest to yours, then move your finger across to the right until it's under the number of years (top row) you have left to invest before you want to begin your PEL. For example, if you've decided you need to save up that $1 million, and you have twenty years left to do it, you'll have to immediately begin putting away $2,397 a month. You'll notice that the numbers in this chart are based on realizing a 10 percent growth rate, while in the previous paragraph I used 6 percent in my example. Here's why.

The table estimates how long it would take your retirement assets to grow. Over any ten-year or longer period, the U.S. stock market has consistently grown in value at an average rate in excess of 10 percent. So using 10 percent as a growth target for your investments is reasonable over time.

However, when it comes time to begin living off those investments, you won't want them subject to the ups and downs of the stock market, so I'll be counseling you to gradually move them into what are called "income-generating assets," such as government bonds and bond mutual funds. These assets are less volatile than the stock market but also generate lower growth rates. Hence, the use of 6 percent as a target for how much your ultimate investment nest egg will generate when it's mostly parked in income-generating assets.

Let's get back to our example of having to build you a $1 million retirement account in twenty years. As I said, you'll have to immediately begin investing $2,397 a month. Why so much? Because compound interest will have only twenty years to work, and to have the same buying power as $1 million today, your Total Savings will have to grow to $1,820,755 twenty years from now because of inflation. Inflation will cause the prices you'll have to pay twenty years from now to be nearly double what they are today, so you'll need nearly twice as much money saved up to pay those prices. It will take $109,245 a year, twenty years from now, to live comparably to today's $60,000 lifestyle.

FIGURE 8

Approximate monthly savings amount needed to reach your Total Savings Goal—assuming that your investments grow at 10 percent annually, and that the Total Savings Goal amount will increase by 3 percent a year due to inflation.

Total Savings Goal (in today's dollars)	Years Remaining Until Starting Your PEL						
	40	35	30	25	20	15	10
$167,000	$88	$125	$182	$267	$400	$633	$1,101
$334,000	$175	$250	$363	$533	$799	$1,263	$2,197

$500,000	$262	$375	$544	$799	$1,198	$1,894	$3,295
$667,000	$350	$501	$726	$1,066	$1,599	$2,527	$4,396
$834,000	$437	$626	$907	$1,331	$1,997	$3,157	$5,492
$1,000,000	$527	$751	$1,088	$1,598	$2,397	$3,788	$6,590
$1,167,000	$613	$876	$1,270	$1,865	$2,797	$4,421	$7,691
$1,334,000	$700	$1,001	$1,451	$2,130	$3,196	$5,051	$8,787
$1,500,000	$787	$1,126	$1,632	$2,397	$3,595	$5,682	$9,886

Okay . . . Let's Start Building Toward Your Total Savings Goal

But first let me be clear that I couldn't possibly give you, in one chapter, the depth and detail that I and other authors could provide in an entire book on investing. What I do intend to accomplish here is to provide you a primer on the most common investment options, and on my preferred "autopilot" investing strategy.

I'm assuming you're not already a sophisticated and knowledgeable investor. If I'm wrong about that, much of what I say in this chapter will be review for you. If I'm right, and—as I was—you've been so busy making bill payments each month you've never had the opportunity to even consider how investing works, this will be an easy introduction to the terminology and process of investing. If you wish to delve deeper into any specific security or investing method, there's no shortage of good books out there. My chief contributions to your wealth in this book will be in helping you to free yourself from Coalition slavery and free thousands of your income dollars for investing. From that point, almost any traditional investing path will get you to your goal.

Which brings me to nontraditional investing paths. Stay off them. In investing, the road less traveled is usually the road less survivable. You don't need any secret investing techniques to build wealth. All you need is sufficient money to invest, month after month. Warren Buffett, the richest investor in the world, just buys solid, unsexy investments and holds on to them for decades. No smoke, no mirrors, just consistency. As the apostle Paul would say, "This one thing I do."

I further recommend you avoid making any statements to brokers or clicking any buttons on broker Web sites with the terms "Put," "Call," or "Option" in them. The only reason to sell "short" is if you're one of Dorothy's Munchkins. If you don't recognize those terms or have no experience with them, that's fine. In fact, I strongly recommend you keep it that way.

Now, if you're a sophisticated investor and have a high level of confidence in your ability to profitably use these techniques, I concede your right to do so. But if you're not an experienced market-timing investor, let's stick to the simple, boring, traditional investing path that has made Mr. Buffett and millions of others wealthy . . . while sleeping soundly.

WE'LL START WITH YOUR EMERGENCY FUND

In the previous section you determined your long-term wealth-building goal. We'll start the journey toward that goal by first shoring up your short-term security with an emergency fund. This is money you'll be able to quickly get your hands on. The common term for this easy availability of funds is "liquidity."

Most financial planners will tell you to build your emergency fund to where it can cover your monthly living expenses for at least six months. Since your emergency fund will shortly be backed up by your long-term investments, I agree that six months' worth of liquid funds is sufficient. Should you lose your income for any reason, you'll have half a year to reestablish that income stream without the pressure that crushes the typical, debt-burdened consumer. Half a year to get your life back together. Half a year to calmly make the decisions that frequently come with an income interruption. *But this money is only for such an emergency.*

Your liquid emergency fund could reside in a money market bank account, a money market mutual fund, certificates of deposit (CDs), or any combination of these. What important benefits do these accounts share? They pay interest, and you can easily get your money out of them should you need it.

Of these options, CDs usually pay the highest interest rate, but that interest rate comes with a string attached. If you need to take money out of a CD before its maturity date, you'll have to pay a penalty, usually the most recent several months' interest. But, if you're following my philosophy of not wasting money on impulse buying and frivolous self-gratification, you won't be robbing your emergency fund anyway, so a CD or two will work just fine.

One technique investors use to avoid having to prematurely cash in a CD is to "stagger" their CDs, meaning they buy a CD with the same maturity period every few months. After they've been doing this for a while, they'll have CDs maturing every few months. This gives them the opportunity to use the money when it becomes available or roll it into another CD, knowing the next CD will mature a few months later. Another option is to split a onetime investment amount into several separate CDs instead of one big one. Let's say you've decided to put $12,000 into CDs. Instead of one $12,000 CD, how about six $2,000 CDs? This way, if you have to prematurely withdraw some money, you'll have to cash in and pay the interest penalty on only one $2,000 CD rather than the larger penalty that would be exacted on a $12,000 CD.

How much would a six-month emergency fund typically require? Let's use the medium-income household from Chapter 5 as an example.

- Medium-Income Family ($60,000 Annual)

  > Mortgage: $100,000

  > MasterCard 1: $1,700

  > MasterCard 2: $3,287

  > VISA: $1,550

  > Discover: $850

> Department Store: $1,122

> Car 1: $12,350

> Car 2: $7,250

> Home Equity loan: $23,500

> Starting Accelerator Margin™: $400

> Debt-free in six years

> Saved $145,597 in interest

> Final Accelerator Margin™: $2,795

> Invested at 10 percent annual return:

$216,437 in five years

$572,542 in ten years

$2,122,436 in twenty years

Let's say the family needs a minimum of $2,000 a month to cover food, property taxes, maintenance, gasoline, insurance, and other ongoing expenses. That means the family members need $12,000 in their six-month emergency fund. As we saw in the last chapter, after paying off all their debts using the Cascading Debt-Elimination System™, their ending Accelerator Margin™ is $2,795. This means that after paying regular ongoing living expenses each month—including setting aside money to build up for expenses that come less frequently, like annual or semi-annual insurance premiums—they have $2,795 left.

Since they need only $12,000 in their six-month emergency fund, and they have $2,795 a month to put into this account, it will take just over four months to build it to $12,000. Even if they decide to use $795 a month for current needs or even recreation, they'll still be able to fully fund their emergency account with $12,000 in just six months. But it would not have worked that way had they tried to build an emergency fund before paying off their debts.

If you'll remember, this sample family's initial Accelerator Margin™ was just $400, and their total monthly expenditures—including all their debt payments—added up to $4,499 ($2,000 a month for their ongoing expenses, plus $2,499 in monthly debt payments). That means a six-month emergency fund in their debt-ridden condition would've had to contain $26,994 in order to provide $4,499 a month for six months. But with only $400 a month available to save, it would've taken them five years, seven months to save up $26,994.

However, following the plan I'm laying out for you in this book, these same family members would be completely out of debt, owning their home and everything else in their lives, in just six years. As I've already shown, their monthly expenses would then be only $2,000 a month, so a six-month emergency fund would require only $12,000 and take only four and a half months to build up.

The bottom line in this comparison shows that by following my plan, these people would be completely debt-free *and* have their six-month emergency fund built up in just *nine months more* than trying to simply build up their emergency fund to cover the way they were paying their bills before they decided to get debt-free. So the benefit of first paying off debt is obvious.

What may be less obvious, however, is that—during this debt-elimination phase—the family is owning more and more of what is being paid off, so its net worth is increasing every month. Remember, net worth is the best numerical measurement of wealth, and you're growing it as you pay off debt. So you're actually *investing* from the very start of this program. It's just that your first and best investments are in your debts. Every dollar you invest in paying off a debt balance moves another dollar's worth of the value of whatever you purchased with that debt directly from the liability column to the asset column on your net worth statement.

An important emotional benefit of this strategy is that by making debt elimination your first investment, your possessions are less and less vulnerable to repossession should you have an interruption in your income. No one will take your house and car away if you own them. And having six months' worth of operating funds available in your emergency account will give you further emotional peace of mind.

Once you have your emergency account funded, your entire Accelerator Margin™ is available for long-term, PEL wealth-building—and there's a hierarchy of investment vehicles you'll want to follow. The idea is to first put your money in investments that will do you the most good, then work your way down through less-favorable investing options.

START AT THE TOP

Have you ever seen someone stack champagne or similar glasses, one sitting inside another in a single vertical column, then begin pouring liquid into the top glass? When the top one is filled, it overflows down into the glass below it. When that glass is filled, it overflows into the next glass down and so on, until they're all filled. That's how you want to build your wealth.

The champagne glasses represent different types of investing accounts, with differing tax statuses. You'll want your top champagne glass—the one you fill first—to be your most tax-advantaged account. Then, when you've maxed out that account, your investment money will overflow down into the next most tax-advantaged account. When it's filled with as much as the law will allow, the balance of your monthly investment funds will overflow down into less tax-advantaged accounts until you've invested the full amount each month. This way, you're making sure you're protecting as much of your money as possible from current income taxes and ongoing capital gains taxes.

In reality, this spread of your monthly investment amount across several accounts is something you'll need to establish only when your debts are paid off and you know how much you'll have available to invest each month. You'll make a plan listing how much of your investment money will go into each account every month, then you'll simply execute that plan, reviewing it annually to make sure you're still getting the most bang for each investing dollar.

This plan might be as simple as:

- Make the maximum allowable contribution to your 401(k) at work, using the money to buy shares in an S&P 500 (America's five hundred largest companies) index mutual fund.

- From the remaining balance, put the maximum allowed amount into your IRA (even if it isn't all tax-deductible), using the contributions to buy shares in an S&P 400 (America's four hundred most consistent midsize companies) index mutual fund.

- From the remaining balance, put some amount into tax-free municipal bonds from your state.

- From any remaining balance, put some into a tax-free municipal bond mutual fund.

- Put any remaining balance into an account populated with the highest-return investments you can find, because you'll be funding this account with after-tax money, and you'll be paying taxes on the interest, dividends, and taxable capital gains events within this account each year.

To give you a better idea of how these accounts would work, let's examine investing as an employee, as opposed to a self-employed income earner.

WEALTH-BUILDING AS AN EMPLOYEE

Start inside a shelter. All but one of the tax-sheltered accounts we'll discuss in this section allow you to deduct your contributions each year from your taxable income. This will save you a percentage equal to your tax bracket on each dollar. In other words, if you're in the 25percent tax bracket, you'll save 25 cents tax on each sheltered dollar. If you're in the

28 percent tax bracket, you'll save 28 cents tax on each dollar, and so on. To find your tax rate, check www.irs.gov. Look for a link to "Tax Info for You."

A tax-sheltered account is just what it sounds like: a shelter from taxes. Think of a shelter like a house, and think of the investments you make within the shelter as the house's furnishings. The house (shelter) is simply a container that protects the furnishings (investments), but the house is not the furnishings. It only holds the furnishings. When you open and fund a tax-sheltered account, you will then be asked to select investments to buy with that money. Those investments will be held in the tax-sheltered account, so their growth and income will be protected from taxes. When I talk about a 401(k) or an IRA, it's only a shelter. You will contribute money to the shelter account and then select stocks, bonds, mutual funds, or other securities to buy and hold within the shelter.

If you're going to invest as an employee, you want your top champagne glass to be a tax-sheltered retirement program offered by your employer, hopefully one into which he will contribute along with you. The advantages of this kind of tax-sheltered retirement account are that money invested in it is sheltered from current income taxes, and the ongoing growth of the investments within the account is sheltered from taxes as well. Income and capital gains taxes are paid only when money is withdrawn in retirement, and only at the tax rate applicable to the amount withdrawn each year.

For most people, the employer-sponsored retirement plan is a 401(k). If you work for an educational institution, hospital, or other nonprofit organization, your plan may be called a 403(b). There is another plan, called a 457 plan, which also shelters income you deposit into it from current taxes, but it has some differences in the way you must take money out when you retire. Otherwise, these plans work pretty much the same, so I'll just use the term 401(k).

When you contribute to your employer's 401(k) plan, he will most often match some percentage of your personal contribution. Some employers match their employees' contributions dollar-for-dollar. This gives employees participating in the plan an instant 100 percent return on their money! But, even if your employer contributes a much lower match percentage, every dollar you have deducted from your paycheck and deposited into your 401(k) avoids current income taxes. When you file your taxes, it's as if you were never paid that dollar. In essence, the IRS is also making a contribution to your retirement plan in the amount of the taxes you would have had to pay on those dollars if they weren't sheltered in your 401(k).

In 2004, 401(k), 403(b), and 457 plans can shelter up to $13,000. If you're over age fifty, you can contribute an additional $3,000 to help make up for the fact that you have fewer investing years left till retirement than younger workers do. These numbers increase every year through 2006 under the current tax law.

If your employer doesn't offer one of these tax-sheltered retirement plans, you can create one of your own. It won't be as good as an employer-sponsored plan because it won't allow you to shelter as much money each year, but it's better than nothing. You're probably familiar with the Individual Retirement Account or IRA. For many years this type of tax-sheltered investment account allowed income earners to invest up to $2,000 each year. Well, the new tax law is more generous to IRA investors as well.

In 2004, most people will be allowed to shelter $3,000 in an IRA. That amount will increase to $4,000 for 2005 through 2007. And if you're fifty or older, you can add $500 to these amounts. These dollar figures are the same whether you're talking about a regular IRA or a Roth IRA.

The difference between a standard IRA and a Roth IRA is simple. With a standard IRA you can deduct the amount you put into the account from your current taxable income each year, but you will pay income tax on the money you withdraw from the account in retirement. With a Roth IRA, it works the opposite. You don't get a current tax deduction, but when you take withdrawals in retirement, ther are no taxes owed. The standard IRA *defers* taxes on the growth and income generated within the account until you start taking out funds. The Roth IRA *eliminates* these taxes. Retirement withdrawals from a Roth IRA are completely tax-free. This is why, for most people, the Roth is the better IRA choice. I would still make any employer-sponsored retirement program the top glass in your stack, but when you get to the IRA level, check with your tax adviser to see whether the Roth is the better play for your situation.

There are income maximums for most tax-sheltered retirement accounts, beyond which the tax deductibility of your contributions is phased out, but even if your income is above these cutoff amounts, you can still make contributions to your tax-sheltered accounts and they'll *grow* tax-deferred. However, the Roth IRA is not available for single taxpayers with annual income above $110,000 or for married couples filing jointly with annual income above $160,000.

Whatever sheltered accounts you decide to invest in, be sure to start immediately after paying off your debts, because *time* is the most powerful lever lifting the potential of your investment growth. Before we move on to Educational Savings Accounts, let me briefly show you just how powerful time can be in building wealth within a tax-sheltered investment account like one of those we've just discussed.

THE POWER OF STARTING EARLY

There were two young men considering their financial futures. When they were nineteen the world appeared to be their oyster, and the major question boiled down to: Should they play first and build for the future later or vice versa?

Young man A decided that he would buckle down immediately and put $2,000 a year into an IRA. But he decided to do this for just seven years, from age nineteen to age twenty-six, then stop investing and use his income to play from that time on. His friend, young man B, thought he'd be more serious and take a longer view. He would get his youthful playing out of the way for those same seven years, then—beginning at age twenty-six—he would invest $2,000 each year into his IRA all the way to retirement.

Here's how the numbers work out. Young man A will invest just $14,000 over seven years. Young man B plans to start investing the year after his friend stops, and he will invest $2,000 a year from age twenty-six to retirement at age sixty-five. That's forty years for a total investment of $80,000. We'll assume their investments each average a 10 percent annual return.

If you're like young man B, you're probably thinking he'll end up with a lot more at retirement, because he's planning to invest nearly six times as much as his friend young man A. At age sixty-five, however, young man A—who will invest just $14,000 over seven years—will see his investments realize *more* growth than those of young man B, who will invest $80,000 over forty years.

Young man A will retire with $944,641, while young man B will have $973,704 in his IRA. That appears to indicate young man B narrowly won. But when you back out their investments, you see that young man A—who invested only $14,000—gained $930,641, while young man B—who invested $80,000—gained $893,704.

Why did young man A's $14,000 grow more than young man B's $80,000? *Because time magnified compound interest.* Young man A started earlier, so his money had more *time* for compound interest to work its magic. Compound interest is indeed powerful, but the earlier you start, the more it can do for you.

For example, every *day* the average American household delays starting on the debt-elimination and wealth-building system I'm teaching you in this book, it's giving up about $400 of future wealth. What I'm saying is that each day it delays starting its investing program will reduce the amount it'll end up with at its investing end-date by approximately $400, because its money will have one less day to benefit from compound interest.

So . . . once you've freed up your monthly cash flow by getting out of debt, you should waste no time beginning your wealth-building program. Give compound interest as much time as possible to make your investments grow. And that's true for investments designed to help put your children or grandchildren through college.

TAX-FAVORED EDUCATIONAL SAVINGS ACCOUNTS

If you have children or grandchildren who will one day want to attend college, and your family's annual gross income is under $160,000, you can invest up to $2,000 a year into an Educational IRA, now known as a Coverdell Education Savings Account. The allowable contribution trails off between $160,000 and $220,000 in family income and is not available to families with annual gross incomes of $220,000 or more. Earnings in these accounts are tax-free if the proceeds are used for educational expenses. These accounts can generally be funded in addition to tax-sheltered retirement accounts.

Another educational savings account is the 529 plan, but it is funded with after-tax dollars, meaning there is no tax deduction for money you deposit in it. The investments within the account will, however, be allowed to grow tax-free . . . if the proceeds are used for educational expenses. Distributions of funds from a 529 plan are also federal-tax-free through 2010. If the exemption is not extended by Congress, distributions will be taxed as ordinary income after 2010. The 529 plan is offered by states, and some states allow the use of pre-state-tax dollars. Many colleges and universities also offer 529 plans. Funds built up in a given state are *not* limited to use within that state, and account balances can be rolled from one state to another as often as annually. Contributions to 529 plans can be over $200,000 in many states. A large number of companies are beginning to offer payroll deductions for 529 plans.

Coverdell and 529 plan contributions can be made in the same tax year.

OTHER EMPLOYEE WEALTH-BUILDING TAX DEDUCTIONS

Some of an individual income earner's wealth-building costs are tax-deductible, but you can deduct only the portion of investment expenses that exceeds 2 percent of your Adjusted Gross Income. In other words, if your AGI is $100,000, you can deduct only investment expenses that exceed $2,000. This calculation shows up on your 1040 Schedule A. Here are some of the wealth-building costs that are considered deductible by the IRS:

- Subscription fees to any Web site, newspaper, or newsletter that helps you invest, like TheStreet.com, Morningstar.com, the *Wall Street Journal,* or *Fortune.*

- Usage fees for your on-line trading accounts.

- Investment books or tapes.

- Accounting, legal, and tax advisory or preparation fees.

- Transportation costs to and from your broker or financial adviser.

- Monthly service fees to participate in an automatic investment service plan.

- IRA fees billed directly to you at home. If the fees are charged to your IRA account, you cannot deduct them. (If you think about it, taking money out of your IRA account to pay those fees means there's less money left in there to grow for your retirement.)

- Some expenses are incurred for both personal and investment purposes, like your telephone, cable, or Internet access bills. These are deductible only to the extent that they're used for investing purposes. For example, if 50 percent of the time on your cell phone is spent talking to your broker, then you can deduct 50 percent of the bill as an investment-related expense. Be sure to keep a concurrent log to record investment usage.

- While you can deduct transportation costs to and from your broker, you cannot deduct the costs associated with attending a shareholder meeting, unless you're a majority shareholder.

- You cannot deduct the costs of attending investing seminars or conventions.

- You cannot deduct trading or broker commissions, but you can add them back in to the cost basis of the security.

The big tax drawback for individuals is that few, if any, of their regular living expenses are tax-deductible. That's one advantage of a business. Rent, vehicle, phone, and other typically nondeductible personal expenses can become partially and even fully deductible within the structure of a business. In the next chapter we'll examine the idea of having a business of your own to increase your income and your tax deductions.

Invest in securities and assets you can comfortably hold for the long term. Most tax consequences arise when an asset is sold for a profit. If you don't sell, you delay many of the tax consequences until you're ready to begin taking the money out of your investments to fund your PEL. When you're in your retirement and enjoying your Post Employment Lifestyle, you can begin to sell some of your holdings as you need the money and pay taxes on the transactions then.

BORROWING MONEY TO INVEST

You may have heard a speaker or read a book encouraging you to borrow money to use for investing. This advice usually involves mortgaging your house to the hilt, but I've even seen such "experts" encourage credit card advances to take advantage of what are touted as sure-thing investments. I believe with all my heart that leveraging and debt are bad investing tools for the *individual income earner.* In fact, they're frequently lethal. It's a different story if you have a business structure through which you're doing the borrowing, and you're borrowing to invest in real estate. I'll deal with that option a little further later on. But right now I want to dispel the idea of borrowing as an individual income earner to invest.

I'll start with my sincere belief that all personal debt is bad. It just makes whatever you're buying cost more. I see no benefit whatsoever for an individual or family to intentionally go into debt when it's possible to avoid it. But there are even more reasons to avoid borrowing to invest than just my financial philosophy.

The typical individual investor is investing in paper assets: stocks, bonds, mutual funds. These securities are just too volatile to purchase with borrowed money. In the short term—one to five years—their value can easily slip below the amount borrowed to purchase them, and their recovery time could have you making payments on the money you borrowed to buy them for a long, long time. Many so-called "sure things" never recover their value after a tumble.

Another strike against this borrowing-to-invest idea is that most borrowing expenses are not as deductible for the individual as they are for a business. Interest is deductible for individual taxpayers only if the money is borrowed against their home equity, which means they're likely putting their only significant net worth components on the line. What little equity or wealth they've accumulated in the value of their homes could evaporate overnight if the investments they buy with the borrowed money move in the wrong direction. You can dress up a pig and take it to church on Sunday, but it's still a pig. For you, as an individual, debt is a pig.

Debt is just the Coalition's siphon hose draining money out of your life. Debt diminishes your wealth; it doesn't increase it. Your goal should be to own your personal assets free and clear. To own your life and everything in it. My goal is to see you building wealth with your personal income, using relatively safe, secure, traditional investments. No goofy, high-risk, high-adrenaline, low-sleep strategies here. Just a steady, commonsense recipe for wealth accumulation.

INVEST IN ASSETS

It's simple to say, "Invest in assets." But, in reality, one person's asset can be another person's liability.

An asset, *as defined by an investor,* is something you own that pays you monthly income, like commercial or residential rental real estate, bonds, high-dividend-yield stocks, CDs, or a money market account; or something you own that can grow in marketplace value, like individual stocks, stock mutual funds, bond mutual funds, or commercial and residential real estate. Pretty simple. An asset, as defined by an investor, is something that builds your net worth and helps you live without having to work for your income.

An asset *as defined by a lender,* on the other hand, includes anything or any part of anything that you "own." This could describe such things as a home in which you have some equity, a car, a boat, a snowmobile, a Jet Ski. This seems to make sense, but hang on.

A liability, *as defined by an investor,* is anything that causes negative monthly cash flow. This can include such things as a home in which you have some equity, a car, a boat, a snowmobile, a Jet Ski. Why are the lender's assets the same as the investor's liabilities? You have ownership in these things; doesn't that make them assets?

Here's why they're liabilities: Even if you own your home, car, boat, snowmobile, and Jet Ski, either they are costing you negative monthly cash flow or they are decreasing in value with time, or both. Your home may be increasing in market value, but it has tax, maintenance, and insurance costs, and you're likely still making mortgage payments. These costs come out of your very real monthly cash flow, while your home's increased market value is only on paper unless you sell the house to capture it. The various vehicles have tax, insurance, licensing costs, and likely monthly payments—negative cash flow. That's why these are liabilities to the true investor. They cause money to move *out* of your life.

Well, then why does your lender consider your home an asset? Because you likely have a mortgage loan on it, from which the lender is enjoying monthly income. See how that works? The house *is* providing positive monthly cash flow to the lender, so to him it is an asset. But to you it's a liability because it's costing you money. I'm not saying you should sell your house to capture your equity and live on a park bench. I'm just showing you how investors see things as opposed to how lenders, and most consumers, see them. You may also have loans on a car, boat, snowmobile, and Jet Ski. These, too, are producing income for the lenders, so they are investor assets for them—but not for you. For you, they are liabilities because they are taking cash out of your life.

Now that you know how to define an asset as an investor, let's examine what kinds of assets are available for you to invest in.

PAPER ASSETS

Stocks. Most people are familiar with the term "stock." They hear about the stock market every day on TV. But what is stock?

Simply put, a stock certificate is a piece of paper showing that you are part owner of the company that issued the stock. The more shares you own, the larger-percentage owner you are of that company. If you start your own corporation, you'd own all the stock and would therefore be a 100 percent owner. If you and your spouse start the corporation, you each might individually be a 50 percent owner. On the other hand, if you buy a few shares of Microsoft stock, you're more like a .0000001 percent owner . . . but you're a part owner nonetheless.

Stock is also called "equity" because, like equity in your home, it's the part you *own.* As an owner you receive a portion of the company's profit each year as a "dividend per share." The company invests most of the rest of its profit into growing the business. This usually causes the business's value to increase in the marketplace, thereby making its stock more "in demand." As demand for the stock rises, its price per share increases, so the value of the shares you own increases. You own the same percentage of the company, but the company is now worth more in the marketplace, so your piece of it is worth correspondingly more. Of course, the reverse also can be true with stocks. Their marketplace value can go down.

A stock's "total return" is the growth in its share price plus the dividends-per-share paid to shareholders. The total return on U.S. stocks has historically grown much faster, over time, than the return on bonds, money market accounts, CDs, or bank savings accounts. When it comes to building wealth, nothing has shown it can dependably or regularly beat the U.S. stock market. In fact, no other paper asset even comes close to the performance of the stock market over time. So, for wealth-building, stocks are the paper asset of choice. You can own them directly, or through mutual funds, as I'll describe a bit further on in this chapter.

Bonds. A bond is a document indicating that you have loaned money to the issuing entity. The issuer of a bond, whether it's a government body or a corporation, is borrowing your money. It promises to pay you a stated interest rate for a specific period of time, called the maturity period. After the bond matures, the issuing party promises to return the full principal amount you loaned it. When you buy a bond you are lending money, you are not buying ownership in the entity. Bonds generally pay a higher interest rate than CDs, money market accounts, or bank savings accounts, but less than the long-term total return on stocks. The same can be said of U.S. Treasury bills and notes. The differences among U.S. Treasury instruments is that a Treasury bill usually matures in ninety days to twelve months, a Treasury note usually matures in one to ten years, and a Treasury bond usually matures in ten to thirty years.

CDs. A certificate of deposit is a savings instrument offered by banks and credit unions that works a lot like a bond. Your principal is protected, you receive a guaranteed interest rate, and it has a maturity period. There is usually a penalty for taking money out of a CD before the maturity date. CDs generally pay lower interest rates than similar maturity bonds and notes, but higher rates than money market accounts or bank savings accounts.

Money Markets. A money market account is somewhat like a mini bond mutual fund. The money you put in this account is invested in short-term bond funds like U.S. Treasury funds, local government (municipal bond) funds, and corporate bond funds. You can open money market accounts at most banks and credit unions. You can open money market mutual fund accounts through most brokers and mutual fund families. To compare bank money market account rates around the country, go to www.bankrate.com. To compare money market mutual funds, go to www.ibedata.com/index.html and click on "Money Fund Selector." Just follow the logical links from there. A money market account pays higher interest than a passbook savings account, but less than stocks, bonds, or CDs.

Passbook Accounts. A plain old bank savings account, also called a passbook account, is at the bottom of the money-growth food chain. It's simply money you're lending to your local bank, for which it will pay you a small interest rate. It then lends the money out at higher interest rate. That's one way banks make money.

In investment terms, money you have in CDs, money market accounts, and passbook accounts is generally called "cash" or "cash equivalents" because it's quickly available (liquid), and—like cash—it's not at risk of principal loss.

Which Should You Use to Build Wealth?

The type of paper asset you use to build wealth depends on what you need the money to do for you, and how easily retrievable you need it to be. If you're saving for your emergency fund, the important considerations would be liquidity and protection of capital. If you're investing to build your long-term wealth, then you're looking for high returns. Here's how stocks, bonds, and cash equivalents have historically performed:

- Over time, stocks have consistently grown in value at a much higher rate than inflation.

- Over time, the total return of interest plus principal from bonds has about kept up with inflation.

- Over time, the total return of interest plus principal from CDs, money market accounts, and passbook savings accounts has fallen behind inflation.

So, if you want your money to grow fast enough to get you and keep you ahead of inflation, the stock market is the place to be. But there is some risk involved with stock investing.

THE STOCK MARKET

When you watch the financial news on TV, you'll hear that the Dow Jones Industrial Average has gone up or down. This number represents a thirty-stock sample of the largest stocks in the market and how they performed that day. The Standard & Poors (S&P) 500 index is a more accurate measure of the overall market's performance, because it tracks five hundred of the largest companies in America. While stock market averages can decrease in value from day to day or even year to year, over time the aggregate value of all the combined stocks in the market has always increased more than decreased. At the end of any historical ten-year period, the overall value of the stock market as measured by the S&P 500 index has always been higher than it was at the beginning of that period. There is no reason to believe this long-term growth trend for stocks will not continue.

For long-term investors, stocks—though they gyrate up and down along the way—are the best bet for building wealth. However, in any short-term period, say, one to five years, stocks could be temporarily lower at the end of the period than at the beginning. For example, for the one-year period ending June 30, 2002, the stock prices of the biggest companies in the U.S. were down compared to the June 30, 2001, prices by an average of 17.98 percent. But they were up from their prices five years prior by 10.7 percent, and they were up from their ten-year prior prices by 12.93 percent. So, even though over short periods you run the risk of your capital investment actually shrinking with stocks, over periods of ten years or longer, history says you're likely to realize a gain.

This is where a Securities and Exchange Commission regulator would jump up and tell me to give the disclaimer that "past performance is no guarantee of future performance." True . . . but it sure beats guessing.

The long-term dependability of the stock market is good news—if you have a long time before retirement. But the market's short-term vulnerability means that the closer you get to retirement, the less of your portfolio you'll want in stocks because—if they take a short-term dive—you won't have much time to wait for them to recover. So, as you approach that day when you plan to start taking money out of your investments, you'll want more and more of it in capital-stable, income-producing securities like bonds, or income-producing assets like rental real estate.

How do you know how much of your portfolio should be in stocks or in income-producing assets at your current age, or at any future point in your life?

ASSET ALLOCATION

"Asset allocation" is a term used to describe the distribution of your investment capital into various types of securities. Asset allocation answers the question "What percentage of your portfolio should be in stocks or stock mutual funds, what percentage should be in bonds or bond mutual funds, what percentage should be in real estate or other hard assets, and what percentage should be in cash or cash equivalents?" But how do you answer these questions for your individual situation?

What you need is a method to help you gradually back out of exposure to the stock market as you age and approach retirement. A good rule of thumb to help you manage this process is called the 110 rule.

Just subtract your age from 110. The remaining number indicates the percentage of your portfolio that should be in stocks. Let's say your age is fifty-three. Subtract fifty-three from 110 and you'll see that you should have 57 percent of your investments in the stock market. As you age, that number will decrease, meaning that less and less of your portfolio will be subject to the stock market's short-term negative risks. You'll notice that unless you live to 110, you'll always have some portion of your portfolio in the stock market. That's because you'll always be fighting the negative effects of inflation, and having some of your portfolio outgaining this incremental thief is an ongoing necessity.

But what do you do with the money you move out of stocks or stock mutual funds?

When you move out of the stock market, the most common destinations are the bonds, CDs, or cash equivalents we've already discussed. These are instruments you can use to generate dependable, consistent income to pay for your Post Employment Lifestyle, while protecting your principal from any decrease or loss.

Now that you know the differences between stocks, bonds, CDs, and money markets, and what the best use is for each of these securities, we can discuss the most popular way to buy them: through mutual funds.

MUTUAL FUNDS

Does the idea of researching individual companies and purchasing individual stocks make you light-headed? Does the thought of buying a lot of different stocks to spread your downside risk (risk of loss of your capital investment) make your head spin? And does the vision of keeping track of the associated documentation make you reach for the antacid? Then you'll want to know about mutual funds.

Mutual funds are just what they sound like: a fund created by people "mutually" pooling their money for the purpose of investing it. Originating in Europe early in the nineteenth century, the first U.S. mutual fund was formed in 1924. When you buy shares in a mutual fund, you essentially become part owner of a company (the mutual fund) that invests in other companies' stocks, in government debt instruments, in corporate debt instruments, in money markets, and in other investment securities.

As a part owner of this investing company, you'll participate in the profits or losses from the mutual fund's investments, proportionately to your number of shares in the fund. Mutual fund shareholders include individuals like you and me, as well as institutions like banks, insurance companies, and pension funds. Mutual funds offer valuable benefits over doing your own individual security buying and selling.

One benefit is that the fund's investments are being guided by a fund manager with years of experience in the market. The fund manager is aided by a staff of specialists who continually research, monitor, and analyze information that can impact the performance of each of the fund's investments. The fund manager's experience and breadth of resources are far beyond what you or I likely enjoy.

Another benefit is built-in *diversification*. The large pool of investment funds at the fund manager's disposal allows him or her to diversify the fund's investments over a number of individual securities. That diversification protects the fund's shareholders from being disproportionately hurt by a downturn in a single security, or even a small group of securities, within the fund.

For example, if you own shares in a fund that invests equally in one hundred different stocks, five of those stocks could lose all their value and your total investment would be reduced by only 5 percent, because those five stocks represent only 5 percent of the fund's holdings. Whereas if you had invested the same amount of money into any one of the five companies that failed, you would have lost *100 percent* of your investment.

Of course, it's unlikely that five companies held by any mutual fund would go out of business, especially all on the same day. What's more likely is that, while some stocks in the fund may go down on any given day, other fund holdings could just as likely maintain their value or go up. The overall gains in the stocks that go up could offset or exceed the losses from those that go down, resulting in a net gain for the mutual fund's share value. Because the fund invests in a lot of securities, your risk is spread out. It's *diversified*.

Most mutual funds are invested in at least one hundred securities. It would take a considerable amount of money for you to accomplish the same amount of diversification on your own. Even if the average price per share across the one hundred companies is just $25, it would cost you $25,000 to buy just ten shares of each stock. On the other hand, you could invest in a mutual fund for as little as $1,000 and get the same one-hundred-stock diversification.

To further assure your protection from being disproportionately impacted by the performance of any individual security within a mutual fund, government regulations forbid funds from investing more than 5 percent of their assets in any single company. And they cannot own more than 10 percent of any company's total capitalization. The benefit for you and me is that no one company's securities can represent a large enough percentage of our mutual fund to sink it. This helps reduce our risk.

Before you start thinking that putting money in a mutual fund is just like putting it in a bank savings account, let me assure you that even with diversification, your investment in a mutual fund can go down. If the overall economy goes into recession, most mutual funds will be negatively impacted. Or let's say you invested in a "high-tech" mutual fund and that entire market sector turned downward for a period. The value of your mutual fund holdings would probably go down, at least until that sector recovered. Diversification provides investors with risk reduction, not risk elimination.

However, it's important to keep in mind that even if your investments appear to go down at any point in time, that change in value is only on paper, or—more accurately—only in your emotions. You wouldn't really experience the "loss" unless you sold your shares at a lower value. But if you hold on to them until you need to begin converting your investments into income for your PEL, you'll likely find they've more than recovered and you've realized a healthy gain.

Another benefit of mutual funds is that fund managers do much of the paperwork for you. For instance, they'll keep track of how all the securities held in the fund perform during the year, and they'll send you a Form 1099 that shows your gains or losses to help you with your taxes. If you own shares in multiple mutual funds, either through a broker or directly through a fund family, you'll get monthly statements showing your holdings and the performance of each fund. You'll get transaction confirmations for each purchase or sale of shares. And with most mutual fund companies and brokers, you can check your account 24/7 on the World Wide Web. Mutual funds fit my approach to life. Relax and let professionals mind your investments—you've got a life to live.

You make money three ways with a mutual fund:

1. When the values of the securities held within the fund increase, the Net Asset Value of your fund shares goes up. This is called capital gains. The capital you invested has grown.

2. When the securities held within the fund pay dividends or interest, you get your proportionate share. This is income. You can have it automatically reinvested into more fund shares.

3. When you sell your mutual fund shares, presuming their Net Asset Value has increased, you'll get back more than you paid for them.

Mutual funds are the perfect buy-and-hold investment. Each month, you apportion your total investment amount into your individual accounts, according to the champagne-glass analogy I described earlier. Just check your monthly statement to see how you're doing, and go back to living your life. Once a year, look over your holdings to see if you need to move money from stock funds to income funds as you approach retirement. That's it.

Mutual Funds Come in Every Flavor. There are mutual funds for every type of security: U.S. stocks, international stocks, government bonds, taxable bonds, municipal bonds, money markets, and more—and each of these can be divided into multiple subcategories. For example, under the umbrella of stock mutual funds there are sector funds for market niches like technology, communications, natural resources, utilities, precious metals, health care, and the list goes on.

There are funds that group companies by capitalization size (large-cap, mid-cap, small-cap). "Capitalization," which is the total dollar value of all outstanding shares, is calculated by multiplying the number of shares by the current market price. This term is often referred to as "market cap." Large-cap companies have capitalizations of $10 billion to $200 billion, mid-cap companies have capitalizations of $2 billion to $10 billion, and small-cap companies are capitalized from $300 million to $2 billion. There are a few other capitalization categories, but these three are the most common and practical for the average investor.

There are also funds that focus on companies by geography (U.S., foreign, global, Asia, emerging markets, etc.). Bond funds can be subdivided by yield, by issuing entity, by maturity term, and by tax status. No matter what type of security you believe would best fit your investing needs, you can find one or more mutual funds focused on that security.

So how do you go about buying mutual fund shares? Well, the first step is to read a little document that tells you—in English—what the fund is all about, and what they plan to do with your money. It's called the fund's "prospectus."

The Mutual Fund Prospectus. Before investing in any mutual fund, be sure to read the prospectus. A mutual fund's prospectus is an explanation of the fund, its objectives, its performance, its costs, and its management, all in a government-mandated format to reduce hyperbole. Let's take a quick tour of what's in every prospectus, so you'll know what to expect when you read one.

The Front Page: Some funds are strategically positioned to undertake higher risks for greater potential gains, while others are not as venturesome and will therefore offer somewhat less upside potential (as well as less downside potential). The front page will tell you the fund's investment objective, such as Aggressive Growth, Growth, or Income. *Growth* speaks of the increase in capital value of the securities owned by the mutual fund. Usually the higher the "growth" potential the fund seeks in its investment choices, the higher the risk of choosing a volatile security that might go down in value instead of up. *Income* is just that, interest or dividends paid by the securities held by the mutual fund, which are passed on to you, a shareholder in the fund.

Key Features: This is a brief description of the fund's objectives, automatic investment features, liquidity, costs, management, shareholder services, and reporting.

Summary of Expenses: Here's where you'll be told about "loads." Loads are sales commissions you pay either when you purchase shares in the fund (front load), upon redeeming shares (backend load), or, in some cases, both. This section will also inform you of the fund's 12b-1 fees. These are charges the fund withdraws from your account to help cover marketing expenses. The 12b-1 fees should never be more than 1 percent, and on money funds or index funds they should be less than .5 percent. Total operating expenses of a money fund should be under 1 percent and should not exceed 2 percent regardless of the fund type.

Condensed Financial Information: This is a table of data and ratios that detail fund performance over a period of previous years. You should always be aware that past performance is no guarantee of future performance, but it is useful information in helping you make an informed decision.

Investment Objectives and Policies: This section explains what the fund does with shareholders' money. It details how they plan to invest and what they expect to achieve. For example, if a fund invests in stocks, its objective will be "capital appreciation." This section also tells you how the fund manager expects to handle volatile market situations. If the policy is to stay "fully invested at all times," you can expect more ups and downs in the fund's performance. But, if the fund's objective also includes "capital preservation," this section will detail how the manager plans to move portions of the fund's assets into Treasury instruments or cash when market forces turn negative. This approach will make the ride smoother, but it will also likely make the fund's potential gains somewhat lower. Risk and reward are inextricably yoked together.

Securities and Investment Techniques: This section defines which types of securities the fund can hold, and what percentage of each type. It also clearly explains the fund's authority to borrow money.

Management of the Funds: The record of the fund manager is an important factor in choosing a mutual fund. Mutual funds understandably advertise their best performance numbers, over their most productive recent years. This is the section where you can verify whether the current fund manager is the man or woman who led the fund through the successful period being promoted. Look for management stability (more than three years). You'll also find information here about the fees and expenses the manager charges the fund.

Distributions and Taxes: When the mutual fund distributes income and gains from its holdings and sales of appreciated securities, you owe taxes on these amounts: when you begin drawing income out of the fund, if it's held in a sheltered account such as an IRA or 401(k); when you next file your income taxes if you own the fund outside a sheltered account. An oddity of mutual funds is that if you buy your shares the day before these distributions are reported, you'll owe the taxes on them—even if you weren't a shareholder when the distributions were actually made or the gains realized. So the information in this section is important to your buying decision. It will explain your potential federal, state, and local tax liabilities from the fund's proceeds. If you see that the fund's distribution date is imminent, you should probably wait until after that date to purchase your shares. This section also explains how the fund determines how much money it makes or loses, how frequently they make that calculation, and how frequently they pay out or reinvest your share of that money.

Share Price Calculation: This section defines how the fund determines a share's Net Asset Value (NAV). The NAV equals the total assets of the mutual fund divided by the total number of outstanding shares. If the fund has assets of $100 million, and there are a million shares distributed, each share has a NAV of $100.

How the Fund Shows Performance: This section explains how the fund's marketing people come up with the performance figures shown in their ads and other promotional materials.

Tax-Advantaged Retirement Plans: Mutual fund companies offer plans through which you can invest in their various funds within the tax-advantaged structure of a standard IRA, Roth IRA, SEP IRA, SIMPLE IRA, Keogh, or other retirement plan. The money you invest in the mutual funds you select grows tax-deferred (tax-free in a Roth IRA). This section will explain any minimum required contribution amounts, as well as any fees charged for maintaining the account.

General Information: This section contains the basic business and contact information for the fund company. It also lists other funds it offers.

How to Purchase Shares: This section will tell you whether you're required to have a brokerage account with the fund company to purchase shares in their funds. It will list addresses, phone numbers, and Web addresses to locate fund shares and will also detail any minimum initial purchase amount requirements and ongoing purchase minimums.

How to Exchange Between Funds: This section details how you can move your money between funds within the company's family of funds.

How to Redeem Shares: This section gives instructions for selling your shares back to the fund, how the redemption price is calculated, and how quickly you'll get your money.

There's a glut of mutual fund promotional information available today, so it's a good thing the government makes all the funds generate at least one document that allows us to compare them as apples to apples. You can request a prospectus by calling the fund family's toll-free number or by going to their Web site. These numbers and Web addresses are listed in ads in every financial newspaper and magazine. You can also find limitless mutual fund sites by searching the term "mutual fund" on the World Wide Web. Another good neutral site for mutual fund information and comparison is www.morningstar.com.

You can also download a prospectus for any mutual fund from the U.S. Security and Exchange Commission's site at www.sec.gov/edgar/searchedgar/prospectus.htm.

Picking mutual funds can be as dizzying as picking stocks. There are actually more mutual funds than there are individual stocks on the New York Stock Exchange. So picking the best mutual fund can be an even more daunting task than selecting individual stocks, bonds, or other securities. But there is an easier and generally more prosperous option than wading through fund after fund to find just the right ones for your portfolio.

THE INDEX FUND ADVANTAGE

When the TV newscasters say, "The Dow Jones average is up (or down), and the S&P 500 is up (or down)," they're reporting the two most popular measurements of the U.S. stock market. These measurements are called "stock market indexes" or indices. These two indexes, and a number of others, measure specific segments of the market.

For example, the S&P 500 is an index based on the combined performance of the five hundred biggest companies in the U.S. economy. If the average of this group's stock prices increases on a given day, the index goes up. On the other hand, if the average of this group's stock prices goes negative, the index goes down. So the S&P 500 index is a barometer of the big-company end of the market. As an example of that barometer, for the period of May 1996 to the first quarter of 2001, the S&P 500 index returned an average annual gain of 14.95 percent.

There are indexes for every possible slice or "sector" of the stock market—technology companies, pharmaceuticals, banks, transportation, utilities, precious metals, and the list goes on. There are indexes that measure the whole U.S. stock market, and there are indexes that track international stocks. So what do these indexes have to do with your investing in mutual funds?

Simple: There are mutual funds—called index mutual funds—that precisely follow these indexes by buying all the securities each index tracks. The exciting news for you is that these index mutual funds actually outperform most other mutual funds investing in the same type of securities.

For example, there are mutual funds that emulate the S&P 500 index. These S&P 500 index mutual funds, offered by several mutual fund companies, consistently outperform 60 percent to 70 percent of actively managed growth funds in any given year. Why am I comparing S&P 500 index mutual funds to "growth" mutual funds? Because a mutual fund that invests in stocks is investing for capital growth. It is expecting the value of those stocks to increase over time. An S&P 500 index mutual fund buys stocks in the five hundred companies listed in the index, so it is a growth mutual fund. In fact, the S&P 500 index is the bar by which all growth mutual funds measure their performance each year, and only about 30 percent to 40 percent beat the index.

Why is this? Why does an S&P 500 index mutual fund outperform way more than half of actively managed growth funds? There are several reasons. One is that an S&P 500 index fund is less volatile because it's much broader based. The average actively managed mutual fund holds stocks in about one hundred different companies, while an S&P 500 index mutual fund contains the stocks of five hundred companies.

Another reason for its superior performance is that there isn't as much stock buying and selling going on in the index fund as there is with actively managed funds, because the S&P 500 index fund just buys and holds the stocks of the five hundred companies listed in the index. This reduces internal transaction costs and capital gains taxable events for shareholders.

Finally, there's the term "actively managed." Most mutual funds have an active fund manager who is buying stocks he or she thinks will go up in the future and dumping underperforming stocks the fund bought in the past. This manager charges the fund's shareholders for his or her services. But an S&P 500 fund doesn't need such an active manager because there's no stock picking to do. The stocks are prepicked by their placement in the S&P 500 index. With fewer transactions and lower management costs, more of the fund's profits are passed on to shareholders, helping it to outperform actively managed growth funds.

Index funds are offered by all major fund families. To find out more about index mutual funds in general, and to research specific index mutual funds, check out http://www.indexfunds.com/.

ETFS

Exchange Traded Funds were developed in 1993. An ETF is essentially an index fund that trades like a share of stock. Whereas most mutual fund shares are purchased directly from the fund and sold back to the fund, ETFs are traded directly between investors through exchanges. Nearly all the more than one hundred ETFs are listed on the American Stock Exchange.

Because they're sold on exchanges, you can buy or sell ETFs at the instantaneous market price, as opposed to waiting until the close of the day for the price to be fixed, as is the method used for establishing a mutual fund's daily Net Asset Value. Because of this instantaneous value setting, you can get out quickly if things start to go bad for your ETF. Correspondingly, if things start to go good, you can get in quickly. You can buy and sell ETFs through regular brokers, including discount brokers.

Because they track indexes, with little turnover in the underlying securities, expenses are extremely low—as little as 12 cents a year per $100 invested. ETFs are more transparent than typical mutual funds in that they are what they are, while the mutual fund is in the hands of the fund manager, and investors have little moment-to-moment knowledge of what the manager's doing with their money.

The granddaddy of ETFs is the S&P 500 Spyders (ASE: SPY). Nearly $2 billion of this fund changes hands daily, so it closely follows the actual index throughout the trading day. For a prospectus, visit www.amex.com, call 800-843-2693, or talk to your broker. To find out more about ETFs in general, and to check on specific ETFs, go to http://www.index funds.com/.

I believe index mutual funds and ETFs are the optimum investment vehicles for average investors. In fact, they are the vehicles I use in my "Autopilot Investing" system. But before I put that system together for you, let me first explain the other key ingredient in the system's recipe: Dollar Cost Averaging.

DOLLAR COST AVERAGING

Investing should be a process, not one adrenaline-packed event after another. The most universally accepted and proven investing process is called Dollar Cost Averaging (DCA). Dollar cost averaging simply means to invest the same amount regularly—such as a fixed monthly investment—regardless of what the market is doing. Pick the best funds to be in based on your investing strategy and goals, and then invest the same or an increasing amount, month after month after month. Do not worry whether the market is up or down when you put your money in each month.

Here's how dollar cost averaging can keep you ahead of the game. Suppose you decide to invest $1,000 a month. When you first start buying shares in a given fund, they're priced at $20. You get fifty shares for your $1,000. Now let's suppose the market goes down, and a month later the share price has slipped to $15. You again invest your $1,000, but this time it buys you 66.7 shares. When the price gets back up to $20, you will have 116.7 shares worth $2,334—*but you paid only $2,000 for them.* Dollar cost averaging, combined with the market's natural ups and downs, put you ahead by $334.

Dollar cost averaging makes you buy *more* shares when the price drops (when they're on sale), so—overall—you come out ahead. The momentum behind dollar cost averaging is that, over time, the stock market has historically continued to rise, despite short-term downturns. Since there is every reason to believe this trend will continue into the foreseeable future, your shares will likely be worth more over time, and you'll have more of them, because you bought some of them cheaply during the market dips.

∞

Okay . . . we've covered a lot of ground so far in this chapter. If you're already a knowledgeable investor, this has been a fundamental review for you. But if this has been your first real exposure to investing's terms and methods, you may be wishing there was a simpler way. Well, there is. It's not the world's most sophisticated investing strategy, but it works.

AUTOPILOT INVESTING

My purpose in writing this book is to help you have a prosperous and *low-maintenance* financial life. To that end, I'm always endeavoring to simplify, simplify, simplify. That's why I practice what I call "autopilot investing," and it's nothing more complicated than dollar cost averaging into index mutual funds and/or ETFs.

This is a no-brainer. Index mutual funds and ETFs outperform most actively managed mutual funds because they simply bet on a broad segment of the market and stick with it. They follow the classic wealth-building maxim of "Buy and hold." As I told you earlier, on average they outperform 60 percent to 70 percent of actively managed funds that focus on similar securities (stocks, bonds, etc.). Since the 30 percent to 40 percent of funds that happen to beat the index are not the same ones from year to year, I'd rather bet on the dependable 60 percent to 70 percent performance of the index fund than on chasing the 30 percent to 40 percent of funds that might beat the index, with no assurance of picking the right ones.

All you need to do is decide what kind of security meets your specific investing need, such as stocks for growth or bonds for income, then find the index that tracks that security, and buy shares in a mutual fund that emulates that index. If you're in the early growth stages of your investing timeline, you could put most of your money into an S&P 500 index fund or ETF. As you approach retirement, simply apply the 110 rule and begin moving money from stock index funds into bond index funds, which would protect your capital and provide income to support your PEL. To compare their performance, check www.morningstar.com.

When you multiply the long-term dependability of index mutual funds and ETFs by the consistency of dollar cost averaging, you have an easily managed system with a relatively high likelihood of success over time. You just make your monthly investments and let the strength of the U.S. market build your wealth.

Will dollar cost averaging into index funds and ETFs protect you from ever experiencing losses? Of course not. Over any short period of time, you could see a decline. The market periodically retrenches to catch its breath and to wring out excesses and illusions. Once everyone's back to reality, the market has historically renewed its climb, and by the end of any ten-year period, it has always been higher than at the start—even if there was a correction or recession during those ten years.

So that's how I invest. I dollar cost average into sheltered accounts, within which I invest in S&P 500 index funds and a few income funds based on my 110 rule percentages. It's a no-hassle way to manage my wealth-building. I use a low-fee brokerage company through which I make the purchases, but I do it myself without the advice or consent of any investment adviser. In fact, I do it all on-line, so it's simple to manage, and I just file the monthly statement when it comes.

But if handling your own investments is starting to sound like skipping rope in a minefield, maybe you should consider letting a good investment adviser take the controls and help you make important decisions. Even if you know a lot about investing but want to enjoy your retirement without having to concentrate on what your investments are doing from week to week, an investment adviser could be just what you need. But how do you find a good one?

FINDING A GOOD INVESTMENT ADVISER

The first place to look is with people you know and trust who use investment advisers themselves. Such personal referrals are the most trustworthy route to a good investment adviser relationship. Unfortunately, most people you know are probably not investing very much, or they're doing it through their employers' retirement savings plan. So you'll likely need to expand the search.

The next place to look would be in quality investment publications, like the *Wall Street Journal, Barron's, Kiplinger's, Money* magazine, and *Worth.* On the World Wide Web, search the term "investment advisers." To narrow it down to your state or a major metro area, just add the name of the state or city to the search parameters, such as "investment advisers

Wisconsin." When you find firms whose names you recognize, call their toll-free numbers or check your Yellow Pages to see if they have a local office.

Regardless of how you narrow down your list of potential advisers to the most likely candidates, you should look deeper before choosing the adviser into whose hands you're going to pour your hard-earned money. Federal or state securities laws require brokers, advisers, and their firms to be licensed or registered, and to make important information public. But it's up to you, the customer, to locate that information and understand it so you can protect your investments. A phone call or Web search may save you from making a bad adviser choice and pouring your hard-earned money into a rusty bucket.

Before you invest with any broker, investment adviser, or investment adviser representative, make sure he or she is licensed to sell securities. And verify that neither he, she, nor the firm has had run-ins with regulators or other investors. This is critical because if you give your money to an unlicensed securities broker or a firm that later goes out of business, it may be impossible to recover your money—even if an arbiter or court rules in your favor.

BROKERS AND BROKERAGE FIRMS

The Central Registration Depository (CRD) is a computerized database containing information about most brokers, their representatives, and the firms they work for. You can use the CRD to find out if brokers are properly licensed in your state and if they've had run-ins with regulators. You can also see if they've received serious complaints from investors. The CRD also contains important information about the brokers' educational backgrounds and where they worked before their current positions.

Where can you get CRD information?

You can ask your state securities regulating agency, or you can ask the National Association of Securities Dealers Regulation (NASDR),

Inc. Either can provide you with information from the CRD. Your state securities regulator may provide more CRD information than the NASDR—especially when it comes to investor complaints—so you may want to check with him first. The North American Securities Administrators Association, Inc.'s Web site (www.nasaa.org/nasaa/abt nasaa/find_regulator.asp) will give you contact information for your state securities regulator.

To get CRD information from the NASD Regulation, Inc., just go to the Web site www.nasdr.com/2000.htm or call NASD at (800) 289-9999.

INVESTMENT ADVISERS

Any persons who get paid to give advice or recommendations about investing in securities should be registered with either the U.S. Securities and Exchange Commission (SEC) or the securities agency in the states where they have their principal places of business. Investment advisers managing $25 million or more in client assets generally must register with the SEC. If they manage less than $25 million, they usually must register with their state securities agency.

Some investment advisers employ investment adviser representatives to work directly with clients. In most cases, these representatives must be licensed or registered with your state securities agency. To find out if they're properly registered, ask to see their registration forms, called the "Form ADV." Part 1 of this form contains the advisers' basic business information, but it also shows whether they've had problems with regulators or clients. Part 2 outlines their services, fees, and investing strategies. Before you give a dime to an investment adviser, ask for and *read* both parts of his or her Form ADV.

If an adviser won't let you see their Form ADV, that's probably a good indication you should look elsewhere. But, if you want to check a form without asking or before you talk with a potential adviser, you can view it on-line at the Investment Adviser Public Disclosure (IAPD) Web site (www.adviserinfo.sec.gov). You can also get copies of Form ADV for indi-

.vidual advisers and firms from your state securities regulator. As I mentioned, you can get contact information for your state securities regulator through the North American Securities Administrators Association, Inc.'s Web site: www.nasaa.org/nasaa/abtnasaa/find_regulator.asp.

If the investment adviser is likely to have $25 million or more under management, the SEC should also have the adviser's Form ADV on file. You can get a copy for 24 cents per page (plus postage) from the SEC at:

> Office of Public Reference
> 450 5th Street, NW
> Room 1300
> Washington, DC 20549-0102
> phone: (202) 942-8090
> fax: (202) 628-9001
> e-mail: publicinfo@sec.gov

Because some investment advisers and their representatives are also brokers, you may want to check both the CRD and Form ADV.

PROTECT YOUR CAPITAL

One more step you'll want to take before writing out your investment check is to find out whether any involved brokerage firm and its clearing firm are members of the Securities Investor Protection Corporation (SIPC) Web site: www.sec.gov/answers/sipc.htm). The SIPC provides *limited* customer protection if a brokerage firm goes out of business, but it *does not* insure against losses caused by a decline in the market value of your securities. Investing with a non-SIPC member means you may not be eligible for SIPC coverage if the firm goes out of business.

Okay . . . here are some questions that will help you get the information you'll need to make an intelligent adviser selection. Ask any adviser candidate:

- What experience do you have, especially with people in my circumstances?

- Where did you get your professional education?

- How long have you been with your current firm, and who were you working for before that?

- What licenses do you hold?

- Are you registered with the SEC, a state, or the NASD?

- Are the firm, the clearing firm, and any other related companies that will do business with me members of SIPC?

- What products and services do you offer?

- Can you recommend only a limited selection or only one brand of products or services to me? If so, why?

- How will you be paid for the services you'll provide me?

- What is your hourly rate, flat fee, or commission rate?

- Have you ever been disciplined by any government regulator or been sued by a client?

- (For registered investment advisers) Will you give me a copy of both parts of your Form ADV?

Any adviser who makes it through all these hurdles is probably legitimate. But there's also the issue of personality and temperament. Spend enough time with a potential adviser to be sure you'll hit it off. The investor-adviser relationship is one that will likely be strained from time to time by the vagaries of the market. Be sure you and your adviser have personalities that can communicate clearly and with a minimum of emotion because when investments underperform, which they will from time to time, your ability to work with this person under stress will be tested.

INVESTING IN REAL ESTATE

Thus far in this chapter, we've concentrated on traditional investments that would be used by most income earners in their 401(k) or IRA. But the stock market is not the only dependable place to build wealth. Real estate is another asset that can generate impressive capital gains and solid income.

There are two ways to invest in real estate: directly or indirectly. Direct real estate ownership is a considerably more "hands-on" investment than just dollar cost averaging into an index fund or sending a monthly check to your investment adviser. On the other hand, owning real estate through a Real Estate Investment Trust is just as "hands-off" as investing in a mutual fund. So let's examine both approaches.

If you're going to own and rent out real estate, I strongly recommend you do it through a business structure, *not* as an individual. Create a corporation or limited liability company that will buy and own the real estate, while you own the company. You'll have full use of all the company's assets, and the company's profits will flow through to you, but you won't be legally exposed to the liabilities attendant to owning rental properties, nor will your personal assets be at risk should your real estate cash flow suddenly turn negative. And, having a business, you'll also enjoy more tax benefits than you will as an individual income earner.

Real estate is an investment asset just like stocks, bonds, and mutual funds, but there are some critical differences. Some are benefits; some are shortcomings. But well-chosen real estate investments can provide income and capital appreciation that paper assets would be hard-pressed to match. A good portion of my income is generated by commercial real estate rent.

One key difference between real estate and paper investments is in the area of leverage. I'm sure I've made it perfectly clear that I'm against the use of any kind of debt when paying for your lifestyle or investing as an individual income earner. However, I'm going to make one tightly defined exception when wealth-building *through a business structure*. Using loans to purchase income-producing real estate *can* make sense if done in a very disciplined and businesslike manner.

The ideal scenario would be that you purchase a piece of real estate but invest only a small percentage of your own money, borrowing the majority of the purchase price as a mortgage loan. Rental tenants would then cover the ongoing costs of ownership, including debt service, while the value of the property increases. Hopefully, rent would actually provide positive cash flow, which could then be used as down-payment money on more properties, or—if you're in your PEL—it could contribute to your monthly income. The original property could then be sold at some later date for more than you paid for it, paying off the mortgage debt and leaving you with a healthy profit.

This use of borrowed money to multiply the impact of your own money is commonly called "leveraging." You leverage the small percentage you actually invest from your own resources with the power of the large percentage invested by the mortgage lender. Let's say you're buying a $100,000 property, using $20,000 of your own money and an $80,000 mortgage loan. A year later you sell the property for $120,000. The mortgage is paid off at closing, and you get a check for $40,000. *You just doubled your money in one year.* That's 100 percent annual growth, and the leverage of the mortgage made it possible. If you had used $100,000 of your own money to buy the property, your return on investment at the sale would have been a healthy 20 percent, but that's a far cry from 100 percent.

I've admittedly ignored the effects of Realtor commissions and taxes in these numbers because I want to illustrate the leveraging concept without a lot of math getting in the way. Do deals really work out as well as this example? Yes and no. Yes, some work out this well; and no, some don't increase in value as much or don't sell so quickly. But some deals work out even better than this one. What makes the difference is the knowledge and savvy of the investor, and these aren't attributes you can develop overnight. You can, however, develop them with the help of books, tapes, video courses, and seminars taught by people who are already doing it. Or, better yet, if you know such a person, you could "apprentice" with him or her to learn the ropes.

DIRECT REAL ESTATE INVESTING THROUGH A BUSINESS STRUCTURE

One thing all the experts will agree on is that this leveraging approach to investing in real estate should be done through a business structure that protects your personal assets. While you could buy rental properties as an individual and get mortgages on each of them, the mortgage lenders would hold you personally responsible for the loans, and if you couldn't make the payments, the lenders could and would come after your personal assets—including the house you live in—to satisfy your obligations.

But when you do this kind of investing through a business structure, you're essentially operating a real estate investing company. The profit from the company's operations can flow through to you, the owner, but the company's liabilities do not flow through to you.

This is done by incorporating (Inc.) or setting up your business as a Limited Liability Company (LLC) or Limited Liability Partnership (LLP). These business structures, which are registered with and regulated by individual states, become what amounts to individual legal entities of their own. This means that if the company owes money, the entity of the company is legally responsible for that debt, not the entity of you. If the company gets sued, your personal assets should not be in jeopardy. Obviously, you should be *willing to make every reasonable effort* to pay all the debts your business would incur, but—legally—they would belong to the company, not you.

As with everything involving the law, there are limits to this protection. If you commit fraud through your business, or if you establish a corporation or limited liability business structure to intentionally avoid paying business debts or to do something illegitimate and then hide behind the corporate shield, it will evaporate in court before your very eyes. If you ever need the protection afforded by these business structures, you'll have to prove that you properly kept all required corporate or limited liability records and that you operated the business in accordance with normal business practices, in good faith, and for the purpose of making a profit.

YOUR REAL ESTATE BUSINESS OFFERS TAX ADVANTAGES

Another advantage of having the business structure feed you the income from your real estate investments is that you can use these flow-through profits to fund a SEP IRA, a SIMPLE, or a Keogh and rapidly build up an enviable paper-asset retirement nest egg with the strong support and help of your friends at the IRS . . . because you'd be getting tax deductions enjoyed only by businesses and retirement plans enjoyed only by the self-employed.

Businesses get to pay with pretax dollars for many of the things individuals have to pay for with after-tax dollars. These include but are not limited to:

- Car(s)
- Plane(s)
- Phones
- Computers
- Travel
- Entertainment
- Health Care
- Education

When these costs are paid by the business, they are expensed or depreciated, so they reduce the business's profit, and it's the profit on which the business or its owners pay taxes. When the government lets you buy part or all of these and other items and services with preprofit dollars, it is, in effect, paying part of the bill. If you're in the 28 percent tax bracket, for example, the effect is that the federal government is paying 28 percent of these costs for you. Because, if you were buying these items or services as an individual—and getting no tax deduction—you would be paying that 28 percent yourself as tax. With the government as your business partner, you're left with more money for investing. So the government is contributing to your wealth-building.

As I mentioned, having a business of your own gives you additional and more generous retirement-plan options as well. This is another way governments tend to favor business owners over regular income earners. Without getting too deeply into the details: As a business owner (self-employed), you can have a Simplified Employee Pension Plan (SEP IRA), which will allow you to shelter up to 25 percent or $40,000 of your self-employed income, whichever is less. If your spouse is also an employee, the two of you can shelter up to $80,000 from taxes each year.

A Keogh plan is another tax-deferral tool for the self-employed. It comes in three flavors, which I won't elaborate on here, but you can essentially shelter 25 percent of your income, up to $40,000 each year.

The third common self-employed/small-business retirement plan is the SIMPLE, which stands for Savings Incentive Match Plan for Employees. It's an IRA that lets you set aside $9,000 ($10,500 if you're fifty or older). In the future, the new tax laws will increase both the maximums you can shelter and the additional "catch-up" amounts allowed to those fifty and older.

These retirement plans are simple, but they all have their pros and cons, so my suggestion is to get a book dedicated to the subject of retirement plans, or talk to your tax adviser, or better yet, both. You can see some of the highlights of these plans on www.simpleirasite.com. I'm not a tax specialist, but I can assure you that the more you can shelter from current and ongoing taxes, the better funded your retirement will be.

So conducting your direct real estate investing through a properly established business not only protects your personal assets, but it allows you tax deductions and retirement program options not available to regular income earners.

THINK YOU'RE A REAL ESTATE INVESTOR?

The benefits of direct real estate investing can be impressive, but before you start scouring the classifieds for your first property, ask yourself whether you're cut out to be a landlord. Some people take to it as naturally as a teenager to a shopping mall, but others don't have the temperament or the skills. Consider all that the title "landlord" implies. As a landlord you'll need to be a cross between a used car salesman and Bob Vila. You'll have to keep your properties rented, which means you'll be advertising, interviewing, schmoozing, checking out, and contracting with tenants. And you'll be Mr./Ms. Fixit—the one they'll call in the middle of the night when the lights don't work or a pipe breaks.

Of course, filling vacancies, dealing with tenants, and making repairs aren't frequent occurrences, but they are periodic and inevitable, so you must inventory your soul to determine whether these hats will fit comfortably on your head. If not, that doesn't mean direct real estate ownership is out of the question for you. It just means you'll have to pay someone else to do these things for you, and that will affect the profitability of your investments.

"Real estate management" is the term generally used to describe people or businesses that will take care of your properties for you. In bigger cities you can find real estate management companies in the phone book. Realtors can also direct you to management companies they've found dependable over the years, but check to see if they're owned by the Realtor's brother-in-law. If you don't live in a large or densely populated area, you may have to recruit management services from local Realtors or building contractors.

No matter the source of your management services, your question needs to be: "How much will management cost me?" Just like the effect of fees charged by a mutual fund manager, your management costs as a real estate investor will have a significant impact on your overall return on investment (ROI). Let's use a quick example to see why.

These numbers aren't necessarily typical, but they're easy to understand for illustration purposes. Let's say you buy a property for $100,000, and you can get $600 a month in rent from it. That's a 7.2 percent annual return on your $100,000 investment. Now let's suppose it would cost you $600 a year for management services. That reduces your $7,200 annual net to $6,600—an 8.3 percent decrease. This means management costs have reduced your 7.2 percent annual ROI to 6.6 percent.

Before you start thinking that doesn't sound bad compared to bonds, CDs, and money markets these days, don't forget that you also have to pay taxes and insurance on your property, not to mention those pesky maintenance costs. Obviously, when you're considering this kind of investment you have to compare it to other investment options, like paper assets. If this was the best real estate deal you could find, you'd have to think long and hard about putting the $100,000 into stock mutual funds instead.

Now, to be fair, savvy real estate investors would never settle for a 7.2 percent return. They're looking for 15 percent to 20 percent before they'll seriously consider a property. They'll tell you that the trick is to buy the right property for the right price. You make your profit when you buy, not when you sell. They look for properties that can easily be improved to justify higher rents. Or they listen for the right seller "story." One that reveals a lowball offer may well be accepted. They're not usually buying properties advertised in the newspapers or listed with Realtors. They've developed the instincts and networks to unearth special buying opportunities that come with the profits already built in.

If you want to try your hand at real estate investing, the first step is to do your homework. Not only do you need to get some good books or audio programs on buying and selling real estate as a business, but you also have to develop a solid understanding of the dynamics of the geographic area in which you're planning to buy. Is it growing? Will demand for residential or commercial space be increasing? Are any major employers in the area making noises about closing down or moving their businesses to another location? Are there any big potential employers talking about moving into the area? Are name-brand retailers moving in, or are they closing their stores and moving out? These questions and others like them will help you determine whether demand for your space would be increasing or decreasing with time. What you want is to get a great deal on a property where conditions are on the upswing.

If you're focusing on commercial real estate, look for buildings with solid, national-sized businesses in them. These are the most stable tenants and the most valuable to have in the property should you later decide to sell it. On the other end of the spectrum, some investors look for properties with few tenants. They believe they can give these properties face-lifts and repopulate them with new tenants paying higher rents. This approach takes a lot of know-how, so consider it only if you're experienced or know someone you can trust who is.

HOW ABOUT "NO MONEY DOWN" DEALS?

You may have seen books or courses offered on TV that will show you how to buy real estate using no money of your own. This practice is limited mostly to residential real estate, although such deals have been struck on commercial buildings.

I bought a couple of those courses some years back. I was going to build my fortune by buying great properties for little or nothing down, and for a fraction of their real value. So I did just what the course told me to do. I went to the county courthouse and looked up people who were in default on their taxes or mortgage payments, and I checked with the sheriff about the next auction. So far, so good.

However, when I started contacting these delinquent owners who were about to lose their homes, I found scared, depressed, sad people. All of a sudden it wasn't an academic exercise anymore. It wasn't just a form with someone's name on it. It was a fellow human being in distress, and

I felt more like loaning that person money than taking their house away for a fraction of its value.

I also found that many of these "distressed" properties needed a lot of work. Even though I enjoy woodworking as a hobby, I didn't feel like spending a lot of my time as a carpenter. Now you may love this idea. Actually, it is a good way of trading sweat equity—your time and efforts—for increasing the value of your real estate. It just wasn't how I envisioned the real estate business working for me. And that's important. Be sure there's no disconnect between your dreams and visions of a real estate business and the actual activities you'll be required to do to make it work.

To be fair in this picture I'm painting, there are situations where even offering a lowball price for a piece of distressed real estate is doing the seller a favor, and that person is grateful. But most of the time you're just putting one of the final nails in his or her emotional coffin. Of course, some of these homes are no longer occupied. They've already been repossessed and are on the block so the lender can recoup some of its losses. You can also find listings of real estate being auctioned by the IRS at www.ustreas.gov/auction/irs. If this kind of opportunity intrigues you, check it out, but don't plan on it being your magic wealth-building bullet unless you know you'll *enjoy* finding properties, cutting deals, fixing up the properties, and filling them with great tenants.

God didn't create you to grind out every day doing something you hate just because it can make money. If you would enjoy this kind of business—and many people do—then do it. But, for heaven's sake, don't get into real estate just because some book tells you it can help you build wealth. Yes, you can make money investing in real estate. But being a direct real estate owner is not a passive investment. It's a business. If you decide to do it, you're becoming a real estate businessperson.

INDIRECT REAL ESTATE INVESTING

The Real Estate Investment Trust is a hands-off real estate investing option. This investment vehicle—usually just called a REIT—allows you to be part owner in commercial real estate, without having any landlord obligations. REITs come with experienced coinvestors and quality property management teams built in.

A REIT is like a mutual fund that invests in real estate instead of stocks or other securities, so it's a good investment for an individual income earner or through a business structure. You're putting your money in with all the other investors', and you're trusting the REIT management team to pick good properties, to manage and maintain them, and to keep them filled with tenants. If the management team succeeds at these three tasks, you will see the value of your REIT shares increase. If management fails, or if the economy in the areas in which your REIT owns property turns down and tenant companies fail, your REIT investment will lose value.

With a REIT, you're getting all the opportunities of real estate but with few of the headaches.

REITs trade on the New York and American Stock Exchanges. Their prices fluctuate daily, they generate regular shareholder reports, and like stocks REITs appreciate and distribute earnings in step with economic growth. Also like stocks, REITs are sensitive to interest rate changes. In that way they behave like an economic sector, such as pharmaceuticals or banks, rather than like a separate asset type, such as rare coins or art.

Just as when purchasing any other investment, buyer beware. Don't cave in to high-pressure sales tactics. Do your homework. Commercial real estate is more of a steady investment than a spectacular one. Don't listen to anyone promising meteoric gains. REITs can be a solid component of your portfolio, but they should never be the bulk of it.

There are REITs designed for income and REITs designed for growth.

If income is your goal, look for REITs that invest in solid, blue-collar, recession-resistant properties. These usually include the suburban shopping mall anchored by supermarkets and large retailers like Wal-Mart and Kohl's.

If you're after growth in the capital value of your REIT investment, you'll also, unsurprisingly, be accepting a bit more risk. These investments include office buildings, industrial parks, and downtown malls. The main risks with these types of properties are that they are more economy-sensitive. For this reason you should seek REITs whose properties are close to where you live, so you'll better foresee potential economic changes. An economic downturn keeps the shoppers home, so would-be entrepreneur tenants stay at their jobs. On the other hand, when the economy is strong, these properties usually outperform their less glamorous "income" cousins.

Like most investment securities, in addition to being available for direct and individual purchase, REITs are also available via mutual fund. Since a REIT itself is like a mutual fund in that its managers buy and sell individual properties within the REIT, buying REITs through a REIT mutual fund is like buying a mutual fund of real estate mutual funds.

There are basically two types of these REIT mutual funds: those that invest exclusively in U.S. properties and those that invest globally. You can find information about REITs on the World Wide Web, in most investing magazines and newspapers, or through an investment adviser.

Okay . . . we've pretty thoroughly investigated getting wealthy using nothing more than the money you already make, so let's turn to Chapter 7, and we'll examine how you can get even wealthier, faster, by making more money.

7

ACCELERATING
STRATEGIES

∞

A sad and rarely known epilogue to *The Wizard of Oz:* the criminal career of Dorothy and Toto.

What they don't explain at the end of the movie—in fact, they cover it up with clever special effects—is that when Dorothy woke up back in Kansas she was still wearing the ruby slippers. At first they were just a trophy of her adventure . . . a curiosity. But one day Aunty Em refused Dorothy a quarter when the Good Humor ice cream man was jingling his way down their road, and the slippers came off the shelf.

Toto was confused at first. He had no idea what "There's no place like the Wells Fargo bank vault" meant. But when he materialized in a room filled with money, he saw doggy biscuits for life. The little furball knew if he just kept his mouth shut, he'd never do without the comforts a famous dog gets used to.

Finding this new 0 percent interest, 0 payment borrowing system to her liking, Dorothy tested the slippers' limits over ensuing months. Regional and worldwide police forces were baffled. And, of course, no one connected Dorothy's new Jaguar with the crime spree. But one day when Aunty Em was pretending to sweep outside Dorothy's bedroom door, she heard the clicking heels and "There's no place like Fort Knox."

The sweet old lady felt plenty guilty as she dialed the Kansas state police to find out if there was a reward and how to collect it.

Dorothy, however, had the last laugh. When Aunty Em finally opened the door to her niece's room, she found that not only were Dorothy and the dog gone, but the girl's new St. John's outfits weren't in the closet, and the drawers of her custom-made armoire were empty. Dorothy never intended to return to Kansas. She'd had enough of feeding chickens who were too stupid to realize they were on the menu.

Neo, on the other hand, found himself unemployed and unappreciated after he freed all the humans from the *Matrix*'s pods into the real world. It turned out that most humans preferred being lied to and taken advantage of. They had little taste for the hard work of actually building futures for themselves. Poor Neo was reportedly seen sitting on a crowded city curb trying to bend a spoon with his mind. Others told of giving a dollar to a down-and-outer who claimed to be "The One."

I'd hate to see you end up like Neo. On the other hand, I can't say I recommend Dorothy's method of providing for your financial security either. What I propose is that we consider more practical and ethical solutions to your long-term financial well-being . . . as well as your near-term security.

This chapter might at first seem out of place in a book about eliminating debt and investing, but when you consider that your employment is nothing more than investing your intellect and energy in a job that provides a return on that investment (ROI), it's obvious that anything you can do either to find a "better investment" or to coax "better returns" out of your current employment investment will help accelerate your debt-elimination and wealth-building process. The more money in, the faster you get there and the more you have when you arrive.

The first and most obvious way to increase your income so you can accelerate your journey to financial freedom is to get a better job—one that pays more.

FINDING A NEW JOB

Employers with jobs to fill have a clear advantage. They can be as selective as they want, meaning the responsibility is clearly on your shoulders to become the candidate of choice—the one they can't pass by. You have to find ways to make yourself stand out from the crowd of applicants for each job.

Fortunately, that's not as difficult as it might seem, because most people don't approach the job hunt with the right perspective. They see it as a simple matchmaking activity, when it's actually a marketing process. A process where the successful job seeker knows that he's both the marketer and the product.

If you're that job seeker, your first order of business is to create a marketing strategy for yourself. And the starting point of a marketing strategy is setting marketing goals. You have to define the target you desire to hit before you can possibly take aim. Your goals include the type of job you want, the salary you're after, the working conditions, the geographical area, and so on.

Be ambitious but also realistic. Take inventory of your previous work experiences, your professional and personal skills, your qualifications and certifications, and any education or training you've received that would prepare you for the job you're after. Look at yourself as a product, and list all the great features you can offer a prospective employer. But don't stop there. Examine each of your *features,* and formulate a way of expressing each as a *benefit* to the prospective employer. Remember, employers looking to buy employees are no different from anyone else looking to buy anything else—they want to know what benefits they'll get for their money.

When you've completed your personal inventory, use it to assess your realistic value in the marketplace. Don't be intimidated or overly conservative. Remember, you are your only salesperson, so you have to be positive and optimistic about your product's value in the marketplace. On the other hand, your marketplace value assessment must be tempered by job market realities in your area, including what others doing the same kind of job are getting paid. If you believe you're worth more than the average candidate, you'll need compelling and easily demonstrable reasons you can present on your résumé and during interviews. Use Help Wanted ads, the World Wide Web, your local chamber of commerce, your state department of labor, and local employment agencies to help you assess your market-place value.

If your inventory shows you're missing something in your skills and capabilities, consider going back to whatever school teaches that subject and get caught up. This can be especially important if you want to change occupations or move into management. For example, a couple of years ago I concluded that no matter what I wrote books, videos, or audio programs about, I would not be a complete communicator with my audience without a presence on the Web. Believing it added to my communications skill set to be able to publish and modify my own Web pages, I went to a technical school and got my certification as a Webmaster. See www.john cummuta.com.

I know full well I'm not in the same league as Webmasters who use their skills every day as professional Web developers, but the capabilities I gained help me manage my own site, as well as a few others for people and organizations I care about. However, if I ever wanted to get back into my original profession of marketing, being Web-certified would put me in line ahead of equally qualified candidates whose skills are not as contemporary. It would give me one more employer benefit to feature.

YOUR RÉSUMÉ

Your résumé is a sales tool, not an autobiography, and it's the first element of an employment marketing campaign. Your résumé's sole task is to get you an interview. The interviews will get you the job. The human resources people who review your résumé should be able to see your potential value to their businesses in ten to fifteen seconds. If it's wordier than that, your résumé will be filed, and you'll get the "Dear Loser" letter.

Start your résumé with a "Career Summary Statement" at the top. This is where you concisely sell the skill and capability package you've become. Remember to state your abilities as *benefits* to the prospective employer, not just as *features* you offer. If you're not sure what the difference is, let me give you an example. Suppose you were selling refrigerators to Eskimos. You might brag that your refrigerator makes ice cubes. That's a *feature*. When one of your prospects retorts that he can make ice cubes by simply laying a water-filled ice cube tray outside his door, you respond, "Ah, yes . . . but the ice cubes created by my refrigerator will never come out yellow, even if the dog team walks by." That's a *benefit* to the buyer.

The rest of your résumé is essentially evidence of what you claimed in your Career Summary Statement. Start with your Work History, from your current position back about a decade or so, if you've been working that long. In most professions, experience more than a decade old is out of date anyway. If you did something exceptional longer than a decade ago, include it. List job titles and accomplishments, but be brief rather than wordy. Imagine you're writing a telegram or classified ad where you have to pay for every letter.

The next important section is Education, especially if you're a specialist or professional for which education is an actual or implied requirement. Again, work your way back from your most recent training. If you have a graduate degree or higher, list it—then don't bother with high school information unless there's something exceptional there. Try to turn each educational entry into a benefit to the employer. In other words, see if you can express what you learned there in terms that sound like they'd help the business to which you're applying. Carefully reading the employer's ad or job description can help you with this.

You could add a section on Professional Achievements and Organizations if you've accomplished any or belong to any. Again, these are valuable only if they can be made to appear as benefits to the prospective employer. If it's just a brag session for you, leave it out. Each statement or sentence in your résumé should be clean and concise. It should read like a brochure, not a novel. Use bullet points, not paragraphs. For more formatting and content tips, see http://www.free resume-tips.com/10tips.html.

Type your résumé on a computer so it's easy to modify, edit, and print a separate version for each job for which you apply. In each, try to make your skills and capabilities match the company's ad. This is more important than you might think. To appreciate why you want to do this, it's helpful to understand how the hiring process works at most companies.

When the manager of a given department needs to fill an opening, he or she writes up a brief job description for the people in the Human Resources Department, asking them to find candidates with certain skill sets and experience. The people in the HR Department generally don't know a thing about the specific skills and capabilities required to do the job. All they have to work with is the description they got from the department manager, so they pull important-sounding words out of that description, and that's how they write their Help Wanted ad.

A few days later, they start receiving résumés. Since all they know about the requirements for the job is what the manager wrote in his or her description, the HR people scour each résumé for the same key words that they put in the ad. The more a résumé matches the ad, the better chance it has of earning an interview. So make your résumé read like you *are* the person they're advertising to find. Don't lie, just use their words, and leave out stuff that doesn't fit what they're looking for unless it's incredibly impressive.

Brutal editing makes a résumé better. Cut out everything that doesn't add to your attractiveness to each prospective employer. Only include facts that will make you more appealing for the specific job in question. Avoid repetition. If you performed the same functions at several jobs, list the duties only once, then highlight your greatest accomplishments at each workplace. Eliminate the irrelevant, such as hobbies, out-of-date skills, and personal information like date of birth and marital status. Nobody's looking for an old married guy who likes gardening. And forget the tired line: "References available on request." It's assumed.

Cut your words to the bone. Eliminate as many personal pronouns, articles, and prepositional phrases as you can. You can even drop phrases like "duties included" and "was responsible for." Just list the important data without all the padding we normally put around it. Use active rather than passive verbs.

THE INTERVIEW

This is your moment to shine. And relax . . . they can't kill you.

Your interviews may be one at a time, or you may face a panel of interviewers in one sitting. Whether they see you individually or gang up on you, the principles are the same. First of all, try to be in a position where you can write yourself notes during the interview. Then, as you meet the persons conducting the interview, ask for their business cards. Spread them out in front of you, matching each card to its owner. If you don't get a card, write each name on your notepaper in the same positional arrangement as they sit across from you. That way, you'll be able to address each by name, and you'll be able to put each question into the context of the asker's relationship to the position being filled.

Make eye contact with each questioner and maintain it as you begin your answer, then move your eyes to the others as you continue. Treat interviewers equally, no matter how they treat you and no matter what their titles. I've known of people who have lost a job opportunity because of how they treated the receptionist. And remember, each person interviewing you will have a different perspective and goal. The HR person will be trying to decide whether you'll fit into the company and its culture. The department manager will be trying to find out if you can do the job and how you'll fit in with the other people in her department. If her boss is also there, he or she may be scouting you for potential to be promoted beyond the initial job you're interviewing for. Remember, they're all hoping to find someone, not to exclude someone. Why shouldn't that someone be you?

In a perfect world I wouldn't have to say this, but . . . tell the truth on your résumé and in all interviews. Shakespeare said, "Oh, what a tangled web we weave, when first we practice to deceive!" Once you tell an untruth, you'll have to tell several more to back it up. Then you'll have to tell even more to support that batch, and so on. Don't weave this web for yourself. You'll be the only one caught in it. And if that's not enough motivation, God said, "All liars shall have their part in the lake which burns with fire and brimstone" (Rev. 21:8). I follow this advice not only because it's practical, but also because I don't look good in an asbestos bathing suit. Seriously, I'm not judging here, I'm just telling you what works—both in the short term and eternally.

Okay, assuming you're going to tell the truth during your interviews, be confident—you're not an impostor. There's a natural human tendency to think, *I'm really not as good as everyone else applying for this job. They all know more than I do about my profession, and they all have a lot more experience.* The silly thing is, they're thinking the same thing about you. And don't let the seeming Superman requirements listed in the Help Wanted ad intimidate you. HR people always advertise for way more than they know they can get for what they're willing to pay. It's a form of prescreening that makes their job easier for them. Don't let it screen you out.

Throughout the interview, remember, you're selling yourself. Concentrate on showing the interviewers what's in it for them (for the company). Constantly and continuously ask yourself, *How can I make myself sound like my chief concern is helping them succeed rather than focusing on what I get out of the deal?*

For example, when you hear them say, "Tell me about yourself," respond with a listing of your strengths and experiences that would contribute to your ability to do the job. Do not tell them about your personal self. It would only make it look as though you're focused on yourself rather than on them.

They may also ask, "If you had to list one fault or shortcoming in yourself, what would that be?" I've actually been asked this question. Here's how I answered it: "I tend to get too focused on my job. Sometimes my employers have had to kick me out the door and send me home at night because I just wanted to keep working." Imagine how interviewers interpret this shortcoming. *Ahhh,* they think. *We'll get an hour and a half's work out of this guy for every hour we pay him for. What a bargain!*

When they finally ask, "Do you have any questions?" don't let your guard down and fall into this trap. Sure, you have questions . . . lots of questions. But, once again, stay focused on the employer rather than your-self. Don't ask a bunch of questions about what benefits you'll be getting, like how many sick days you'll get and when they become available, or how many vacation days you'll get the first year, or whether you'll be expected to work overtime. Instead, ask about job issues, like:

- What projects will I be working on?
- What kinds of people will be on the same team, or in the same department?
- May I see the job description?
- Why has this job become available?
- What qualities are you seeking in the person for this job?
- What's the next step?
- When will you be making your decision?
- When will you want this person to start?

Sooner or later, someone from the company will bring up pay and benefits. That's when you should ask questions about those issues.

Where can you find job openings? The best place is through a per-sonal referral. If you know someone who knows the person doing the hiring, that's a real benefit. If not, there are the usual sources, like the newspaper Help Wanted section, state employment agencies, headhunters, as well as classified ads in trade publications for your industry. But there are also some good World Wide Web sites that can help you with your job search and résumé/interview preparation. Here are just a few:

- www.careers.msn.net

- www.jobsearchpro.com

- www.usjobnet.com

- www.monster.com

MAKE MORE MONEY AT YOUR CURRENT JOB BY GETTING PROMOTED

If you are happy with your current employer, but you'd like more opportunity and compensation, the best way to achieve both is to become indispensable. This is also the best way to avoid the proverbial pink slip when times get tight.

I was once CEO of a company experiencing a downtime, and I remember that there were a few people I knew I'd hang on to until the end, if need be. They knew how everything worked, they knew where everything was, they knew our business, and they knew our customers. They could handle multiple responsibilities because they knew *why* those jobs were being done and *how* they affected the company's overall ability to serve our customers.

That should be your goal if you want to be indispensable. Know as much as you can about your company's business, not just your job or department. Check out its Web site. Read the annual report. Know what its challenges are. Know what the company believes to be its biggest opportunities. Know the principal benefits it provides its customers. Then let your superiors know, in ways subtle and not so subtle, that you know and care about these things. You can do this by engaging in conversations on these subjects, or by asking relevant questions. Asking questions and making suggestions by e-mail or memo allows for copies to be made and retained by those above you in the business. This will keep your name before them. Just don't make yourself a pest. It's a delicate art.

Another way to give yourself upward opportunities is to concentrate on making your immediate boss or supervisor successful. This might sound like brownnosing, but it's just smart business—and you need to think of yourself as a business. Your customers are your boss and his or her boss. Keeping this perspective will help you choose between important and unimportant tasks. After all, satisfying the customer is how everyone succeeds in business, right?

When you focus on helping those above you succeed, everyone will notice your loyalty. Loyalty is a rare virtue these days, and it will help you stand out from your fellow workers, but don't let your loyalty compromise your integrity. Do good. Do right. Even if the president of the company asks you to do something illegal or immoral, say no. Either she will respect your integrity and know she can trust you in the future, or you'll go right to the top of the layoff list. If it costs you your job, you'll know that it wasn't a good place to work anyway. On the other hand, God blesses integrity, and so does the marketplace. Sooner or later you will be rewarded.

One obvious benefit of focusing on your boss's success is that he will likely remember you on the way up. As he gets promoted—in part because you helped him succeed—you will be promoted along with him. Of course, I can't guarantee this, but loyalty is normally a two-way street. Even if the boss doesn't get promoted himself, he may reward your loyal efforts by recommending you for other opportunities within the company—maybe not above his position, but often equal to it. I was once the Manager of Membership Marketing for a well-known national nonprofit organization. After less than a year of practicing these help-your-boss-succeed principles, I was promoted to Director of Membership Marketing . . . on the recommendation of my boss, the Director of

Membership Services. We became equals on the organizational chart . . . and it was her idea.

As you focus on the needs of the company, as you learn everything you can about its operations, problems, and opportunities, and as you help your boss succeed, you're actually conducting a marketing campaign. You're marketing yourself as the indispensable, eminently promotable superemployee. Part of this campaign is to create a paper trail that evidences your exceptional performance.

One way to start this trail is to ask your boss for more frequent reviews than required, so your employee file gets fat with good stuff. If you get complimentary correspondence from outside or inside the company, see if you can have it put in your file. If you write anything for trade publications, teach a class at the nearby community college, or volunteer your time to charitable organizations, ask to have articles, releases, thank-you letters, or any other evidence of your activities placed in your file.

FIND A MENTOR

If you're serious about growing your career and building your perceived value, you'll greatly aid your cause by finding a mentor to coach and challenge you each step of the way. Your immediate supervisor might make a good mentor, but you may well find that someone in a completely different department or area is better suited to help you craft yourself for indispensability and upward mobility. Look for an experienced company veteran. It's more important to find someone who can teach you the cultures of the company, the industry, and the market your business serves. If you work at a nonprofit organization, everything I say about companies here applies to your organization as well.

Your mentor must have a great attitude. Don't even consider a whiner, complainer, or gossiper. These people will only fill you with negatives, and that won't help you achieve your goals. Attitude determines altitude. So it's obvious you can't learn how to move up from someone whose attitude is always down.

It's usually best if your mentor is higher than you on the organizational chart, so he or she can advance your name for promotion. The mentor will often be your "sponsor" for bigger and better things within the business. But focusing above your present position in the company hierarchy should not stop you from considering less-visible mentor candidates. You may find the wisest person in the building is the janitor. He may know more about the history, culture, and methods of the business than the president. Whomever you choose, let the person decide whether he wants to take on the responsibility of mentoring you. It won't work if the person is not enthusiastic about sharing what he knows and imparting it to you.

WATCH FOR TURMOIL

Volatility creates opportunities. When conditions inside or outside a business or organization cause confusion, uncertainty, or chaos . . . therein lies opportunity. Upper management is always looking for people who can solve problems—people who aren't afraid to take on difficult and messy situations. If you can present yourself as such an employee, you'll win management's admiration and an opportunity to tackle some troubles. When you succeed, you'll be indispensable.

While this might sound scary, even crazy, be comforted by the fact that most problems are not nearly as ferocious as they first appear. Once you're in the middle of it, ideas will come to help you tame the beast. Of course, these problems/opportunities may not reside within your current job description or department, so be flexible and willing to move to a different area of responsibility. This is especially true during layoff periods. Only those willing to cross departmental and even professional lines will become indispensable heroes.

Such opportunities aren't limited to solving problems. If you see opportunities not being pursued, make suggestions, and be willing to be tasked with their accomplishment. When you get the nod to pursue an opportunity, remember to stay bottom-line focused, and that means holding the line on costs as well as bringing in new revenue. You'll have to become sales-oriented to maximize a growth opportunity, but that's not all that complicated. Sales is simply about trading value for dollars. A sale is made when the stack of value the business is offering appears higher—in the customers' minds—than their stack of dollars. So pursue your opportunity by concentrating on showing the customers how much value your company can offer them.

In fact, if you're going to undertake any opportunity or responsibility within a company, you should always be thinking *customer*. The customer is everyone's boss and every business's most valuable asset. All money in a business or nonprofit organization—including your paycheck—comes from the customer. It might help you "think customer" to put a photo of a typical customer in a highly visible place in your work area, so you can regularly look at it and ask, "How'm I doin'?"

KEEP YOURSELF CURRENT

If you want to be indispensable in today's economy, don't limit yourself to yesterday's knowledge. I can't think of many jobs that don't deal with new equipment, methods, or technologies on a regular basis. The employees who keep up with these changes are much less likely to get the pink slip than those who fall behind. I know that keeping up can be challenging, because nearly everything seems to be changing with each passing day, in nearly every profession. But it's a choice you have to make. During your income-producing years, you can't give up. You have to keep challenging yourself to grow in pace with your industry—actually faster than your industry—so you can be the last person your company would lay off. Don't stick your head in the sand and pretend change isn't happening.

That's what the coal firemen who worked for the railroads in the 1930s did. Instead of learning skills used on new diesel-electric locomotives that were replacing coal-fired steam engines, they had their union fight to mandate the retention of coal firemen on the new diesel engines . . . even though there was no coal to shovel. Of course, it wasn't long before the rail-road companies worked these requirements out of their labor contracts, and the coal firemen joined the dinosaurs in the unemployment line.

You can't hold back the tide. You can't stop or reverse time. As much as you and I might like to, we can't go back to simpler days. If we're going to maintain our marketplace value, we have to keep in step. Actually, we have to stay one step ahead of our competition—the other people doing our kind of work. We must always be more appealing than the other options our employer has. And that's our responsibility, not our employer's. We may ask the boss to pay for any training we need to help the company stay current, but it's our responsibility to initiate that process.

I don't believe in evolution, but there's one place the "survival of the fittest" model seems to apply: the marketplace. When examined in the macro—the big picture—the marketplace is devoid of emotion or senti-ment. It doesn't favor anyone. It rewards people in direct relationship to the value of the service they're providing at that moment in time. If you don't feel you're being fairly compensated, you can take your case to the marketplace. If the marketplace agrees with you, there will be other employers willing to pay you more. If the marketplace doesn't concur with your evaluation, you won't get any offers, and you might even lose the paycheck you have. The humbling thing is: Your vote doesn't count. Your only options are to resign yourself to your current pay level and opportunities or increase your skills and knowledge—your value in the marketplace.

If you're really aggressive, you won't look only to increase your value to your employer and the marketplace, you'll look to get a piece of the pie for yourself. Here's one way to do that within your current employer's business.

BE AN INTRAPRENEUR

"Intrapreneur" is the label for someone who creates a business within a business. This person has the same "growth hormone" as an entrepreneur. He just chooses to create and grow his business idea within the structure of an already existing business. The intrapreneur creates a business model that *could* be spun off into a separate business. It's a stand-alone idea for a business that's simply operated as a division or department of an existing business to take advantage of the cost benefits and infrastructure already in place.

The intrapreneurial idea is presented to ownership as an internal opportunity to grow the business and its revenues. Part and parcel of this presentation is that the intrapreneur propose himself as the new unit's senior manager, who also gets a piece of the profits. Creating a new business operation and making it profitable is not a nine-to-five process. It will take an ownership attitude and commitment, which should be rewarded with an ownership reward.

Even with a piece of the profits, intrapreneuring is not as profitable as being the owner, but there are fewer downside risks. It's a more secure way of starting and running a business of your own . . . because it's not completely your own. I've seen such "businesses" eventually spun out as separate companies and even sold to the intrapreneurs who started them. So the person did end up moving from intrapreneur to entrepreneur-owner.

SELF-EMPLOYMENT AND FREE-AGENCY

Self-employment is a sort of half step between being an employee and a true business owner. I make this distinction because it's an important one to understand. When I say "self-employed," I'm talking about the engineer who moves out to become a consultant, the graphics designer or writer who goes freelance, the computer programmer who steps out on his or her own to take on clients. These self-employed free agents are not so much business owners as they are job owners. I'm not putting down this mode of income-building. It can be very lucrative. I'm simply distinguishing it from a business owner, as I'll describe.

The self-employed person trades one boss for many bosses, called customers or clients. However, going self-employed is usually the easiest way to make the step from employee to employer because you're doing the same thing, just for more people. The self-employed professionals' first clients are often their employers, and they build their client list from there. Or maybe they've been freelancing on the side, and the work gradually builds up to where it can support them.

If you're considering this route to self-reliance and more money, keep a couple of things in mind. First of all, your paycheck is not the only money your employer spends on your behalf. Be sure you factor such costs as health and life insurance, sick days, and vacation days into your profitability analysis. Second, consider the fact that your employer paid you the same amount each pay period *whether the business's income was up or down.* That won't be the case for your self-employed income. It will be linear. You'll essentially be trading time for dollars, just like an hourly job, and if you don't work, you don't make any money.

On the other hand, if your services are in demand, you can set your rates to potentially pay you much more than your employer did. As a self-employed professional, you're in charge of your own income level. But, as I said, be careful to figure in the costs of all the benefits you'll now be paying for yourself. And don't minimize the cost of overhead, even if you're working from home. Be especially mindful of your costs when setting your pricing.

Here's a basic formula for establishing what you need to charge your customers:

- Consider all your costs, including health insurance, business insurance, any utilities, and rent. If you're using space in your home, you should figure in a reasonable rent to pay yourself. Then estimate how many billable hours you'll actually be working during the month. Divide your costs by this number of billable hours. The answer will tell you how much of your hourly rate will go to covering your costs each month.

- Now decide how much you want to earn as the employee of your business each month. Divide that number by the billable hours figure. This will tell you how much of your hourly rate will pay your wages each month.

- Now determine how much profit you'd like your business to make each month. *Your wages are not the business's profit.* They are a business expense. Divide this monthly profit amount by the billable hours figure. This will tell you how much of your rate is for profit.

- Now add the three components of your hourly rate together, and you'll see how much you need to charge to cover your costs, pay yourself, and make a profit. You can compare your rate to those of competitors, but if some others are offering substantially lower rates, they have obviously not done these calculations to assure they're really making money. If you find your prospective market won't pay your rates, either you need to do a better job communicating the value you will provide for the money you're asking, or you need to reconsider your business altogether.

As I mentioned earlier in the section on real estate investing through a business of your own, as a self-employed business owner you can have your business pay for a portion of, or in some cases all of, many of the expenses you'd normally pay 100 percent for as an individual. These can include such things as phone, automobile, utilities, furniture, clothing, travel, entertainment, and more. Talk to your tax consultant to determine what expenses are legitimately deductible for your business, and ask whether it would be in your best interests to take the home office tax deduction. This is a deduction for using a set portion of your home principally for business purposes. He or she will know whether you meet the IRS's tests for taking this deduction.

Even though it can just be you doing services for a few clients, you'll need to choose a legal structure for your business, and *under no circumstances* should your personal and business finances be mixed. You can start your business as a sole proprietorship, but once it's up and going, you should choose a stronger, more defensive structure such as a limited liability company or a corporation. You can choose any of these structures, even if you're always going to be the sole employee. I'll cover these business structure options in a moment.

Now let's look at having a true *business* of your own.

BECOME A SMALL-BUSINESS OWNER

If you're entrepreneurial, the best answer—from a wealth standpoint—can be to become a business owner.

Business owners enjoy tax deductions for things employees don't, they enjoy income that is generally produced by the efforts of employees other than themselves, and they enjoy the growth in the business's value. It's much easier to sell a true business being operated by employees than it is to sell a self-employment business built on your performance alone.

Let's look at the tax benefits first. As a business owner you get to reduce your personal expenses by making them business expenses. That way you can live the same lifestyle on less personal income—because you don't have as many personal expenses. The idea is to live the lifestyle, but have the business pay for some of it with deductible money. Again, check each expense with a trusted tax adviser, so as not to run afoul of the IRS.

It takes a certain kind of person to be an entrepreneur or a business owner, and there is a difference between the two. An entrepreneur is a pioneer. He or she breaks new ground and starts a business idea from scratch. An entrepreneur is great at making something from nothing, but he's not usually built for maintaining a business that's been running for a while, because it has lost its start-up excitement. It's boring.

A business owner, on the other hand, buys and operates a business started by someone else. This person is good at operating an already proven business, but not usually as good at starting something from scratch.

Regardless of the label you give yourself, when you're on your own in business, no one's going to coordinate your activities for you. You have to be self-directed, whether you're an entrepreneur or a business owner/manager. You also need to be able to sell. If you're an owner, "salesperson" is automatically part of your job description.

If you have business start-up and operating experience, that's great. If you don't, you'll have to learn and build experience. And if you're not already working in a business that does what you'd like to do in your own business, you should probably find a job in the right kind of business and work there for a year or two. It'll be a priceless education because the experience you'll gain will help you not become a business failure statistic, and it will likely help you save and make thousands of additional dollars over the course of your business operation.

When it comes to successfully operating any kind of business, all the experts and veterans agree on what's most important. Getting and keeping customers is the critical job in any business. It doesn't matter how efficient your operations are or how precisely your books are kept. If you don't have enough customers, you'll go out of business. So everyone's focus, especially in the early days, must be on customer acquisition and retention.

That means marketing, and marketing is both a proactive and reactive process. You must be aggressively searching out customers and giving them your pitch, as well as responding to their feedback over time. Word of mouth will never get a new business going. It requires proactive marketing, which includes advertising, public relations, and sales. Too many businesses have come and gone because the owners believed the old *Field of Dreams* promise: "If you build it, they will come." Sorry . . . they won't. You have to follow the biblical admonition to "go out into the highways and hedges, and compel them to come in" (Luke 14:23). If you're not good at those tasks, you'll have to learn them or hire someone to do them.

Another attribute you'll be happy you're blessed with, or you'll have to develop, is patience. New businesses start slowly and don't produce much excess revenue in the early years. Every marketing campaign will cost twice as much as you expect, take twice as long to generate business, and it'll produce half the revenue you anticipate. So, if you have a job, keep it during the business's infancy and let revenue fuel growth instead of using it up to pay yourself. Any available profits should go into marketing in the early days.

Does it sound like I'm trying to talk you out of having a business of your own? Well, in a sense I am. If you find yourself easily scared by what I've said so far, you probably aren't composed of the free radicals necessary to make a go of it. There's nothing wrong or inferior about that. It's a simple DNA issue—either you match or you don't. On the other hand, if you're feeling up to the challenge, and you're willing to bet on yourself to make it work in spite of the odds, you probably are afflicted with the entrepreneurial bug and are compelled to venture out on your own.

When you take the plunge, know this: You'll work the hardest at the beginning and early stages. You'll have to put in more than reasonable hours and resources up front, so that someday you can work few or no hours and continue to enjoy an income stream from the business. It's a lot like taking off and climbing to cruise altitude in an airplane. It requires full power to overcome inertia, begin moving, and eventually defy gravity. Power can be reduced slightly during the climb. However, once the plane reaches cruising altitude, power can be substantially reduced and the plane will maintain cruising speed and altitude, using far less fuel than was required during the takeoff and climb.

Once at cruising altitude, a properly designed business model should produce income for you, as the owner, whether or not you're working. This is the principle distinction I've been making between owning a business and being self-employed. A true business is one where you are the owner and senior manager, but the plan is that your employees will eventually run the business with decreasing direction from you. You want the business's income to eventually become independent from your day-to-day involvement. If you take a vacation, the revenue should continue coming in unabated. Self-employment, on the other hand, operates on a linear relationship between your work time and incoming dollars. If you stop working or take a break, revenue stops.

To achieve this miracle of walk-away income, your business must be based on duplicable systems. You, the business owner, must develop or purchase systems that will manage the business's operation for you, so that you don't have to be there telling everyone what to do from moment to moment or situation to situation. In fact, the successful operation of your business should not be dependent on you or any particular employee. It should be totally dependent on the systems in place to control every function and every employee operation.

McDonald's and other franchises are good examples of system dependency versus individual dependency. You can order a Big Mac in Seattle, Sydney, or South Hampton, and it will taste the same. You can walk up to a McDonald's in any of those cities, and you'll be treated the same, likely asked identical questions, and the environment will be similar. The burgers and fries will be cooked the same way, the products will be handled and delivered the same way in each location . . . all because the McDonald's corporation operates on systems. You won't find a better Quarter Pounder in Sydney just because some guy there really knows how to fry, or a worse burger in Seattle because they can't find a good cook. The quality is consistent worldwide because systems, not individual skills, dictate how the products are prepared.

Systems include:

- Policy manuals
- Operations manuals

- Human resources manuals
- Job descriptions
- Task descriptions
- Automation
- Business plan
- Marketing plan
- Sales plan
- Organizational chart
- Quotas
- Training
- Vision statement
- And anything else that will control the business's operation and output.

Why is it so important that your business be able to operate with or without you? Because financial independence is most accurately measured in time, not dollars, meaning: How long can you live without having to work? How much freedom have you really achieved if you have a great business income, but you're a prisoner of the business? This is the reason I view the *business* model as superior to the *self-employment* model. Of course, the self-employment model can easily grow into a true business model, where employees are eventually hired to take over the bulk of the work. This can be a good way to start and grow a business to where it can live without you.

BUSINESS STRUCTURE

Whether you choose to operate as a self-employed professional or a business with employees other than yourself, one decision you'll have to make is what legal form your business will take.

The most prevalent form is the *sole proprietorship*. This is the easiest form to establish because it's just you, as an individual, doing business as (DBA) the business. Nearly 75 percent of American businesses operate in this form. The upside is that sole proprietorship is the simplest form to implement. Just open a business bank account, print some business cards, keep separate books from your personal funds, comply with any licensing and zoning requirements, and you're in business. The downside is that you're completely exposed to any liabilities the business may experience.

For example, if the business gets into a position where it can't pay its debts, you're personally responsible. If the business gets sued, you personally get sued. This is the main reason many businesses either grow into a *limited liability* form or they *incorporate*.

The next most popular business structure is the *partnership*. This is essentially a divided sole proprietorship. Most of the people who opt for partnerships do so because they don't want to go it alone. Each partner's percentage of ownership is set forth in the partnership agreement, and this division covers both the partnership's assets and liabilities. When the partnership makes money, the profits are owned by the partners in proportion to their ownership as stated in the agreement. When the partnership has debts, or gets sued, the liabilities are also proportionate to the relationships laid out in the agreement. Because a partnership does not provide any real protection of personal assets, many partnerships also grow into limited liability partnerships, limited liability companies, or corporations.

The *corporation* structure offers a business owner many benefits and a few drawbacks. What's unique about a corporation is that it is a separate legal entity from the owners, almost like another person. Since it's a separate entity, it maintains its own relationship with creditors, lenders, vendors, and customers. This provides what is called a "corporate veil" between those the company does business with and the owners of the corporation. Technically, this veil should protect owners from personal liability and debt responsibility, but, like most veils, it can be flimsy.

For starters, even if you incorporate, most lenders and creditors are going to require you to personally guarantee loans and credit in the business's early days. That way, if the corporation defaults on any obligations, creditors will be able to come after your personal assets to satisfy the business's obligations to them. The corporate veil also provides no protection if the company is not operated as a real business with all the paperwork and record keeping attendant to such a business. Finally, the corporate veil understandably provides no protection in cases of criminal or fraudulent business activities.

If you own a corporation, your taxes will depend on which type of corporate form you choose. The subchapter C corporation is the traditional form and the one used by most large businesses. A subchapter C corporation pays taxes on its profits, and then shareholders pay taxes on their individual distributions and capital gains from any profits they take out of the company. The subchapter S corporation operates similarly, except the corporation itself doesn't pay income taxes. All profits and losses flow through directly to shareholders and are filed on their individual Form 1040s, whether or not they actually take the money out of the company. Of course, if they later do take money out of the company on which they've already paid taxes, they won't have to pay taxes on it again.

Limited Liability Companies (LLCs) and Limited Liability Partnerships (LLPs) are sort of half steps between a sole proprietorship or partnership, and a corporation. You could think of them as "corporation lite." They afford most of the same liability protections as corporations but are less complicated and expensive to set up and operate. All profits and losses flow through directly to the owners and are filed on their individual tax returns. Talk to your lawyer and accountant to choose the best form for your business and your individual needs and circumstances.

WHERE TO FIND SMALL-BUSINESS OPPORTUNITIES

There are many good books at your library and local bookstores on starting a business of your own, as well as on buying and operating an existing business. I've developed a program called *Wealth Machine* that includes sixteen audio sessions, a workbook, a database marketing software program, the software user manual, and a marketing video. You can find out about it at my Web site: www.johncummuta.com. There are also several good magazines, available at most newsstands and bookstores, that specialize in home-based and small-business opportunities, like franchises. *Entrepreneur* magazine is the premier example. If you're thinking of a business of your own, browsing your local bookstore for books and magazines can be an energizing and educational experience.

Check out these sources on the World Wide Web:

- www.johncummuta.com

- *Entrepreneur* magazine on-line: www.entrepreneur.com

- *Business Opportunities Handbook* on-line:
  http://www.busop1. com

- *Business Opportunities Journal* on-line: http://www.boj.com

- Franchise business opportunities: http://www.franchise1.com

- Federal Trade Commission—franchise and business opportunity rules and regulations: http://www.ftc.gov/bcp/franchise/netfran.htm

- Do business with the U.S. government:
  http://www.sba.gov/expanding

- Buy and sell businesses:

  http://www.usbx.com

  http://www.bizbuysell.com

  http://www.br-network.com

Of course, all you have to do is search the Web with terms like "entrepreneur," "small business," or "business opportunities," and you'll be overwhelmed with information. If you have Internet access, I invite you to try it because a real education awaits you out there. But, as always, buyer beware. If an opportunity is not wrapped in a brand name you recognize, be very wary. There may be more wolves in sheep's clothing out there than genuine sheep. Never give anyone a dime of your money or sign any agreement without much counsel and review by a trusted attorney, preferably one who specializes in franchises or business opportunities. Your accountant should also be a part of your precommitment business counseling.

I know I've said a lot of complicated and possibly intimidating stuff in this section, but the truth is that starting and/or operating a business of your own can be one of life's real adventures. If you approach it as such, you can have fun. On the other hand, if you're not designed to enjoy the emotional altitude changes that come with this lifestyle, keep your job, and build your wealth that way. You'll live longer.

By the way, if you're ever tempted to use debt to build your business (other than a real estate business where it can be a benefit), be aware: According to an August 2002 *USA Today* article, the businesses that made it through the recent recession in the best health and in the best position for future profits were the ones that were *debt-free* going in. On the other hand, CEOs who thought they could use debt to leverage their growth either went out of business, went bankrupt, or went to jail.

WORK/PERSONAL LIFE BALANCE

Don't ever lose the things money can't buy just to get the things money can buy. Building wealth can become pretty empty and meaningless if you lose the people with whom you were planning to share your secure and prosperous days.

Never lose sight of what you're working for. I can remember that early in my marriage and fathering days, I was a classic workaholic entrepreneur. And my excuse to myself, my wife, and my kids was "I'm doing it for you." Baloney! Sure, they benefited materially from my success, but I was doing it because I wanted to. I enjoyed the challenge and the rush when I succeeded. It was mostly about me, not them . . . and I nearly lost them. So take it from one who knows: Keep your future lifestyle, and its planned coparticipants, in mind as you either climb the corporate ladder or build your own enterprise. Celebrating alone wouldn't be fun.

Another "doing it for them" trap often catches single parents who work two or more jobs to put kids through college or otherwise give them a better future than the one the single parent is living. While the end is noble, the means may well undermine the purpose of the effort. If your children grow up as "latchkey" kids because you're always working, more damage may be done by the lack of a loving, nurturing parent in their everyday lives than from lack of tuition when it comes time for college. No children ever died from having to work their way through college, but too many kids die from joining gangs or looking to drugs to fill the void left by an empty house.

Please understand that I have the utmost respect for people raising children on their own. I'm not trying to judge your motives or your actions. I'm simply posing questions that only you can answer for your life and the lives of your children. I pray the Lord helps you find just the right balance for your family. For my part, I intend to help relieve your financial pressure, so you can accomplish all your hopes and dreams for yourself and your children.

The plan I've shown you in this book should eventually allow you to do all the things working like a dog prevents you from doing now. When you're a working machine, you're unable to spend sufficient time or give sufficient mental attention to your spouse. But as you follow the plan in this book to financial freedom, you'll have increasing time and resources to spend with and on your spouse. When you're working sixty or more hours a week, you're not spending enough time with your children. A bad result of that is, their lives can be permanently damaged by your absence. Another bad result is that they may end up calling someone else Daddy or

Mommy. But when you follow the plan in this book, your children won't have to look at photos to remember who you are.

And don't forget to spend time with yourself. Yeah . . . you! When I was working around the clock, either physically or mentally, I had practically no time for John either. I literally told myself that I'd make it up to me later, when I was rich. Phooey! I was missing some of the best years of myself life for something as fleeting and temporary as money. What a knucklehead!

Spend time with your hobbies. Remember the guy or gal who used to love to fish, play tennis, garden, fly? Be careful you don't lose that inner person, because too much focus on achieving financial goals can squeeze him or her out of existence. Don't always be building a life—have a life. Am I saying goals and diligence are wrong? Of course not. I've already discussed their importance earlier in this book. The heading of this section is "Work/Personal Life *Balance*." Balance implies that everything important is present, properly positioned, and in the right weight. Just make sure that as you build financial freedom, you schedule in a little time for each of the important people in your life—so they're all still available to you when you get there. And that includes the real you.

One of the most currently relevant work/personal life balance questions is whether both parents in a two-parent household should work. Many couples come to a point where they decide they either want to buy more stuff or pay off their debts, and the logical conclusion appears to be that if both of them work . . . Well, two incomes are better than one, aren't they? Not necessarily. Don't assume that having a stay-at-home spouse go to work will significantly add to the household *net* income. It may add to your gross income, but you can spend only your *net* income.

In her book *Two Incomes and Still Broke?* (Times, 1996), Linda Kelley says:

Second incomes are often overrated in terms of net value or spendable income. Spendable income is what remains of a paycheck to spend on financial goals after all job-related expenses are subtracted. It's not generally recognized that second incomes are subject to larger and more job-related expenses than first incomes. This may be because identifying job-related expenses is such a complex undertaking. You've doubtless budgeted for the easy-to-see expenses, such as childcare and an extra wardrobe. Most other expenses are intangible and often stem from a lack of time to spend and manage assets with thought and deliberation. But Uncle Sam's pickpocket tactics on second incomes are the real scandal. He meticulously camouflages the fact that second incomes almost always pay higher effective tax rates than first incomes, and his well-hidden take is often the decisive factor in measuring a second paycheck's worth.

Often a second income is just a way to get new clothes or to buy consumer stuff you probably don't really need . . . at least not as much as you need the domestic tranquility you may lose with both parents working. This being the case, you have to ask yourself if the reasons for working are worth the cost when measured against the impact on your children, if you have any. Recent research has shown that having at least one parent available full-time during the formative years is a leading determinant of intelligence in children.

I acknowledge that many couples work for professional or career-satisfaction reasons, and I'm not criticizing that. However, if the two incomes are being sought for financial reasons alone, break out the calculator to see if it really pays. A friend and his wife were considering her going back to work. But after daycare, clothing, transportation, increased taxes, and other related costs, she would have ended up working for a net of just 60 cents an hour.

And the times, they are a'changin'. According to the U.S. Census Bureau, in 2000, 55 percent of mothers with children under one year old were working or looking for work. That's down from 1998, when the labor force participation rate was almost 60 percent. This represents the first decrease of working mothers since 1976. In a study by New York research group Catalyst, 86 percent of Generation X women said that having a loving family is extremely important, while only 18 percent of these women responded that earning a great deal of money is what matters. Many young women are reacting to having watched their mothers struggle to balance career and family, and they don't want the same stress.

A March 2002 *USA Today* article reported,

> These days, even part-time work can mean full-time stress. That's partly why Edie Hofmeister left. The lawyer used to travel around the country and work on insurance coverage litigation on behalf of multimillion-dollar corporations. Now she's taking her 4-year-old daughter, Alexandra Sasse, to Chuck E. Cheese's for her birthday. The trade-off, she says, is worth it.

It's not within the scope or purpose of this book to come down on either side of the working mother issue. I'm simply saying that when you're debt-free and have substantially lowered monthly requirements, one spouse staying home with the children becomes a viable option. If that's the goal of your heart, you bought the right book.

SOME PROFESSIONS MAY MAKE IT HARDER TO ACHIEVE DEBT FREEDOM

Professions that push you to "act" prosperous are dangerous to your financial health. Lawyers, accountants, investment advisers, and doctors are examples of these kinds of professions. When you're in one of these perceived-affluent professions, you have to belong to the right country club, the right bridge club, and the right social circles. To join, you have to "look" the part. You're also led to believe (by the Coalition of Four) that you have to "look" successful in these professions to attract clients.

What this leads to is nothing more than a high-level "keep up with the Joneses" trap. These people are ripe pickin's for the Coalition. They're "Consumers Supreme." They not only spend as if there's no tomorrow, they buy the most expensive stuff. The Coalition laughs all the way to the bank, and the poor doctors, lawyers, investment advisers, senior executives, and the rest just turn up the speed of their working treadmills and hope their hearts, marriages, and sanity will hold out.

That's no way to live.

Your ultimate career goal should be to be doing what you love to do, living where you love to live. So far in this book, I've shown you how to stop the unnecessary bleeding of money from your life, I've shown you how to pay off your debts, I've shown you how to build your wealth with paper assets and real estate, and I've given you ways to build your wealth by increasing your job income or by building a business of your own—all so you and those you love can reach a point where you live where you want, how you want, doing what you want, every single day. That's how I define being wealthy.

In the next couple of chapters, we'll examine the two biggest expense areas in the average family's life. They also happen to be the two biggest money traps in which the Coalition of Four wants to catch you.

8

WHAT YOU DRIVE

∾

What you drive will, in large part, determine the quality of your financial journey and its destination.

If Dorothy wanted to go somewhere, she just clicked her heels. When Neo needed to travel, he only had to find a phone so someone back on the *Nebuchadnezzar* could zap him to wherever he needed to go. We, on the other hand, have to drive. But, in today's Coalition-crafted world, *what* we drive has been manipulated into a lot more than just transportation. It has become a facet of who we are . . . and thereby a prime opportunity for the Coalition partners to capture a major slice of our lifetime income.

But we're going to look under the hood and see what they're doing to us. In this chapter we'll consider . . .

- What part automobiles play in our lives
- How they can help us
- How they can financially hurt us
- How to buy cars and trucks

ORUKTOR AMPHIBOLOS: AUTOMOBILE

In 1792 Oliver Evans applied for a U.S. patent in Philadelphia on a steam land carriage, which he called the "oruktor amphibolos"! Then in 1887

George B. Selden, a Rochester, New York, attorney, received a patent for what he called a "road machine." In 1895 the Duryea brothers started manufacturing their "motor wagons." In 1896, Henry Ford introduced an experimental car he dubbed the "Quadricycle." In newspapers of the times, these self-propelled vehicles were called such names as "autometon," "motor-vique," "oleo locomotive," "autokenetic," "buggyaut," "motor carriage," "autobaine," "automotor horse," "diamote," "otoring," "mocole," and, of course, the "horseless carriage."

To break the tie, in 1895 the *Chicago Times-Herald* offered a $500 prize for the best name for motorized vehicles of the day. The winning entry: "motorcycle." The word *automobile* didn't even get an honorable mention. But, in 1897, the influential *New York Times* cast the die with its line: "The new mechanical wagon with the awful name—automobile . . . has come to stay."

Although some of these early names were poetic if not pronounceable, for the purpose of this discussion, I'm going to use the term "car" to represent cars, light trucks, SUVs, or any other current label for the vehicle you drive each day. And though the names have changed, one thing hasn't. We're still being seduced into believing our personal transport vehicle can do more for us than just get us from here to there.

THE CAR'S PURPOSE

Since this book is about helping you avoid wealth-draining traps laid by the Coalition of Four—and thereby help you achieve true, debt-free financial independence—I have no choice but to confront the American love affair with the car. Because our lover, the car, is cheating on us and lying to us, telling us that it will deliver far more than dependable transportation. But it's not just the car's fault. You see, we earnestly want our car to mean more, and that's the paradigm I'm here to dethrone.

I know this may hurt, but your car's true purpose is to transport you wherever you want to go, whenever you want to go. That's it. You get into trouble when you begin ascribing other values and purposes to it. When you see your car as an extension of your personhood, you're in trouble, because you'll then be vulnerable to paying too much money in an attempt to buy the personhood of your dreams. Whether you're a man trying to look macho or a woman trying to project success, you're going to spend too many of your hard-earned dollars trying to buy that quality through a car. The result is that you fail on two counts:

1. The car will not contribute anything to your personhood.
2. You'll do serious damage to your ability to achieve financial independence.

This whole issue is less about cars than it is about psychology. Watch TV car commercials. In many you don't even see the car until the last few seconds. What they show you is a person or several people being sexy, or cool, or macho, or successful, or sophisticated, in other words, being what you'd like to be. Then they show the car and imply that sexiness, coolness, machismo, success, or sophistication comes as standard equipment with it. All you have to do is buy the car, and you'll become like one of those people in the commercial.

The sad reality is that you're not one iota changed when you drive off the lot with the new car. You're just poorer. And the car is worth as much as 20 percent less when the tires hit the street in front of the dealership.

Do the math. You're going to bring in only so much money in your life. No matter what your profession, there's a limit to how much you'll make during your income-producing years. Every dollar you blow on more car than you actually need is a dollar that cannot build your wealth. Let me be clear about exactly what dollars I'm talking about here. You likely need a car. The question is, *How much* car do you really need, and how *new* does that car have to be to look good and provide dependable service? If you're buying more than you really need, or you're buying a brand-new car, *how much more are you paying for the unnecessary part?*

Those are the wasted dollars. Dollars that will never get to multiply in your investments.

So the battle is over those "more car than you really need" dollars, and that's where psychology comes in. There's psychology to the car's design. There's psychology to the images shown in the ads and the soundtrack behind those images. There's even psychology behind each car's name. Here's what a *USA Today* article said about today's car naming schemes:

Names using just letters and numbers are all the rage in the auto industry. Acura has transformed its lineup to initials: TL, RL, MDX, RSX. Mazda is studying a change to a letters-and-numbers system, so soon there may be no more Protegé, Miata or Millenia. Even South Korean upstart Hyundai is looking at upper-crust initials.

Naming experts say alphanumeric names make consumers think of technology and luxury.

Hyundai had no intention of initialing its first vehicle priced over $20,000, the XG300. One name up for consideration was Concerto, which would play off the Sonata name Hyundai uses for another sedan. But consumers hated it.

"XG300, they told us, sounded more technological and deserving of a higher price," says spokesman Chris Hosford.

Unlike their American SUV counterparts, Acura, Lexus, BMW, Mercedes and Infiniti have all stuck to letters and numbers for their SUVs: Acura MDX, Infiniti QX4, Lexus LX and RX and BMW X-Series.

They are probably correct to do so, says naming expert Joe Selame of BrandEquity in Newton, Mass. "Young people relate to alphanumeric names . . . There is so much abbreviation and coding on the Internet that it seems natural to them," he says.

Given that Cadillac is desperate to attract those young, tech-savvy buyers, CTS probably makes more sense than Catera, its predecessor, which was named after a city in Spain.

See . . . there are even people who earn a living by finding just the right names to make you part with your money! It's all part of the Coalition manipulation, and they're better at perpetrating it than we are at resisting it. They reshape the bodies of their cars, film them in seductive settings, give them new names, and we fork over our money.

MY 'VETTE STORY

When I was in my fast-lane days, driving my gold Corvette, I didn't recognize the real cost of its $549 monthly payments. I did, however, gradually recognize that the Corvette was special only for the first few months; after that, it was just my car. The car I went to the store to get a gallon of milk in. The car I drove my kids to school in when they were late. The car I drove to work.

When I first got the 'Vette, I remember that each time I drove up to people I knew, they'd say, "Wow, John, cool car." But every time after that when I'd drive up, they'd just say, "Hi, John." It really didn't hit me until my financial crisis magnified the weight of those $549 payments that I had been paying more than $1,000 every couple of months to get one "wow" out of each person I knew. That was a lousy return on investment.

Although it may have been an ego booster, the little gold car was a bust as efficient transportation. It couldn't carry anything besides me and Lois. And even when I wasn't moving, the police thought I was speeding . . . or at least thinking about it.

It was useless in winter. I remember that after one six-inch snowfall, it took me more than an hour to get out of the parking lot by my office, because the low-to-the-ground Corvette kept compressing snow under the chassis to where the wheels weren't making contact with the ground. Even when they did get traction in the snow, the torque in the power train caused the rear wheels to spin every time I touched the accelerator. It was a gold, plastic coffin in the winter.

Another fond memory was when I took it in for its one-thousand-mile "checkup." It cost $1,000! That's right—a dollar a mile. A grand to look her over, tweak the fuel system, and vacuum out the interior. Why so much? Because anyone who could afford a Corvette could afford expensive maintenance. It was one of those implied situations where if you had to ask about the price of maintaining the thoroughbred, it was too rich for your pocketbook. So I paid the $1,000 and smiled as if it were nothing. How stupid was that?

Pretty stupid. But I was caught in a psychological trap: I had been telling everyone that I was a successful entrepreneur, so I had to play the part, and that included "acting wealthy" to the Chevy dealer who was gouging me out of $1,000 for doing practically nothing. Peer pressure and image maintenance—they're deep, destructive Coalition traps, and they're more prevalent today than ever, especially when it comes to our cars.

∞

WHAT'S OUR MONEY BUYING US?

People increasingly wear their cars like ID badges. "This is who I am," they believe their cars say. Yeah, they do—but what's your car saying? Is it saying you're gullible? Is it saying you're insecure to the extent that you have to prove you're somebody, or that you're still sexy, or that you're still young, or that you're sophisticated? Are you crying every time your correspondingly expensive monthly payment or insurance premium comes due, while the car manufacturer, advertiser, dealer, and finance company are laughing all the way to the bank?

Or are you one who thinks that your car tells the world what you're worth or how successful you are? Do you believe that if you're driving a Ford Taurus and I'm driving a BMW, I must be more successful than you? Well, not only is that a Coalition deception, but the reverse is more likely true. In a study of American millionaires, it was found that fewer than 25 percent own a new car, less than 20 percent lease a car, and more than 80 percent own American-brand cars. So much for the image that millionaires are driving new foreign luxury cars. No, the only people driving new foreign luxury cars are the poor suckers the manufacturers, Media, Advertisers, and finance (or lease) companies duped into believing it would make them look like millionaires.

Unless you're among the Microsoft superrich, you have to choose between *looking* wealthy and *being* wealthy—at least during the bulk of your income-producing years. Later, when your investment balances have commas in them, you can be a bit more adventurous. Again, it's a matter of making only so much money in your lifetime. You can either consume it, trying to appear to have money, or invest it so you really will have money. Pick one.

FILTER OUT THE ADVERTISING

Car manufacturers know exactly how to frame a commercial. If they want you to buy a car for its snob appeal, they'll position it that way. If they're selling you youth, you'll see the car breaking the speed limit down a winding road or sliding sideways on a rain-slick surface. Young men are subtly told that the right car will reap a harvest of beautiful women. You'll see attractive women's heads turn as the car goes by, or the lone male driver will have a bevy of beauties with him as he cruises down the road.

So what happens to a young male watching this kind of commercial? He gets the subliminal message that "car equals girl." From that point in the commercial, his brain is no longer functioning. The price, the monthly payments, the interest rate—all are irrelevant. He simply marches, like a robot, to the car dealer with a voice in his head leading him on: "Car . . . girl, car . . . girl, car . . . girl."

I'm exaggerating (a little), but it really is a master manipulation, and I'm not the only one who's noticed the Advertising Industry pushing familiar gender buttons in its car commercials. Here's an analysis of a TV truck commercial I found on the Swarthmore College Web site:

THE RUGGED ALL-TERRAIN VEHICLE

Synopsis: No people are shown in this commercial; a voiceover is only used to heighten the message the music is relaying. Without directly divulging the brand of car in this commercial, the music playing is the ubiquitous "Like a Rock" theme. The voiceover is male, highlighting the rugged, powerful features of the car we see during the commercial. The car itself turns, drives, and splashes through small streams, traversing a rocky, mountainous landscape with relative ease. The car shots are shown in slow motion, presumably to make the car look more stylish and capable. Though we never see a driver, the association of the voiceover with the automobile suggests that were we to see one, the driver would be mal. . . This commercial plays off our pre-existing gender stereotypes to sell its product. Of the eight people present in the room at the time that this commercial came on, only one of them that I polled thought the driver "might" be a woman. The rest all assumed, without giving the matter much thought, that the driver was male. This simple association alone speaks volumes to the work the car industry, as well as other technological industries, have already done to gender-type their products. Whenever we see a rugged sports utility vehicle with a powerful V6 engine, we assume (usually correctly) that the target audience is male. The wording of the commercial also codes for a male audience: words used in the voiceover, such as "powerful," "rugged," and "adventurous" all ring more masculine than feminine. The industry would be well-served, I think, to find more neutral words or to create more ground-breaking commercials in the hopes that these gender stereotypes and strong associations lessen in the future.

I wouldn't hold my breath, because the Advertising Industry isn't interested in fairness or changing cultural stereotypes; it's interested in selling stuff. And if it works to puff up men and boys into thinking they'll be more masculine by buying the manufacturer's rough, tough pickup truck, the Advertisers will keep doing it until it stops working. They know, with certainty, who buys or is likely to buy the product being advertised, and they play that audience segment like a fiddle, manipulating emotions and egos until the actual facts of the purchase no longer compute. It becomes a completely emotional process.

Here's another take on how it's done, from a professional photographer. It's an excerpt from an article published in the October 1994 issue of *International Photographer* magazine:

> *We see her in the distance, shimmering in the changing light. As she moves closer, individual shapes become more apparent, more enticing. The play of light and shadow across her smooth and silky skin is so inviting, as the lens caresses every line and curve of her elegant, youthful body.*

Welcome to a car commercial. You could change the gender and a few of the adjectives and make the subject masculine, but the purpose would be the same. Sex appeal. It sells and it's the main theme of most automobile advertising in one way or another.

These commercials are so good, so artistic, they not only sell cars . . . they sell themselves as entertainment. There are myriad sites on the World

Wide Web that offer car commercials for sale on video. That's right. People are paying $19.95 and more for videos of car commercials. Only in America!

Instead of watching the commercials as entertainment and letting them play their little games on your subconscious, what you should do when you feel a tug on your emotions is, first of all, warn yourself that you have entered the manipulation zone; and second, ask yourself if you really need *any* new vehicle, much less the one being advertised. I know that's a radical concept, but it could save you thousands and thousands of dollars.

That's what we all *should* do. Unfortunately, most American consumers just salivate and do as they're told by the Advertisers. They don't do a cost-benefit analysis to determine whether the car or truck they're buying will perform any of their normal driving tasks better than the vehicle they already have, or one they could buy for a lot less. They just trot down to the dealer and sign away the next four to six years of their incomes, totaling tens of thousands of dollars. Dollars that should be building their future financial security, but instead are building GMs, Fords, Mitsubishis, or some other auto manufacturer's financial security.

Here's the cold, hard truth: No matter what the ad promises, when you click the seat belt closed around you, you're not a bit more successful, you're not a bit more attractive, you're not a bit wealthier. In fact, the opposite is true. So whatever psychological fulfillment you thought you were buying, you did *not* get it. Unless you truly needed the car and made a wise buying decision, you just got poorer. That's all that was accomplished at the car dealership.

YOUR WEALTH IS NOT MEASURED BY WHAT YOU DRIVE

As I've said several times already, true financial wealth is measured by how long you can live without having to work. I don't drive a $40,000-plus foreign luxury car, I drive a five-year-old American-brand pickup . . . but I can live indefinitely without working because my monthly requirements are low, and passive investment income pays me enough to meet those expenses. My expenses are low because I have no payment on the pickup, no payment on the house, no payment on any debt. And, because I don't have to work, I do whatever I decide to do—like writing this book in my home office. My morning commute is thirty seconds, the weather's always fine, and because I don't need the truck to get to work, it has less than sixty-five thousand miles on it. See how all that works together?

The important point here is that my *freedom* is my real wealth, not the truck. If I were leasing a Mercedes to look wealthy, that would just increase my expenses and make it harder for my investments to generate enough income to sustain my wife and me. So I'd have to work harder . . . maybe even go back to having a regular outside job. The net effect: The Mercedes would actually be *reducing* my wealth, not increasing it.

And forget what the Joneses or any of your other neighbors are driving, because they're just driving to the poorhouse. They're trading real long-term wealth for temporary illusions of wealth. If you envy what they're driving now, just wait. They'll be envying how well you live during your decades of retirement, while they have to keep working to pay their latest list of debts. You'll be the enviable one because you followed the system I've shown you in this book, and you didn't fall prey to the Coalition's car commercials and peer pressure.

Maybe Benjamin Franklin best captured what I'm trying to say in his little book *The Way to Wealth:* "These are not the necessaries of life; they can scarcely be called the conveniences: And yet only because they look pretty, how many want to have them? By these, and other extravagancies, the genteel are reduced to poverty, and forced to borrow of those whom they formerly despised."

LET'S GET DOWN TO SOME SPECIFIC CAR GUIDELINES

For starters, never, never, never buy a brand-new car. Sounds almost un-American, doesn't it? But unless you're a Bill Gates heir or you've won the lottery, forget about new cars. The reason is simple: They're a rotten value for the money. New cars lose half their value in the first two to three years. So the most cost-efficient way to get ahead of the depreciation game is to buy two- to three-year-old cars, preferably for cash. Let someone else take the initial depreciation bath. You'll get a solid car with many tens of thousands of miles still in it for half the price. And many of the warranties will still be in effect.

Here's how the editors of MSN's Carpoint Web site see it:

> These days, a car bought several years into its life span has stabilized greatly in value but has neither declined significantly in mechanical reliability or appearance nor increased in ownership costs. (In fact, insurance costs and other fees often are considerably less than when the car was new.) Therefore, if your main goal as a vehicle buyer is obtaining reliable transportation for a good price, the used-car market can be the best place to shop.

And if you're hooked on that new car smell, they sell it in spray cans at the auto parts store.

A two-year-old car can actually be more dependable than a new car because any bugs have likely been addressed by the original owner, and today's cars are capable of more than two hundred thousand miles if cared for. I know of a limousine operator who routinely got three hundred thousand miles out of his vehicles. When asked how he did it, he said, "Maintain the fluids. Keep the oil, transmission fluid, and all other fluids fresh, and keep the car clean." Pretty simple.

Okay . . . you agree. You'll buy used cars rather than new ones. But, even then, be certain of your motivation. Some reasons are valid; some are more emotional than substantive. For example, watch out for the repair bill motivator. If you hear yourself saying, "I've had to take this car to the repair shop twice in the past few months. I should just get a new car, so I won't have these repair bills," get a hold on yourself. Take a cold shower or something. Then settle down with a calculator. See if you can get the calculator to tell you that $3,000 to $6,000 a year in new car payments is cheaper than $500 to $1,000 in annual repairs.

The unfortunate irony is that people usually start saying this about the time they've already fixed all but the last major item needing repair. Right when they're one repair away from a period of dependable service, they trade or sell the car instead of fixing that last thing. Trust me, maintaining most cars that are a decade or less old will always be cheaper than buying a new one, especially if the new one comes with payments.

For more information on taking care of your car, see Appendix E: How to Make Your Car Last. Keeping the car, we have in good shape also helps keep our finances in good shape. Remember, it's not rocket science. It's all about spending as little as reasonable now, so you can spend as much as you want later.

LEASES STINK

I've set this issue apart from *buying* a car, because leasing is a completely different animal . . . and not a financially friendly one. As an individual income earner, you should never lease a car. It makes no sense to me to pay the leasing company thousands of dollars and end up owning nothing! The company has thousands of dollars of your money, and you have nothing! It gets your hard-earned cash, *and* it gets the car back! Who's winning that game?

Before you jump up to object, I acknowledge that if you own a highly profitable business, leasing a car might make financial sense, although I'd have to see the numbers to be convinced. But that's a *business* financial decision. I'm talking about your personal finances here. For the average-income earner, leasing a personal vehicle makes no sense. The fatal flaw in leasing is that you can *never* pay it off. It's like rent. The cash continues to leave your life, while you build no equity in anything. It's negative cash flow without any corresponding gain in your net worth.

Yes, I know that leases have buyout clauses at the end, but you'd come out a lot better if you just financed a straight purchase than you would taking a lease and buying the vehicle at the end. Like I said, leases stink. Of course, I firmly believe financing a car stinks. It's just more debt, and it only makes the car cost more than it's worth. I use it as an example only to show how bad I think leasing is.

HOW TO BUY A GOOD USED CAR

The two best times of the year to buy a used car are the Christmas season and late summer to early fall.

At Christmastime, dealerships are ghost towns because most people are at the malls, Wal-Mart, and Toys R Us buying gifts. Plus, many dealerships and salespeople are competing in year-end sales contests. Dealers may also have tax incentives to get inventory off their books before the end of the year. The July through October opportunity is caused by dealers trying to make room on their lots for the new-model-year inventory.

Buying a used car today is not what it was a decade or longer ago. In the olden days you'd travel from dealer to dealer trying to find the best price, you'd haggle with some guy in a leisure suit, then you'd drive home with the feeling you could've done better. Not anymore . . . because today's used car buyer is easily armed with information yesteryear's buyer could only dream about—although the initial information has to come from you.

Before you even start shopping, establish how much you're willing to spend. And don't forget to allow some extra for licensing and taxes. Once you've set that amount, ignore cars whose cost is above it, and even those that just barely squeeze under the bar. Your goal is to try to find yourself a real bargain that probably deserves to be near your upper limit but can be had for less.

Next, decide what you want in the car. This can include both accessories and capabilities. Do you want air-conditioning at any cost? Will you be using the car to haul the kids off to school or to wine and dine clients? What kind of mileage do you need it to give you? Start with the must-haves, then move on to the like-to-haves, like the CD player, paint color, convertible top, and so on. The like-to-haves are negotiable; the must-haves are not. Another way to say this is: The like-to-haves are the first things you'd sacrifice if you found an otherwise perfect car.

This list will help you immediately eliminate certain models and types. You can't take six kids to the Little League game in a two-seat sports car, and you can't expect frugal gas mileage from a big SUV. Your list of must-have capabilities will pare your search down to only those cars that can do the job.

Once you've narrowed your search down to the models and years that fit your requirements, it's time to find out what they're worth. Today's car buyer has the World Wide Web to help in that regard, and the best site I've found that shows used car values is the Kelley Blue Book site (www.kbb.com). It has a pricing guide that will walk you through the process of identifying a specific vehicle through a series of mouse clicks, ending with the car's current retail value and an offer to find a nearby (within fifty miles) dealer with such a vehicle in inventory.

Not bad . . . let your mouse do the walking. Here are some other good World Wide Web sites that will help you make a better used car purchase:

- http://www.vehiclesonline.com
- http://autos.msn.com
- http://www.carfax.com
- http://www3.nadaguides.com
- http://www.carprices.com

Of course, once you find a car, you have to know if it's in decent shape before you hand over your money. In Appendix D: How to Buy a Good Used Car, I've compiled a checklist that will literally walk you around the car and through a test drive, so you can have a high level of confidence you're not buying someone else's problems.

That's it. You're now psychologically prepared for car commercials and their manipulations, you know that used cars are the vehicles of choice for wealth accumulators, and you know how to find and buy your next used car. Now it's time to determine where you'll drive to at the end of each day.

In the next chapter we'll discuss hearth and home. A home can absorb the bulk of the money that could otherwise make you rich, so this is a crucial subject, and I promise we'll examine it from all sides. Turn the page, and let's go.

9

WHERE YOU LIVE

∞

A man's home is his castle."

"Home is where the heart is."

"There's no place like home."

These and other homey aphorisms paint warm and fuzzy pictures of the typical family home. But if you put a home in the hands of Dorothy and Toto, it becomes a lethal weapon. If you put a home in the hands of the Coalition of Four, it becomes a powerful wealth siphon. And if you put a home in the hands of a typical consumer, it can become a lethal, self-inflicted wound, devouring the bulk of what should become a retirement nest egg.

It's common knowledge that for most people, homes are their largest single purchases. Unfortunately, homes are often their largest single ego statements as well. Manipulated by the Coalition's constant urging, many people purchase way more home than they need, condemning themselves to lives of mortgage company servitude. Working month after month to metabolize huge mortgage, insurance, and tax payments, they have no lives. . . but they look good doing it.

"House poor" is the term used to describe these people. They spend too much on their houses and their associated costs, so they're poor people living in big houses. They live "for" rather than just "in" their home. Even with two incomes they barely make it, and there's little or nothing left over for building a financial future or having a current life. So how much house is too much?

Most financial professionals will warn you not to buy a house with a price more than two and a half times your *current* annual salary. Your house payment, including principal, interest, taxes, and insurance, should add up to no more than about 28 percent of your monthly *take-home* pay. You can generally count on maintenance, taxes, and other house costs to be about equal to your monthly principal and interest (P&I) amount, so your home will actually cost you about twice your P&I each month. Unfortunately, many people are violating these rules of thumb, some by great amounts. They buy more house than they need . . . and more house than their lifetime incomes can afford.

Why?

For the same reasons we talked about with cars in the previous chapter. They believe their houses make a statement about their value as persons, as well as their financial value. We live in a highly competitive society, and that carries over to the house races conducted among siblings, coworkers, and neighbors. Consumers are trying to "out-house" each other, spiraling their finances into the outhouse. And to make matters even worse for the poor home-buyer, prices are getting out of reach. Home prices in some areas are growing faster than income. From 1991 to 2001, the rise in family income trailed gains in home prices—45 percent vs. 52 percent—despite a surge in the number of two-income-earner families.

"The run-up in single-family home prices is crowding out solidly middle-class households from buying," says Bruce Katz, director of the Center on Urban and Metropolitan Policy at the Brookings Institution, in a *USA Today* article. The median price of a U.S. home rose more than 6 percent in 2001 to $147,500. That's fabulous news for a home owner looking to sell, but it's devastating for households looking to buy. And when those households put both adults to work to qualify for a big mortgage, they expose themselves to the vulnerability that should one income-earner lose his or her job, the remaining income may well be insufficient to continue paying the mortgage.

THE MORTGAGE COMPANY MAKES IT EVEN WORSE

As I mentioned in earlier chapters, the damage done to your lifetime finances from buying too much house will be compounded by your mortgage company—because you're going to pay it back at least two and a half times what it lends you. Want to see how much you're really scheduled to pay the mortgage company for your loan? Just multiply your monthly payment amount by 360 . . . that's thirty years of twelve payments a year. If you have a shorter mortgage, multiply the number of years times twelve, then take that total times your monthly payment. For most people, the result is two and a half to nearly three times what they borrowed.

The word *mortgage* comes from the root words *mort* (death) and *gage* (engage or grip), so "mortgage" = "death-grip." Nothing could be more appropriate, because if you die—either physically or in terms of losing your income—the mortgage company has a grip on your home. If you or your heirs can't pay for it, the mortgage company maintains its grip, and it gets to foreclose and sell your home for whatever it can get. And that's happening to a record number of today's home owners.

We are currently experiencing a foreclosure rate of more than two hundred thousand a month! And yet millions of Americans continue buying too much house and end up living right on the edge of foreclosure. They need everything to go right—every month—or they risk falling behind financially. This kind of pressure is more than most people can bear, and many don't. They give up, hand the keys over to the mortgage company or the sheriff, and walk away . . . often homeless. Imagine going from owning a big, fancy house to being homeless in a matter of months, just because something unexpected and unplanned-for happened. Unfortunately, this is more than imagination for hundreds of thousands of families.

But it doesn't have to be that way for you. No matter what size your home mortgage, the debt-payoff method I described in Chapter 5 will eliminate tens of thousands to a hundred thousand dollars or more in mortgage interest, and it'll get the note paid off in a relative handful of years—four to five years on average. If you have the income to get a mortgage, my system will use that same income to eliminate it in an amazingly short time. Which begs the question: If such incredible savings are right there for the taking, why doesn't the average home owner ever think of accelerating his mortgage payoff?

JAN AND JERRELL'S STORY

When I first met Jan and Jerrell Herron, they were in their early fifties and lived in central Texas. They'd known each other since the first grade and were childhood sweethearts. Jerrell was a procurement manager at Dell Computers. Jan, after raising two children and working for many years, was focused on keeping their home and fulfilling the couple's substantial commitment to assisting local churches.

The Herrons received information about my system in 1994. Jan was somewhat skeptical, but Jerrell wanted to test the principles the book taught. The couple had the usual credit card debts and two fairly new cars, but their biggest concern was that they had no retirement savings. "I had changed jobs a few times over the years," Jerrell explained. "I was at Texas Instruments and later at IBM, and each move brought a promotion, but I didn't accumulate a company pension. Jan and I started to worry about our senior years."

After studying the plan, Jan and Jerrell decided to focus on paying off their debts and saving for retirement. *In just one year, using the Cascading Debt-Elimination System™, they had managed to pay all of their credit cards to zero, totally pay off their late-model cars, and pay a substantial amount of their mortgage. During the following year, they succeeded in paying the rest of their mortgage.*

The two have also accrued a substantial retirement fund in the form of Dell stocks, tax-free bonds, mutual funds, and a 401(k) plan. Both Jerrell and Jan feel much less worried and more relaxed since they started making the best possible use of their money.

The couple also convinced their thirty-two-year-old twin sons to begin following the Cascading Debt-Elimination System™ principles. "One of our sons now has his home entirely paid for," Jan proudly says, "and the other is within a year of truly owning his home."

∞

WHY AREN'T MORE PEOPLE ACCELERATING THEIR MORTGAGE PAYOFF?

Most people aren't trying to pay off their mortgage faster because no one they know is doing it. It's not important to friends and family, so it never seems important to them. Thanks to the Coalition's pervasive brainwashing, there's no peer pressure to pay off your mortgage. The peer pressure is all in the opposite direction—to use up any surplus monthly income on self-indulgences. If the average-income-earning household does hear about or try a mortgage-reduction method, it's usually either the extra-payment-a-year or the biweekly scheme. These have some impact, but not nearly what my system does. Those plans can cut a thirty-year mortgage down to twenty to twenty-three years, depending on the interest rate, but my plan will cut the same mortgage down to four to six years.

When it comes to the old "death grip," the smart play is to pay it off as fast as possible. That way thousands—in many cases more than a hundred thousand dollars—that would have been interest going to the mortgage company becomes your money flowing into your investments.

BUT ISN'T MY INCREASING EQUITY
IN MY HOME AN INVESTMENT?

First of all, look at your mortgage payment coupon. See how much of your monthly payment goes to interest and how little goes to principal reduction—to building your equity. Pitifully little of the average monthly mortgage payment goes to paying down principal, usually something like 5 percent to 10 percent, and this is true regardless of the loan's interest rate. But even the little slice that does go to the equity side of the ledger is not really an investment.

Many people think their homes will provide nest eggs for their old age, so they look at the money they're pouring into their mortgages as investment dollars. They think their homes' appreciating equity will bail them out after lifetimes of financial irresponsibility and mismanagement. Well, it used to work that way in the 1950s, 1960s, and 1970s. Many homes that were bought for ten or twenty thousand then are worth hundreds of thousands today. But since that time, things have changed. Homes are not appreciating at the incredible rates they did for the World War II and early baby-boom generations. And what appreciation there is, isn't following predictable patterns.

For instance, it's no longer a given that homes in the North and East will experience little or no appreciation, while those in the South and West will. According to a 2002 report by Case Shiller Weiss on annual home value appreciation/depreciation: In Los Angeles and San Francisco, medium and larger homes were losing between .4 percent and 6.3 percent. While in Boston, medium- and low-priced homes were increasing in price 5.5 percent and 10.1 percent respectively. The average appreciation in residential real estate across the nation is just under 5 percent, and when you figure in maintenance costs and taxes, it's considerably less than that.

This growth percentage has recently been pushed up by abnormally low interest rates that make higher prices easier to pass off on buyers, but as sure as gravity, real estate value growth rates will come back down to the 5 percent or lower range as soon as the economy resumes dependable upward movement and interest rates bounce back to more historic levels. Don't base your housing strategy on temporary market conditions, letting lower interest rates seduce you into buying more house than you should. And, again, don't be maneuvered into buying too much house on the advice that it's "a good investment."

Your home is not really an investment. As I explained in Chapter 6, a true investment asset is one that pays you a regular income or increases in value *with the intention of being sold to capture that value*. But you have to live in your home, so how can you sell it to capture the value? You likely won't sell it. You'll just live there until you die and pass the home to your heirs as part of your estate. However, if you're not locked into leaving your home as an inheritance, there is one possible way to get equity out of it without having to sell and move out—it's called the "reverse mortgage." As you can certainly tell by now, I'm against mortgages and all other personal debt, but in certain retirement circumstances, this tool might be a way to benefit from personal wealth that's tied up in your home's equity. It's not a tool to be used lightly, but if it can make the difference between enjoying or simply enduring your final years, it might make sense.

A reverse mortgage will let you pull equity out of your home by way of a loan that does not require you to make any payments as long as you live there. The loan amount can be paid to you in one lump sum, as regular monthly advances, or at times and in amounts of your choosing. You won't have to repay any of the loan as long as you live in the home, but your estate will be required to pay back the money—plus interest—when you die. This means you won't be leaving the home to your heirs, you'll just be leaving them the job of selling it to retire the reverse mortgage obligation, or paying the loan off out of their own resources if they wish to keep the house. By the way, you'll have to pay the reverse mortgage back yourself if you sell or permanently move out of the home before you're gathered to your ancestors.

A reverse mortgage is considerably different from other kinds of debt, and it can be complicated, so it's important to understand how it works before pursuing one. Rather than going into all the nuances of reverse mortgages in this book, I recommend the AARP's detailed and complete explanation at http://www.aarp.org/revmort/.

MOVING UP BY DOWNSIZING

Let's get back to the people who buy more house than they need, because it's an epidemic problem today. Do you ever find yourself driving through a neighborhood or subdivision, asking yourself or your spouse, "How can these people afford these homes? How much money do they make?"

Probably not much more than you do. They've just been seduced by the Coalition into impressing people with their square footage or their address. I know several families who took advantage of good times in their income streams to saddle themselves with whopper houses, and all of them—yes, *all* of them—ended up regretting their decisions. A couple have already lost their big homes, and the others either are trying to sell or are working themselves to death to maintain the payments.

One of these situations happened more than a decade ago when I was working with a friend who had his own business. The business appeared to take off, and his income spiked. Up to this time, he and his young family had been living in a small apartment, and their low expenses and increasing income made them feel rich. But instead of conservatively stepping up to a modest house and paying it off, this dynamic, entrepreneurial go-getter built a house that could've qualified for its own zip code. You could literally come in the front door and yell for him, and if he was over the horizon in his bedroom, he couldn't hear you.

Unsurprisingly (to me, anyway), the business took a dip. You see, businesses do that. From mom-and-pop shops to General Electric and

Microsoft, they all have up times and down times. So his business hit a downtime, and he eventually lost the big house. Had he purchased and paid off a more modest house when his income was stratospheric, he may have been disappointed when he went home each night while his business was down, but he would have had a home to go to. Instead, he ended up back in an apartment, scrambling to cover the payments on his Jaguar, expensive furniture, and other trappings of success.

It was about the same time that Lois and I went through our financial crisis. We lost two cars and an airplane, but we did manage to hang on to our house. However, even though we could cover the payments from month to month, our increasing awareness of how the house was consuming our future wealth led us to a fork in the road. So we did something you may want to consider if you're carrying more house than you need: We downsized.

If you're in too much of a house for your lifetime financial plan to metabolize, and you'd like to downsize, now might be a great time. Then pay your new, smaller home off according to the plan I showed you in Chapter 5, and you'll be well on your way to debt-free financial independence. If you know you're not going to stay in your current house, selling sooner rather than later may be the smart play because our changing population and culture will likely hold down home equity gains in the future, regardless of interest rates.

THE LAW OF SUPPLY AND DEMAND

Many of the homes purchased in the past twenty years have been bought by women entering the workforce. But when these women marry, they frequently marry men who also own houses. The newlyweds either move into one of the houses they already own, or they sell both and buy a new home. Two homes are replaced by one. Supply begins to exceed demand, and that puts downward pressure on prices.

Another cyclical change affecting this imbalance is that baby boomers are beginning to retire, and many are selling their homes to move into retirement communities. The so-called "bust" generation following the baby boomers is smaller, meaning there are fewer people coming along to buy all the houses the boomers are starting to sell. This potential glut of homes will likely have some depressive effect on prices, so if you're going to be a seller, waiting may not bring an increase in what you'll get for your house. In terms of a strong selling price, it may be as good as it's going to get for a while.

Just focus on your ultimate goal: to own the house you want to end up in, and to pay off its mortgage as rapidly as you can.

But If I Pay Off My Mortgage, I'll Lose the Tax Deduction

So? As a homeowner you get a small tax break for paying mortgage interest, but it only serves to slightly reduce your effective mortgage interest rate. It certainly doesn't turn your home into a winning investment, and it's no reason to resist paying it off.

For every dollar you pay in mortgage interest, your income taxes are reduced by that portion of a dollar equal to your tax bracket. In other words, if you're in the 28 percent tax bracket, each dollar of mortgage interest you pay reduces your income taxes by 28 cents. So you're paying a dollar to get 28 cents back. If that sounds like a good investment to you, just let me know. I'm sure I can find volunteers who will gladly give you 28 cents for every genuine U.S. dollar you want to "invest" with them.

The truth is you'll be way ahead to pay off your mortgage and give the government their 28 cents in taxes on each income dollar. You get to keep the remaining 72 cents because you won't be sending that dollar to the mortgage company as interest, and the last time I checked, 72 cents was worth more than 28 cents. You'll still get the mortgage interest deduction while you're paying off your mortgage. It will only disappear when you've eliminated the beast! And don't forget, in Chapter 6 I told you how you can shelter many dollars from 100 percent of income taxes, not just 28 percent.

On another note: Mortgage interest payments and your home's value are not among the criteria used to determine your children's eligibility for financial aid for higher education, so paying off your mortgage won't make any difference there either.

THE BOTTOM LINE

You've probably figured out by now that my goal is for you to be insulated from life's ups and downs as soon as is mathematically possible. That's particularly true when it comes to hearth and home. If you lose your job, I want you to be confident you'll still be able to go home each day while you search for a new job, because you own that home. Your job hunt won't be compounded by the stress of wondering when your house will be repossessed. If you get sick and can't produce income, I don't want your family's concern for you to be exacerbated by their fear of being evicted.

If you think I'm overdramatizing the possibility of this happening in your life, listen carefully for news stories of people who had high-paying jobs, then unexpectedly lost them after being laid off. These stories are more prevalent than you probably realize, and many of the people in them quickly use up all their reserves, then use up their unemployment benefits, and, finally, they're thrown out of their homes—with no resources. In less than a year, they go from well paid and living the Coalition's version of the high life to unpaid and homeless, or to working at McDonald's and living with relatives. It's no fantasy. It's brutally real.

But if you buy no more house than you need—and pay it off quickly—you're raising the floor of your life. You're limiting how far you can fall in hard times. It's a lot more than a financial issue. It's an emotional "security" issue, and that's increasingly important as you age. It's also somewhat of a gender issue.

Men are somewhat more likely to see the home as an asset against which money can be borrowed to buy or do other things. Women, on the other hand, frequently see the home as the family's nest—an important place of safety and security. This mismatch in perspectives has caused many a marital clash and even disintegration of the marriage. So, if you're a husband reading this book, please pay attention. You'll earn lots of points by paying off the house.

Marriage is like a bank account. You can make an occasional withdrawal if you regularly make enough deposits. Paying off the house, and assuring your wife she now owns her nest, is a *big* deposit. I'm not trying to get into a gender war here. I realize that many couples don't fit this profile, and sometimes the attitudinal positions are reversed. But the important point is that a mismatch on this issue can cause serious problems.

WHAT IF YOUR CURRENT HOME ISN'T WHERE YOU WANT TO END UP?

What do you do if both you and your spouse agree that the house you live in now is *not* the one you want to retire in? Obviously, the answer is that you'll have to move. But when? If you're talking about twenty years down the road, I recommend you pay off the house you're living in now according to the debt payoff plan I explained in Chapter 5. When you're ready to move, sell your house and move to your new location. Use the money you get from selling your paid-off house to buy your new home.

But if you plan to move in seven years or less, I recommend a different strategy. Use my Cascading Debt-Elimination System™ to pay off all debts *except your home mortgage.* Just continue paying the minimum-required monthly mortgage payment. Once all your nonmortgage debts are paid off, begin investing all your Accelerator Margin™ into guaranteed-return investments, such as bond mutual funds, CDs, or money markets. When you're ready to move, sell your house and use the proceeds from the sale—plus the money you've built up in savings—to buy your new home.

Why this different strategy if you know you'll be moving in seven years or less? Because putting the money in guaranteed-return investments or putting it in your current home's equity won't make a dramatic financial difference over such a time period . . . but it will make a difference in your flexibility. When you begin house hunting at your new location, putting earnest money down on the house you want to buy, renting moving trucks or hiring a mover, and taking care of all your other transitional expenses, it'll be nice to have some of your assets accessible as cash rather than tied up in your house's equity.

MONEY'S NOT THE ONLY ISSUE WHEN YOU PLAN TO MOVE

When a future move is a certainty, you'll also need to plan all the other facets of your new life. For example:

- Are you going to be working in your new location?
- Have you started researching the job market?
- Have you begun building any local relationships that would help you get the job you want?
- Are you thinking about starting a business in your new location?
  - > Have you begun researching zoning and other requirements?
  - > Are you qualified to run such a business?
  - > Do you need any resources you now don't have?
  - > Do you need training?

Think of all the potential issues involved in such a life change, and begin mapping out a strategy for each one. Your transition will be much more successful, and your stress level dramatically lower, if you know you've got all contingencies covered. Peace of mind comes from being ahead of the game.

Once the move is over and you've begun generating your new income stream, get back on your debt-elimination plan and pay off everything. The equity from the house you're selling, plus your savings, may be enough for you to buy your new home with cash. But if it does take a mortgage, put it right into your debt-elimination plan and pay it off as quickly as you can.

Watch out for the natural urge to furnish your new home with everything that would make it "perfect" before you've achieved debt-freedom. Get what you need, but hold off on major furnishing projects until you can pay for them with cash. I know this will take discipline, but I urge you to find it because way too many people dive back into debt in order to "start out fresh" with new stuff around them. Unfortunately, their "fresh" start is really nothing more than a stale old Coalition trap. When your new home is paid for, you can afford to spend real money on furnishings.

Of course, before you can furnish your new home—maybe even before you can buy it—you have to sell your current home. Appendix F: How to Sell Your House, is a step-by-step checklist for successfully doing just that. Now let's get down to more detail about getting you into your ultimate retirement home.

FINDING AND BUYING YOUR RETIREMENT HOME

You may be perfectly happy living right where you do now. That's great! But, if you're not, the question becomes: Where would you love to live? Remember, this book is about getting you to your ideal life, not just about solving your debt problem. So where would you love to live? A recent study showed that more than half the people living in American cities would move to the country if they could. That being the case, there's better than a fifty-fifty chance you're one of those people, so let's talk about that.

When you start inventorying possible new locations, the key is to focus on the quality of an average day in the life you want to live. Don't pick a location because it would allow you to do something you'd do only once in a while. For example, if you like to ski a few times a year, that doesn't mean you have to move to Aspen. You can always vacation in Aspen, but live somewhere else where the cost of living is a fraction of what you'd pay right there in the mountains. The key to making a good choice is thinking about your *average* day.

What time do you want to get up on an average day? What do you want to do first? What do you see yourself doing during the bulk of the day? Is climate a factor in doing that? How do you see yourself spending a typical evening? Look for a home in a place that allows you to do all those things with the most convenience for the least cost. You can always travel to do the things you'll want to do only occasionally.

Once you've narrowed your list of potential destinations, check them out.

Lois and I took little vacations throughout the year and drove through all our prospective retirement areas to experience them. We had decided to leave the hustle and bustle of the city behind and go rural, so these trips were scenic and somewhat like reverse time travel. We saw images from days gone by, like three generations eating breakfast together in the local restaurant. The kids in these small towns dressed and acted like normal, happy young people. Their hair was not all the colors of a rainbow, and most of them would likely make it through today's airport security without setting off any detectors. The local newspapers weren't filled with murders, drugs, and strife, but rather with local government issues, and the successes of local residents, high school sports teams, and students. One of my favorite front-page headlines was "Cat Bites Woman." If that's the worst thing that happens in a week, I want to live there.

If leaving the fast lane and taking the exit ramp sound right to you, too, you'll find a wonderful, inexpensive world in the country. But buying a rural home or piece of property on which to build can actually be more complex than buying a city home. In the city there are strict and pervasive building codes to protect buyers. These are not as prevalent in the country, particularly in less-populated areas outside the towns. So if you find a house you like, get a trustworthy building inspector or contractor to examine the structure and mechanicals. And make sure this person isn't related to the seller (sometimes hard to do).

You'll also be dealing with a less-structured real estate profession in many rural areas. Don't misunderstand what I mean by "less-structured." These people are not stupid or simple. They can outmaneuver a city slicker in a minute and sell them a sinkhole no locals would touch. It's just that you're less likely to see a Multiple Listing Service or even shared listings in the country. Often each Realtor sells only his or her own listings, so you'll be dealing with more Realtors if you want to see all the properties a rural area has to offer.

ONCE YOU'VE SETTLED ON A LOCATION . . .

You should plan on visiting the area at least once during each season. This will slow you down from doing anything on impulse, and it will give you an opportunity to see each property at its worst. That beautiful pasture in the summer could be underwater in the spring, or under five feet of snow in the winter. Some sellers will even let you camp on property you're considering, so take advantage of such opportunities to get really close to the land before you buy.

Before you buy a specific property, try to find time to take an extended vacation in the area. Better yet would be to rent a place to stay for a month or two. That way you can become a regular at the local restaurant, where you'll begin hearing of properties outsiders never find out about. This will also give you a chance to see if you really do fit into the environment and culture as well as you've been thinking you would.

While you're doing all this planning and investigating, be sure to consider any emotional questions such a move might raise. For instance, would you be moving away from close friends and family? I've known several couples who retired and moved halfway across the country—mostly for better weather—only to come back a couple of years later because they missed their kids, grandkids, or old neighbors. That wasted a lot of money.

Lois and I deal with the weather question every Wisconsin winter. Sometime right after Christmas we say, "Boy, Florida, Arizona, Texas, or some other warm place would be nice." But, after a momentary thought about living somewhere else, we think of our six grandsons, who all live right around us, and any notion of moving dissolves away. Actually, I like the four seasons. It's just that our Upper Midwest winters seem to get longer every year. The solution for us: vacations, not moving.

Actually, my travels have shown me that the grass is usually not any greener on the other side of the fence . . . or the country. If you think it is, you're probably just looking at it through grass-colored glasses. Every location has its good points and its not-so-good points. Places that are warm in the winter are often stifling in the summer. Once you're financially independent, when things aren't so good where you live, just vacation where they're better. Then go home to where they're just fine most of the time. Both your quality of life and your finances will be better for it.

LET'S RECAP THE PLAN FOR YOUR HOME

Buy the right house for you . . . for the right reasons. Don't let the Coalition manipulate you into more house than you really need. Compete with your friends, family, and neighbors in the size of your retirement accounts, not the size of your houses. Once you're in the right house, pay if off as quickly as possible.

Don't look at your house as a retirement investment. With some regional exceptions, real estate just doesn't appreciate fast enough to be a good investment. Besides, you have to live somewhere, so your house will likely be just the place where you live, rather than an investment against which you draw income. It's usually best to simply look at your house as your nest . . . the place where you make wonderful memories.

Since, in most cases, your home won't be a retirement investment, your plan should be to have it cost as little of your lifetime income as is reasonable. This will leave the maximum amount for investing in assets that will pay you retirement income.

If your current home is the one you want to stay in for the duration, just pay off the mortgage along with your other debts, as explained in Chapter 5, then begin investing for retirement. If, on the other hand, you know you won't be staying seven or more years in your present home, begin investing as soon as you pay off all your nonmortgage debts, while you continue making minimum-required mortgage payments. When you do decide to make the move you know you're going to make, you'll have more cash available for earnest money and other relocation expenses.

During the time before you move, spend your vacations checking out potential retirement areas. When you find the one you want, spend extended time there. As soon as you're ready to make the transition, use the money you've been investing since you paid off all your nonmortgage debt for earnest money on the house you'll be buying, as well as for paying other relocation expenses. Then sell your current house, combine the proceeds from the sale with what's left of your savings, and buy your new home—with cash, if possible. Because cash talks.

I remember one of the many radio interviews I've done on this subject, where a young man called in to say he'd read my first book and had been following the principles for years. He just wanted to tell me that a week earlier he had purchased a $30,000 piece of real estate for $10,000—because the seller needed cash, *and he had some.* You can make better deals when you have the money. No matter what you're buying, being a cash buyer puts you in a much stronger bargaining position than someone who also has to find financing. The cash sale is more immediate and more certain in the seller's mind; therefore, it's more emotionally valuable to him, so he's often willing to make more concessions to get the cash in hand.

See, it all starts with getting out of debt. If you take only one life-changing principle from this book, that's the one you should appropriate.

Getting completely debt-free is the gateway to everything from less stress, to more time with your family, to more time with your God. When your life is less chaotic, priorities can come back into divine balance.

In the next chapter we're going to briefly cover a subject that you may or may not need assistance with: making sure you don't spend more than you make each month. Some people are really good at managing the inflow and outflow of their monthly and annual incomes. Others are in a constant fog about where their money goes. Chapter 10 will help them . . . and maybe you too.

10

A PLANNED
SPENDING SYSTEM

∞

An old Japanese proverb says, *"He who buys what he needs not, sells what he needs."*

That was my experience. I bought a lot of stuff I didn't really need because I thought my income stream could indefinitely support that level of "consuming." The result: I ended up selling two cars and an airplane just to save my house.

In retrospect, I realize I had been a free-form spender. I had little idea where random chunks of my monthly income went . . . they just went. I was enjoying a typically consumptive lifestyle, but the expenditures required to sustain that enjoyment were frequent and impulsive. I wasn't directing the spending of my income; it was as if I were watching it happen on a wide-screen TV—a TV on which I was making payments. Then, all of a sudden, I put my hand in my pocket and it was empty.

Ooops!

As my financial house of credit cards came crashing down around my ears, I realized the necessity of knowing where every dollar was going, and why it was going there. I suddenly had to plan my spending instead of just letting the dollars fall where they would. When I developed the Cascading Debt-Elimination System™, I saw the incredible power not only of knowing where the dollars were going, but of focusing as many of them as possible on debt elimination and wealth-building. So I became an avid planned spender.

To this day, I plan my spending rather than just letting it happen as my impulses dictate, and that's why I'm still debt-free and doing fine, even after the horrifying early years of this brave new millennium.

Not a Budget . . . a Planned Spending System

This is a Planned Spending System, not a nonspending system. Most people use the term "budget," but I don't like the negative, restrictive implications of that label. The idea of this Planned Spending System is to buy what you really need—and can truly afford—on purpose, not just because you saw an item on TV or saw your brother-in-law with something you wanted. It's about managing your spending with a longer-term mind-set. This means you'll make choices about where you'll spend your money, but you will still spend. That's what they print money for. The important point is, as you spend, you'll keep your long-term interests in mind. You won't sacrifice your future for a quick feel-good today. And that means you'll have to accept the reality of your income.

The simple Planned Spending System form (Appendix G), which is really the Accelerator Margin Finder Form extended out over a year, is based on the fact that you're going to bring home only so much money each month. You have to decide on what to spend that income. And you must continually recommit yourself to the reality that *you cannot spend more than you bring home.* The Credit partner of the Coalition of Four wants you to believe that it's easy and harmless to spend more than you bring home, but the result is credit debt slavery. To avoid that outcome, use the Planned Spending System form to help you make choices—choices to say, "Yes," and choices to say, "No."

Setting Up Your Planned Spending System Is As Simple As 1-2-3

1. Determine how much you bring home each month.

2. Determine what expenses you need to spend your money on.

3. Determine how much to spend on each expense.

DETERMINE YOUR INCOME

Include all household take-home income. If both spouses work, you'll achieve your common goal of debt-free financial independence a lot quicker with both incomes in the game. If children in the home work, it's not unreasonable to call on them to commit a percentage of their incomes to the common household good of becoming debt-free. If any of these incomes vary from week to week or month to month, average them for a year and use that number. Be conservative and round down to whole dollars.

When you have the final number for your total household income, enter it into the Monthly Household Income box at the top of column 2 on the Planned Spending System form in Appendix G.

DETERMINE YOUR EXPENSES

Create a category for each expense. Some expenses will be major categories, while other expenses will logically fit under major expense categories as subcategories. For instance, the "Automobile" major expense category could include subcategories such as:

- Loan payment
- Gasoline
- Insurance
- Maintenance

I put auto insurance as a subcategory in the "Automobile" major category, but it could just as easily be a subcategory of an "Insurance" major category, along with home-owner's insurance, medical insurance, boat insurance, liability umbrella insurance, life insurance, and so on. It's up to you. Set up your major categories and subcategories however they make the most sense to you. Let's look at a couple more sample major categories and possible subcategories under them.

The "Recreation" expense major category could include:

- Dinner out

- Movie out

- Baby-sitter

- Vacation

- Golfing

The "Clothing" expense major category could include:

- Footwear

- Dresses and suits

- T-shirts, shirts, pants

- Your favorite team's hat that you bought at the game

- Anything you can wear

Tracking your expense categories will quickly show you where spending might be out of proportion or even out of control. Major expense categories can include (but are not limited to):

- Automobile

- Child care

- Children
- Clothing
- Eating out (both at work and after work)
- Education
- Entertainment (outside and inside the home)
- Family allowances
- Gifts
- Groceries and household supplies
- Other household expenses
- Home repair
- Insurance
- Medical
- Miscellaneous
- Mortgage
- Personal
- Pets
- Recreation
- Rent
- Savings
- Telephone
- Transportation (other than automobile)
- Utilities

These category names are the most common, but they are only my suggestions. Use whatever labels work for you. Just make sure that when you're done, everything to which you regularly commit money is in your plan as an expense category. Now write your expense category names in the left-most column of boxes on the Planned Spending System form in Appendix G.

Start with major categories, and then add whatever subcategories seem logical to you. The more precise your subcategories, the more you'll come to understand your spending patterns, and this is valuable knowledge. On the other hand, don't make it too hard on yourself to maintain your Planned Spending System by creating a monster with fifty categories and a half dozen subcategories under each. You want to end up with a system that achieves its money-management goal but is easily maintainable so you'll actually use it.

DETERMINE HOW MUCH TO SPEND

Once you've decided on your monthly spending categories, it's time to determine how much of your income you'll spend in each category. Here's where reality hits. As we've already agreed, you have only so much money coming in each month, and you can't spend any more than that, so your Planned Expense Amounts for all the categories, when added together, *cannot exceed your monthly take-home income.* Let's put some numbers to your major and subexpense categories and work out your Spending Plan.

Start with Fixed Monthly Expenses. The journey to determining how much you *must* spend to meet your obligations each month begins with those expenses that are not reducible. These fixed expenses are the ones that require the same amount each month, such as your tithe, mortgage payment, car payment, rent, insurance, child care, and the like. You can't trim these expenses, so you must be sure to cover them first. Of course, your tithe is not an expense, it's worshipping God, but it should come at the top of your monthly financially commitment list.

Next in line are fixed expenses that are paid less frequently than monthly. Home owner's insurance is a good example. In many cases this premium is paid annually, semiannually, or quarterly, but not monthly. You may also have other nonmonthly expenses that come up only periodically. The challenge is that you have to account for these in your monthly Spending Plan. If you don't, you'll continue to be surprised when they come due, and you'll be short of income to cover them because they weren't worked into the monthly plan.

The way to include a nonmonthly expense in your monthly Spending Plan is to first figure out the number of months between payments, such as three, six, or twelve, and divide the expense's payment amount by that number. This will give you the monthly component of that nonmonthly payment. For example, let's say you had an insurance premium of $300 that came due every six months. Just divide $300 by six, and you'll see you need to put $50 in your monthly Spending Plan, so it can build up to $300 every six months.

I not only recommend you put the monthly amount in your Spending Plan, I recommend you actually write a check for the amount each month and deposit it in a money market account you open for the purpose of accumulating each month's portions of nonmonthly bill payments. This will allow the partial payments to accumulate, while earning some interest, until each bill's complete payment is due. Then, when a payment does come due, just write a check from the money market account to cover it.

Earning interest is one reason to move the money out of your regular checking account into a money market account. The other reason is that if you let these partial payments accumulate in your regular checking account, you risk feeling too prosperous as your balance appears to increase, and spending money earmarked for an upcoming quarterly, semiannual, or annual payment.

Another way to solve the nonmonthly payment problem—at least for insurance premiums—is to ask the insurance company to bill you monthly. This service will likely cost you a small fee, but some insurance companies are beginning to waive that fee if you pay your premium online. If you make this change, your premiums simply become fixed monthly expenses, and the amount goes into the appropriate category or subcategory box on the Planned Spending System form.

Just to see where you are at this point, subtract the total of your fixed expenses from your take-home income. This will give you a better picture of how much you have left each month to pay your variable expenses— the ones you *can* control.

Variable Expenses—Where Discipline Makes a Difference. You don't have any monthly control over your fixed expenses. They are what they are. Of course, you could sell something you don't really need to eliminate its fixed monthly payment. But, for the most part, your real leverage to reduce your monthly costs is limited to variable expenses. Here you're not simply entering a fixed amount determined by someone else. You get to decide how much you *should* spend in each variable category and enter that amount in your Planned Spending System. Of course, then it's up to you not to consume more than the planned amount in each variable expense category.

The easiest way to estimate the amount for a variable monthly expense is to add up the past twelve months' payments for the expense and divide the total by twelve. This will give you the average monthly cost for that variable expense category or subcategory for the previous year. If you know that rates or other considerations may affect the category's costs for the year ahead, factor that knowledge into your estimate. Or if you know that certain expenses will vary widely from month to month or season to season, make your best educated estimate for each monthly Planned Expense Amount.

"Utilities" is a common variable expense category, and its typical sub-categories include: electricity, gas, fuel oil, and water. Changing seasons cause these expenses to vary widely over the course of a year, so they're obvious candidates for determining an average amount for your Spending Plan; then in months when an expense runs below average, any excess in the average planned amount would be deposited into your money market account. This accumulated amount could then be tapped to help cover the expenses in months when they come in above average. However, many utility companies today will establish an annual budget for you, based on your prior year's usage, and bill you for the average monthly amount throughout the year. This gives you a stable monthly payment, even though your usage may vary widely across the year.

Enter each fixed and variable expense amount in the Planned Expense Amounts column (second column) of the Planned Spending System form in Appendix G. These should all be minimum required payments. If you're in the habit of adding something extra to certain bill payments, don't do that on this Planned Spending System form. The purpose of this form is to help you clarify how much you can realistically count on each month for your Accelerator Margin™, so payments shown for all expenses must be the minimum required. No more.

Add up all your Planned Expense Amounts, and enter the total in column 2 in the box to the right of Total Monthly Expenses. Now just subtract your Total Monthly Expenses from your Monthly Household Income, which you entered at the top of column 2. The balance is your available Accelerator Margin™. Hopefully it will be 10 percent or more of your monthly household income, but even if it's not, the plan will accelerate your debt elimination, so don't get demoralized. Enter that amount in the bottom box of column 2. If you've been totally honest with yourself, the resulting Accelerator Margin™ should be a realistic amount you can use for the Cascading Debt-Elimination System™ calculations in Chapter 5.

How Close Will You Stick to the Plan?

As you go through the months of the year, simply enter the actual amounts for each expense category in the labeled column for that month. Compare the actual amounts with those you projected in the Planned Expense Amounts column. If the expenses for any category routinely run either higher or lower than you projected, adjust its Planned Expense Amount accordingly. And remember, each time you pay off a debt, remove it from the Planned Expense Amounts column and recalculate your Accelerator Margin™. If your income increases, make the adjustment in the Monthly Household Income amount at the top of column 2, and recalculate your Accelerator Margin™ at the bottom of column 2.

WHAT ABOUT PLANNED GIFT SPENDING?

Whether you plan to include seasonal gift expenses in the generic "Gift" expense category or break it out as a separate subcategory, you should handle it the same way I explained for other nonmonthly expenses. Establish your total holiday spending amount, then divide it by twelve. This is how much you should put in the Planned Expense Amounts column for this monthly expense. And, as with your other nonmonthly expenses, I recommend you actually write a check for that amount each month and deposit it in your money market account so it can earn interest until gifts are purchased.

When holiday shopping season arrives, just write a check from the money market account to the checking account you'll use to do your shopping. Your shopping will be a lot more fun when you know the money is there, and you won't be enduring the credit hangover most other people suffer in January.

ACCURACY COUNTS

This Planned Spending System will do you no good if you don't accurately record your expenses. Earlier in the book I recommended keeping a Spending Journal—at least until you have a handle on how much you're really spending, especially on cash purchases. You have to know where your money is going, and if you lie to yourself about it, you're both the liar and the fool who believes the liar. The Planned Spending System is somewhat like a diet, in that cheating only hurts you.

On the other hand, you may be a bean counter by nature, and you already have a system on your computer with printouts filed away for reference. If you have a system that works for you, use it. But if you don't have any planning and tracking process in place, I highly recommend that you use this simple Planned Spending System form. You'll have much more confidence in your debt-elimination and wealth-building journey if you have confidence in the numbers it's based on. The Planned Spending System form in Appendix G can easily be replicated in Excel or any computer spreadsheet program. So, if you like automating your life, feel free to do that.

11

THERE'S NO PLACE
LIKE HOME

∞

Remember how we started this book . . . with Dorothy and her friends facing "the Great and Powerful Oz"?

You'll recall that the successful conclusion of Dorothy's adventure was her heal-clicking journey home, and that's what we're going to do in this chapter—bring it all home for you. Although transforming your debts into blessings and financial independence won't be as simple as clicking your heels together, neither will it be as hard as slaying the Wicked Witch of the West.

There are basically two parts to your successful journey home to debt freedom and prosperity:

1. A *plan* to get you there.

2. Your *effort* to work the plan.

In the preceding chapters I've given you the plan:

- *Understand the Coalition of Four's brainwashing and manipulation campaign* against you, so you can perceive its attacks and defend yourself.

- *Stop making new debt.* Cut up the credit cards, and close the accounts. Maybe freeze one card for an emergency backup, but learn to use real money, checks, and a debit card for your purchases. If you can't afford to pay for it with cash, you can't afford it right now.

- *Follow my Cascading Debt-Elimination System*™ and get rid of all your debts—including your home mortgage—in about five to seven years.

- I showed you ways to *find Accelerator Margin*™ *money* to speed up your debt-elimination process.

- *Once you're debt-free, invest* most of your newfound monthly cash flow through mutual funds, principally index mutual funds, and real estate (if it fits you) to build financial independence for your future years.

- *Redesign your life* to match your dreams and your understanding of God's plan for you, and live that life without using credit for the rest of your years.

Now it's time for you to begin putting that plan to *work.* Yes, there's that four-letter word. But there's no other way. Here's what the Bible says:

"But do you want to know, O foolish man, that faith without works is dead?" (James 2:20).

Notice that the verse is a question. I believe it's phrased that way because God knew when he inspired James to write these words that many men and women don't really want to know that faith without works is dead. They'd like to think they can simply believe their way out of the consequences of financial irresponsibility. But God doesn't bless irresponsibility. He uses its consequences as teaching moments—opportunities to help us learn how not to be irresponsible again.

If you really believe God wants you to be debt-free, then your works will evidence that, and they'll move you from debt prison to debt freedom.

In the preceding chapters I showed you a complete plan to get you from being an indebted servant of the Coalition to being a free man or woman, able to live the life God created you to live. I hope my argument was sufficiently convincing that you have a level of faith that it could work for you. Now you have to add works to your faith. And when you do, you can be confident you'll succeed because you have so great a cloud of witnesses.

HUNDREDS OF THOUSANDS HAVE PRECEDED YOU

I've taught my debt-elimination and wealth-building strategies to nearly a half million people over the years through my books, audio programs, videos, software, and seminars. Let's hear from a few of them:

John! You Rock!

We should be out from under $164,000 of debt in about 4 years just with my husband's income! Every day we "find" more income to add to the Accelerator Margin, chipping away at that four year figure . . . and WE'RE EXCITED!

When I prayed for God to help us get out of debt . . . now John Cummuta is a part of our lives. Thank you, John.

—Rick and Marcie Palmer

I am a recent John Cummuta convert and my husband and I are already starting the plan. We will be debt-free in June or July of 2007. Unbelievable! You have both of us so excited that we are having FUN paying off our debts instead of feeling denied. It is a genuine pleasure. You have really opened our eyes. Thank you, thank you, thank you!

—Karen May

It's only been two months since working the plan, but already we have paid off two cars (and are working on the third and final one). I can't wait until all our debt is gone, including the mortgage (by my calculations we should be debt free in 54 months).

—Martha Shea

You saved my life, because for quite a number of years I had been searching for a way to get out of debt.

—Chico Villagran

I am an IT consultant who was "caught" by the recession in the sector which happened in mid-2000. The rates halved but the bills just kept coming. I will never get caught like that again. I am currently in the process of selling my big city flat to clear ALL my debts. As a result of your course, I have learned how things really work and what's important.

When I see people driving in their big BMW's and Merc's, with their big mortgages, I now feel sorry for them! They are spending their futures to try and impress (equally misguided) people now.

I will never have credit in my life again.

—Gary Brennan (UK)

You are the man! Thank you for your program.

I am single with no children. I have made over 110k in the past 3 years and yet I was still broke. I mean it is a struggle to just get 500 in the bank. I have a mortgage of 98,000, student loans of 42,000, and 6,800 in siding I have to have done. The credit cards, well I am only 2,800 in debt.

Since I have started to listen to your program I understand better how and where I am goofing. I had no clue as to an Accelerator Margin, or even where the income leaks were. With your program

and a lot of discipline on my part, I think I can . . . without hurt-
ing too much . . . I can be debt free in 5 years if not sooner.
Thanks.

—Scott A. Neff

Wow! What a program! Last week I had been in a state of depression and very anxious because of our huge bills; but, no more! In
just one week, we've done a 180° turnaround. We're headed to the
top of the world!

This program is so simple it's unbelievable! But, when worked
out, there is no way anyone who gets the program wouldn't use it.
We've already paid off the first bill (after just five days), and will
have $77,000 in bills paid off in less than four years, if we only add
$200 a month and don't cut corners on spending. We hope to only
take two to three years, and then start wealth-building.

I only wish we had known about your program years ago. Keep
up the good work.

—Bonnie Bowles

Isn't it encouraging to see the hope and excitement in their words? But are
you questioning whether you could really join these people in their successes? If you are, your problem is the person asking the question.

The Principal Obstacle to Your Success Is Between Your Ears

Little dialogues are constantly running in your mind, and they're either
reinforcing or obstructing the behaviors that would get you to your
desired financial freedom goal. Some of them actually make it out of your
mouth as mumbles or "talking to yourself," some only rattle around in
your head, but every one of them either builds you up or tears you down.

Stop reading for a moment and ask yourself whether your self-talk is uplifting and encouraging or negative and self-defeating.

Okay, now let's focus on just the words that actually make it out of your mouth, intentionally or unconsciously. Are they positive and reinforcing or negative and damning? Proverbs 18:21 tells us that "death and life are in the power of the tongue." Our words create our outcomes. In Matthew 21:21, Jesus tells us that if we "say" to the mountain, "Be removed and be cast into the sea," it will be done. He didn't tell us to pray to God to move the mountain out of our way. He instructed us to use the power of our own words to move obstacles from our paths.

So your internal self-talk and mouth-talk can be solving your problems or complicating them, removing your obstacles or making them bigger. Which is it for you? If you find that your vocabulary, especially your financial vocabulary, is negative, change it. Make a prayer-assisted effort, as the old song goes, to "accentuate the positive, eliminate the negative." You'll be amazed at how the seeds of good words will blossom into harvests of good outcomes in all areas of your life, not just your finances.

And while we're clearing out negative self-influences, let's not forget the "Big A": *Attitude.* If you have a negative attitude about money that doesn't allow you to really believe you deserve to be financially successful, it will hold you back. In fact, it may even cause you to self-destruct each time you approach success. God did not create you for failure. It doesn't matter how you grew up, whether your parents were prosperous, or how much reinforcement you received as a child. You can ask God to deliver you from all that baggage and start fresh. A better attitude is only a prayer away.

I'm not saying that faith and prayer automatically equal financial prosperity. What I am saying is that if you operate on God's prayer-assisted level playing field, your honest efforts to improve your finances will not be subconsciously undermined by your own attitudes or emotional baggage from the past.

For example, I grew up poor. I can still remember as a first and second grader having to put cardboard inside my shoes because the soles had worn through. To this day I have to catch myself and pray my way out of piling on work out of a spirit of fear, a spirit of lack that says, "If I don't work, work, work, I'll somehow slip back into that not-enough life I lived as a child." That lack attitude is not from God. It's Satan's way of marginalizing me out of God's plan for my life by keeping me on an unnecessary, fear-driven money treadmill. Don't let that happen to you.

Conversely, don't let yourself be dissuaded from working toward financial independence by outside influences or inside attitudes that say you're not worthy. Pray them away.

KICK BAD FINANCIAL HABITS

Actor Errol Flynn once said, "My problem lies in reconciling my gross habits with my net income."

Most of us in this Coalition of Four culture feel frequent pressure to push our habits beyond our net income. Even occasional surrenders to these pressures can damage the stewardship of our lifetime finances, but habitual surrenders are almost always financially fatal.

So how can you break bad financial habits? Well, first you have to identify what triggers them.

Many of your negative financial habits are likely connected in some way to people, places, or things. In other words, interacting with certain *people,* being in certain *places,* or being tempted by certain *things* can cause a bad financial habit to kick into gear and damage your finances.

For example, let's say you have friends at work whose spouses make a lot more money than yours. Whenever you go out to lunch or shopping with them, they freely spend money beyond your ability to match. But because your subconscious mind doesn't want to accept the fact that you have less disposable income than they do, it prompts you to keep up with their consumption level. It's a habit triggered by being with those people.

Or even tougher, when your children plead for the latest doll or superhero toy they've seen on TV, you feel compelled to get it for them. Mostly out of love, but also out of a sense that you wouldn't want your kids to be the only ones on the block without a laser-blasting karate-chop-me Elmo.

Take a moment and make a list of the people in your life who trigger excessive spending. I'm not suggesting you cut them out of your life. What I propose is that you control your responses to them, working toward a win-win outcome. One method to help you accomplish this is called the "sandwich technique." It allows you to say no to the negative situation you're trying to avoid by sandwiching your refusal between two positive statements.

For example, you could say to your well-off friends at work, "Thanks for the invitation. I'd love to lunch with you at Tiffany's Emeralds 'n' Escargot, but I brought my lunch today, and I'm really looking forward to it. How about if we get together at the afternoon coffee break in the cafeteria?" See how you sandwiched your negative response between your appreciation of the invitation and your suggestion to spend time together at the afternoon break?

With children each request for spending offers a teaching moment. You could explain that what they want is okay (positive), but you don't really have extra money right now to buy it (teaching fiscal responsibility); however, you'd be happy to discuss ways they could earn the money to buy it themselves by doing chores around the house, or by getting a paper route, mowing lawns, etc. (positive).

This technique can almost always work out for both parties, while maintaining control over your spending.

Which brings us to *places* that trigger your spending.

You probably know the usual suspects in your life. They might include the mall, Orlando, the jewelry store, the theater, the power tools department, the car showroom, or anywhere else your brain shuts down and your spending gland pumps out of control.

Take a moment and make a list of these places. Then avoid them unless you've made a rational, planned purchase decision, for which the long-term consequences have been considered. If you really want to maintain control of your finances, you have to cut out places that trigger out-of-control or impulse spending. Just like the person who wants to maintain a healthy weight doesn't hang around the refrigerator!

Which brings us to *things* that trigger your spending.

Each of us has areas of special affinity where we're weak when presented with an opportunity to buy more of certain items. These areas of weakness include such *things* as tools, shoes, jewelry, golf accessories, clothes, home entertainment equipment, gardening stuff, art, and on the list could go. For me it's pilot/airplane stuff. I have everything I need, but when a pilot magazine comes in the mail, I'm drawn to the ads and frequently tempted to buy stuff I don't need.

Many times the temptation to buy things you don't need is thrust upon you by a commercial, magazine ad, or catalog. Regardless of the source, your best defense is delay. As I mentioned earlier when discussing how to decode commercials, I take the ad from the magazine or write down the information from the TV commercial and place it aside for at least three days. If I still want the *thing* just as much when I review the offer three days later, I give myself permission to buy. But almost without exception, I have trouble figuring out why I was so fired up just three days earlier, and I throw away the ad or information.

Our favorite *things* are seductive to us . . . but seduction wears off with time.

It's a Wonderful Life

Living debt-free and able to choose my own path each day is truly a blessing. I can't explain how unburdened and in control I feel. And you can live this way too. Don't only dream about it. Go after it, achieve it, and live it. Many others have used the principles in this book to break free of the rodent derby and fashion lives that give them freedom to enjoy the people and accept the callings God has placed in their lives.

When the weight of financial dependence rolls off your shoulders, you'll blossom like a flower to become all you were created to be. Financial pressure causes you to retreat inward. You get into an emotional fetal position, protecting yourself from everything outside because most of what's out there is unpleasant. But when the unpleasant is removed, you can expand to enjoy all God has placed before you. It's exhilarating . . . and a lot more rewarding than the junk you can buy with a credit card.

You'll be free to be the father, mother, spouse, son, daughter, friend you were created to be.

So . . . What Are You Waiting For?

You're in control. The answers are right here in these pages. I suggest you read this book at least twice. There's a lot in here, and it won't become part of you from just one reading. Your brain leaks, you know, and you have to refill it periodically.

Check out www.johncummuta.com on the Web for other resources I've developed that could help you succeed in your debt-elimination and wealth-building efforts. If you see something you think you need, print out the page and set it aside for at least three days. If you still feel the same way after that, get it—you must really need it! You can also e-mail me at john@johncummuta.com to let me know how you're doing.

I'll be praying for you, asking God to bless your efforts and give you a tailwind in your journey from debt to blessing. Prayer works, and I pray for those who are working hard to apply the principles I've been entrusted to pass along in this book. I'm pulling for you, and I sincerely hope you're going to start toward your new life today!

However, if for some reason you're still on the fence and not ready to commit to the plan I've laid out for you here, let me ask you two questions. If you care at all about yourself and your future, answer them, because choosing to do nothing is choosing to fail.

1. If not this plan . . . what plan?
2. If not now . . . when?

Appendix A

ACCELERATOR MARGIN™ FINDER FORM

∞

STEP 1: TOTAL HOUSEHOLD INCOME

Income Source	Earner A	Earner B
Salary (net, take-home pay)	$	$
Part-time or self-employment income	$	$
Home-based business income	$	$
Investment income	$	$
Social Security	$	$
Pension	$	$
Veteran's benefits	$	$
Other	$	$
Individual totals	$	$
Total Income (Earner A + Earner B) =	$	$

STEP 2: REDUCING YOUR MONTHLY EXPENSES

List all your current monthly expenses in the Current column below. In the Reduced column, write the lowest amount you can reasonably spend on each expense item. *Don't forget the monthly share of any annual, semiannual, or quarterly expenses.*

Total all Reduced amounts at the bottom of column 3, then subtract that amount from your Total Income above. The resulting number is your maximum possible starting Accelerator Margin™. If you feel you need to use a lower Accelerator Margin™ to give yourself some breathing room each month, that's your decision. It will just take you a little longer to become debt-free.

Monthly Expenses	Current	Reduced
Retirement plan contributions		
Other savings contributions		
Going out for lunch at work		
Dining out (other than work lunches)		
Groceries		
Telephone (including cell)		
Heating fuel		
Water/sewer		
Electricity		
Car costs (fuel and maintenance)		
Parking, tolls, etc.		
Car 1 payment		
Car 2 payment		
Insurance—automobile		
Insurance—health		
Insurance—home		
Insurance—life		
Insurance—other		
Home equity loan payment		
Other loan payment		
Child care		
Cable or satellite TV		
Movies out and video rentals		
Other entertainment		

Sports (golf, fishing, etc.)

Health club

Lawn maintenance

Laundry/dry cleaning

Pet food and care

Subscriptions

On-line computer services

Credit card 1 payment

Credit card 2 payment

Credit card 3 payment

Credit card 4 payment

Total Reduced Monthly Expenses =

    Total Income – Total Reduced Monthly Expenses =

        Your Accelerator Margin™

Appendix B

CALCULATING YOUR DEBT PAYOFF

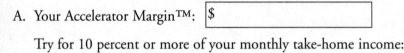

A. Your Accelerator Margin™: $ [   ]

Try for 10 percent or more of your monthly take-home income:

B. Write each debt name in the first column below, its total balance in column 2, its minimum monthly payment (excluding tax, insurance, or any amount you might typically add to it) in column 3.

C. Divide the total balance of each debt by its monthly payment, and put the answer in column 4.

D. Prioritize your debts in column 5, beginning with the debt with the lowest division answer in column 4 as priority debt 1, the next lowest division answer as priority debt 2, and so on.

E. Column 6 is where you add your Accelerator Margin™ (from A above) to the monthly payment amount for priority debt 1, and put this total to the right under Accelerated Monthly Payment. Now divide debt 1's Total Balance by this Accelerated Monthly Payment. The answer goes in column 7.

F. When debt 1 is paid off, add what used to be its monthly payment amount to its Accelerated Monthly Payment. Then add this amount to the monthly payment of debt 2, and put the total in column 6 as debt 2's Accelerated Monthly Payment.

G. Continue adding each paid-off debt's monthly payment amount to its Accelerated Monthly Payment and rolling the total to accelerate the payoff of the next debt.

Name of Debt	Total Balance	Minimum Monthly Payment	Division Answer	Payoff Priority	Accelerated Monthly Payment	Months to Pay Off
1	2	3	4	5	6	7
___	___	___	___	___	___	___
___	___	___	___	___	___	___
___	___	___	___	___	___	___
___	___	___	___	___	___	___
___	___	___	___	___	___	___
___	___	___	___	___	___	___
___	___	___	___	___	___	___
___	___	___	___	___	___	___
___	___	___	___	___	___	___
___	___	___	___	___	___	___
___	___	___	___	___	___	___
___	___	___	___	___	___	___
Totals:	___	___	___	___	___	___

I. **Total Debt** (total of column 2): $_____

J. **Total Monthly Payments** (total of column 3): $_____

K. **Total Accelerated Payments** (A+J[A is the Accelerator Margin™ amount in the box across from A at the top of the form.]) $_____

L. **Years to Debt Freedom** (divide column 6 total by 12): _____

Appendix C

WEALTH-BUILDING PLANNER

∞

MONTHLY AMOUNT AVAILABLE TO INVEST

Total Amount Needed	$1,000	$2,000	$3,000	$4,000
$400,000	16.3 yrs	10.6 yrs	8.0 yrs	6.4 yrs
$500,000	18.4 yrs	12.3 yrs	9.4 yrs	7.6 yrs
$600,000	20.2 yrs	13.8 yrs	10.6 yrs	8.7 yrs
$700,000	21.8 yrs	15.1 yrs	11.8 yrs	9.7 yrs
$800,000	23.2 yrs	16.3 yrs	12.8 yrs	10.6 yrs
$900,000	24.4 yrs	17.4 yrs	13.8 yrs	11.5 yrs
$1,000,000	25.5 yrs	18.4 yrs	14.7 yrs	12.3 yrs
$1,250,000	28.0 yrs	20.6 yrs	16.7 yrs	14.1 yrs
$1,500,000	30.0 yrs	22.5 yrs	18.4 yrs	15.7 yrs
$2,000,000	33.4 yrs	25.5 yrs	21.3 yrs	18.4 yrs
$3,000,000	38.2 yrs	30.1 yrs	25.5 yrs	22.5 yrs

Assumed: 8 percent annual growth rate

Appendix D

HOW TO BUY A GOOD USED CAR

∞

Okay . . . you'll stick to buying two- to three-year-old cars. So how do you do it successfully?

- The first rule is to leave your emotions at home.

- Never buy a car on impulse.

- The CD player, or how good your girlfriend looks in it, is not a reason to buy a car.

- When you find an acceptable car, take it to your mechanic. Pay him or her to give it a complete checkup, which will probably cost you around $50. It'll be some of the best money you'll spend in the transaction. If the seller resists your mechanic's checking it—run.

- Dress down when car shopping. You'll feel more comfortable crawling around the car, and the price won't creep upward.

A STEP-BY-STEP USED CAR CHECKOUT:

- Inspect the exterior:

  ❑ Look for signs of major damage or rust.

  ❑ Do the colors of all the fenders and doors match *exactly*?

  ❑ Are there signs of hail damage?

  ❑ Are there signs of repainting, like overspraying inside doorjambs, inside the gas filler-cap area, around the front and rear glass, on exterior moldings, and inside wheel wells? Some people paint for cosmetic reasons, but more frequently it's to hide repaired damage.

  ❑ Look down the sides to check alignment.

  ❑ Watch for sagging, uneven door alignment, or waves in the flat surfaces.

  ❑ Stand at each corner and push the bumper up and down until the car is bouncing. When you stop pushing, it shouldn't bounce more than a couple of times. Otherwise, negotiate for the price of new shocks or struts.

  ❑ Check the tires for uneven wear and tread damage. Don't forget the spare.

  ❑ Check a vinyl roof for fading color, bubbling, or loosening.

  ❑ Check for glass damage.

- Inspect the interior:

  ❑ Look for splitting or tearing of leather/cloth coverings.

  ❑ Check the condition of the headliner.

❑ Power seats should function properly.

❑ An excessively worn brake pedal could mean the driver was hard on the car.

❑ Do all the gauges operate?

❑ Look under the dash for hanging or taped wiring.

❑ Make sure everything electrical works.

- Now let's pop the hood.

❑ Look under the car for fluids leaking on the ground.

❑ Fresh oil on the engine is not normal, but dirt is.

❑ Check the coolant for a fresh green color.

❑ Check for soft or worn hoses and belts.

❑ Check the oil. It should not be black or very dark brown, and the amount should obviously be within the safe range.

❑ Check battery electrolyte (cover the plates), brake fluid (no more than a half inch from full), and transmission fluid. Transmission fluid that smells like burned coffee can indicate trouble.

❑ Remove the air filter and check for oil, which would indicate a cylinder problem. Dirt is normal.

- Start the car:

❑ Before you start the engine, turn off the radio and everything else.

❑ When it starts, check the mirrors for smoke.

❑ Have the seller or a friend rev the engine, while you get behind the car and watch for smoke. A little is okay, but blue smoke indicates burning oil, which is always bad.

❑ Listen for clinking, tapping, or any other abnormal noises. They're rarely harmless.

- Take the car for a test drive:

  ❑ Before test-driving, turn the wheel from one extreme to the other. There should not be any squeaking or resistance.

  ❑ Then, with your foot on the brake, move the gearshift through all the gears. There should not be any knocking, grinding, or clunking sounds. The louder the sound, the more expensive the repair.

  ❑ Keep the radio down and other people in the car quiet while driving.

  ❑ Try a hard stop from 30 mph. Does the car stop in a straight line? Does the pedal feel mushy? Are there any noises?

  ❑ Next try accelerating. Does the car jerk or hesitate?

  ❑ Does the transmission properly drop down a gear when accelerating to passing speed?

  ❑ Make sure you drive over all the types of surfaces you'll encounter when you own it.

  ❑ After you've had the car up to highway speed for ten minutes, check the gauges for overheating or other problems.

  ❑ While on the highway, drop down to about 10 mph under the speed limit, then punch it. Watch for blue smoke in the rearview mirror.

  ❑ Then, while at the speed limit, take your foot off the accelerator, and watch again for blue smoke.

  ❑ There should be no shimmying or shaking in the steering wheel.

❑ When you're back on slow streets, take your hands off the steering wheel and check for straight tracking.

❑ The best situation is to have your mechanic with you during these tests.

Appendix E

HOW TO MAKE
YOUR CAR LAST

∞

Now that you own the car, let's keep it in good shape.

- Keeping the transmission in good shape will hold down the repair bills.

  ❑ Stop completely before shifting between drive and reverse.

  ❑ Turn off overdrive unless you'll be driving over 45 mph on level ground. This may require shifting to D3 or third gear.

  ❑ To check transmission fluid, drive for about fifteen minutes, park on a level surface, apply the parking brake with engine at idle, and carefully shift from park to drive to park.

  ❑ Now check the transmission fluid dipstick. Wipe it clean and check again.

  ❑ If the fluid is dark or smells like burned coffee, replace it.

  ❑ If low, add fluid in the dipstick hole. Check your owner's manual for the correct fluid type.

❑ If you drive more than fifteen thousand miles a year, change transmission fluid annually. If you drive fewer miles, change it every two years.

❑ You can reduce strain on the transmission by using the parking brake when parked on an incline.

❑ Test your brakes by pressing the pedal three times, then hold it down. The brakes should feel firm and should not sink.

❑ While holding down the brake pedal, slide your other foot under the pedal. If it doesn't fit, the pedal needs adjustment.

❑ A low or sinking pedal means the brakes need checking.

❑ A pulsating pedal can mean a warped or damaged brake disk. This comes from frequent hard-braking.

❑ A pulsating pedal when hard-braking with antilock brakes can be normal.

❑ Have the brakes inspected every six months or six thousand miles. A good time to do this is when rotating the tires. Waiting for noises or problems can be expensive.

❑ Save money on brakes—drive at a steady speed. Don't speed up and brake frequently.

❑ Start using the parking brake. This often adjusts the braking system for pad wear.

❑ Never drive with your foot touching the brake pedal.

• Now let's check the oil.

❑ Change the oil every three months or three thousand miles, whichever comes sooner. This is the best way to lengthen engine life.

❑ Brand-name aftermarket filters, such as Fram, Motocraft, STP, and Purolator, are as good as OEM, and much cheaper.

❑ There is no proven need to use synthetic oils. Use regular oil, and change it regularly. Waiting longer may void warranties.

❑ Be sure to run the engine for at least fifteen minutes before an oil change, so the sludge softens and drains out.

❑ Replace the drain plug gasket annually.

• Now let's look at the battery.

❑ Batteries hate cold weather; it cuts power capacity in half. At the same time, oil is thicker and fuel does not mix as well with cold air.

❑ Loose battery connections can give poor starting performance.

❑ Inexpensive washers, available at auto parts stores, impede corrosion.

❑ You can also coat battery terminals with Vaseline.

❑ Check the battery hold-down bracket to make sure it's tight, but not too tight, which could crack the battery.

❑ Although most new batteries claim to be "maintenance-free," they occasionally need a sip of distilled water. Keep the plates covered.

❑ Wear eye protection whenever working on a battery.

❑ If adding water in winter, drive the car for fifteen minutes to mix the water so it doesn't freeze on top.

❑ A discharged battery also can freeze.

❑ Batteries don't last forever. Plan on replacing the battery every four years. This is cheaper than a roadside breakdown.

❑ Always exchange your old battery for the new one. This ensures environmental disposal.

❑ When shopping for a new battery, get equal or greater CCA (Cold Cranking Amps).

❑ Avoid buying batteries after nine months from the date of manufacture.

❑ Fill out the warranty card.

• Finally, keep the car clean. That keeps down corrosion and other problems.

❑ Wash your car regularly. Dirt, leaves, berries, bugs, bird droppings, and salt will damage the finish if left unattended.

❑ Wash your car in a shady spot.

❑ Rinse the car before washing with a mild soap.

❑ Soak any areas that have stubborn spots. Don't rub them hard.

❑ Start at the top and work down.

❑ Wax your car twice a year: spring and fall.

❑ Be sure to use the appropriate wax for your car's finish—especially clear-coat finishes.

❑ Plastic or rubber areas can benefit from treatment products. Make sure the area is dry before applying.

• Check your car carefully for rust. If rust is evident:

❑ Rust should be sanded down to shiny metal.

- ❑ Next apply a rust-preventive primer.

- ❑ Then apply touch-up paint. Many new cars come with a small container.

- Now let's move inside.

  - ❑ Don't use your car as a trash can.

  - ❑ Vacuum the carpet on a regular basis.

  - ❑ Clean the carpet and upholstery, including upholstered side panels, annually with protective cleaner.

  - ❑ Replace worn floor mats.

  - ❑ Inspect sun visors, the headliner, and vinyl parts. Repair or replace damaged parts. If you don't, the damage will only get worse, which might motivate you to get a new car—and that's expensive.

  - ❑ Avoid using cleaners on the dashboard that may cause glare.

  - ❑ Use a sunscreen in your windshield if you park your car in the sun. Heat destroys synthetic interior materials.

Maintaining your car will keep you happy with it longer. But when you do decide to sell, it will make your car worth more. That's dollars in your pocket.

Appendix F

HOW TO SELL YOUR HOUSE

∾

USE A REALTOR

People who try to sell their own homes are thinking like owners, but you must learn to look at the real estate sales process from the perspective of the buyer. Don't forget, the money you want is going to come from a buyer. Because buyers go to Realtors, that's where all the buyers are. So, if you want to sell your house, go where the buyers are.

BUT THE REALTOR'S GOING TO TAKE A COMMISSION!

So will the buyer, if you don't use a Realtor. Buyers know you're saving the commission by selling yourself, so they want deeper discounts.

IT'S ALL ABOUT MARKETING

Selling a house is like selling anything else. It's the marketing that makes the difference. Professional real estate firms have continuous marketing budgets built into their commissions. You'd have to pay that out of your pocket to put your house on the market as FSBO (For Sale by Owner).

Even with a Realtor, some of the marketing responsibility is yours. Your first responsibility is to be gone, or at least out of sight, when your house is shown. Your other obvious responsibility is the appearance of your home.

THE APPEARANCE OF YOUR HOME

Let's take a walk around your home to see what *you* need to be taking care of. You're preparing your home to be *viewed* by prospective buyers. So we'll start with what's called "Curb Appeal." How will the home appear to the buyer as he first drives up?

- *The front walk.* If it is cluttered with snow, toys, tree leaves, or overhanging shrubs, clear the path.

- *The front door.* Lay out a nice, inviting mat. Make sure the key works easily and the door opens easily—no Addams family creaks.

- *Pets.* Keep them out of the house when the Realtor is showing it. Many people are not only afraid of animals but allergic to them as well.

- *Light switches.* They should operate lights, and *only* lights—not blaring stereos, TV, coffeemaker, etc.

- *Closets.* The doors should work freely. No one should be hurt by falling debris.

- *Kitchens.* The cleaner, more organized, and odor-free, the better. Keep trash out. Don't make sauerkraut, fish, cabbage, or anything with garlic or curry right before the house is to be shown. "The Realtor can't sell it, if the buyer can smell it." Bake bread or cookies. Put a drop of vanilla extract on a lightbulb.

- *Other odors.* Pets are in a class of their own. Litter boxes and other pet odor issues must be cleaned often or removed to the garage.

- *Bathrooms.* They must be immaculate at all times, especially toilets. Fix any leaking faucets or toilet tanks.

- *Storage areas.* If they're stuffed full, rent a storage space and get most of the stuff out of the house.

- *Mechanical equipment.* Make sure the areas around the furnace, water heater, and electrical panel are clear. Wipe them off, so it at least looks as if you pay attention to them. If the furnace rattles, get it fixed. If you use fuses, keep boxes of spares out of sight.

The better kept your home is, the more often the Realtor will show it. And, obviously, the better it looks, the more likely it is to sell—and the higher the price a buyer is likely to offer. Once you get that offer, you're entering the negotiation zone.

NEGOTIATING THE SALE

You actually need to start this process long before you receive an offer. Start by looking at your home from a buyer's perspective. The buyer is never going to be willing to pay you for the sentimental value of your home. He or she is also going to be considering other homes in the area.

From your perspective:

- Why are you selling?

- How motivated or desperate are you?

These are all factors of the price you'll eventually settle on with any buyer.

Is the competition level of other similarly priced homes in your area increasing or decreasing? How does the condition of your property compare to those homes?

WHEN YOU GET AN OFFER . . .

- Weigh it objectively.

- Control your emotions.

- Will this amount allow you to move forward with your plans?
- If you don't accept the offer, how will that affect your plans?
- Are there any advantages to selling now vs. later?
- Is this a good, qualified buyer who is likely to be funded?
- How much earnest money is he or she offering?
- Does he or she have a house to sell?
- You can respond in one of three ways:
  - ❏ Accept the offer.
  - ❏ Counteroffer with acceptable terms.
  - ❏ Tear it up.

I suggest one of the first two. Offers are not as easy to come by as you might think.

A DEAL WILL BE REACHED ONLY WHEN . . .

- The seller is motivated.
- The buyer is excited.
- They both find the deal acceptable.

Any terms that are unacceptable kill the deal: The seller will then have to look for another buyer; the buyer will then have to look for another home. It's either a win-win deal or no deal.

Both buyers and sellers back out of deals because of second thoughts about some unacceptable term. The time for second thoughts is *before* you agree. Know ahead of time how far you'll go to make a deal.

WHAT IF YOU'RE NOT GETTING ANY OFFERS?

If your home has been on the market for months and hasn't sold, it's time for action:

- Determine how many homes in your general area have sold during the time you've been in the market.

- Are they similar?

- How many competing homes are still on the market? More or fewer than when you listed?

- Find out how many in your price range sold last year. That will give you an idea of how many of the available homes will sell this year.

- Make sure yours is one of the homes that will sell. Yours must be the best priced, the best marketed, the best maintained, and offer the best terms compared to your competition.

- If things are really slow, to differentiate your property you could offer to pay some of the buyer's expenses and offer a home warranty.

- You could also offer to take a second mortgage. That way, instead of giving money away in a price reduction, you get it back . . . with interest.

- Another way to get a competitive edge is to improve the home by painting, replacing worn or outdated carpeting and flooring, and replacing old-style lighting fixtures.

> To have the first home sold, make the best value in the eye of the beholder.

Appendix G

PLANNED SPENDING SYSTEM

MONTHLY HOUSEHOLD INCOME =

EXPENSE CATEGORIES	PLANNED EXPENSE AMOUNTS	ACTUAL MONTHLY EXPENSES											
		JANUARY	FEBRUARY	MARCH	APRIL	MAY	JUNE	JULY	AUGUST	SEPTEMBER	OCTOBER	NOVEMBER	DECEMBER
TOTAL MONTHLY EXPENSES													
MONTHLY ACCELERATOR MARGIN													

ACKNOWLEDGMENTS

∞

This book is the result of more than a half century of living and learning, so I must first acknowledge God, who ordered my steps through the experiences that won me the knowledge I share in these pages.

It would be impossible to recognize everyone who has had an impact on me in the area of money and thereby contributed something to this book . . . but I'll try to hit the highlights: Jesus, Solomon, Benjamin Franklin, Charles J. Givens, Keith L. Russell, Ralph Nader, Suze Orman, Robert T. Kyosaki, Larry Burkett, Thomas J. Stanley, William D. Danko, Bill Staton, Earl Nightingale, Russell H. Conwell, Zig Ziglar, Dennis Waitley, Brian Tracy, Napoleon Hill, Og Mandino . . . and my dad.

In terms of writing this book I must acknowledge my proofreader and copy improver: my wife, Lois. I thank Chip MacGregor and the folks at Alive Communications for representing me and helping me focus this project. And, of course, Brian Hampton, Kyle Olund, and the troops at Thomas Nelson who aided me in polishing an idea into a book.

ABOUT THE AUTHOR

❧

JOHN CUMMUTA is the author of the best-selling Transforming Debt into Wealth® system, the Debt-FREE & Prosperous Living® Basic Course, the Wealth Machine™ business startup system, Customer-Focused Direct Marketing, and the Sales Machine™ PC database marketing program. He is a popular financial and small-business seminar leader. Since 1991, Cummuta has been a tireless voice for the stress-free and option-filled life of complete debt-freedom. Through his seminars, books, audio- and videotapes, and computer software, he has helped countless families get out of debt and begin to build new, financially free lives.

Experience for yourself the freedom of owing *nothing* and owning *everything* in your life... sooner than you ever thought possible.

Transforming Debt Into Wealth

Just using the money you already earn, within 5 to 7 years you can pay off your home mortgage, your loans, and your credit cards and retire a debt-free millionaire!

Have you had enough of working hard to make money... just to find that your paycheck comes in one day and goes out the next to pay your mortgage, your loans, and your credit card bills? How much disposable income do you have left over to enjoy life and invest for your retirement? What would happen if, through no fault of your own, your paycheck stopped coming in? Would your bills stop coming in as well? Or, like most people, are you two paychecks away from financial disaster?

You don't need to wait 15, 20, or 30 years to pay off your mortgage. Even if your credit cards are maxed out and you have a huge mortgage to pay off, you don't have to wait 15, 25, or 30 years to become debt-free. Following a few simple steps, you can pay off all your debts in 5-7 years or less and retire a debt-free millionaire over the same time it would take you to pay off your mortgage. What's even more impressive is that you can do all of this without an increase in income, just using the money you already earn.

■ Eliminate your debts, don't consolidate them.
■ Live stress-free knowing you really own everything in your life!
■ Pay back a 30-year mortgage in 5 to 7 years or less!
■ Pay off your loans and credit cards faster than you ever thought possible!
■ Use the money you are wasting on interest payments to retire a debt-free millionaire!
■ Quickly increase your monthly disposable income!
■ Experience once and for all the freedom of being debt-free!

Find out more at

www.johncummuta.com

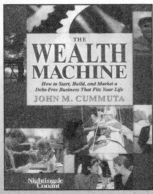